Gemstone of Paradise

Gemstone of Paradise

The Holy Grail in Wolfram's Parzival

G. RONALD MURPHY, S.J.

UNIVERSITY PRESS

2006

OXFORD
UNIVERSITY PRESS

Oxford University Press, Inc., publishes works that further
Oxford University's objective of excellence
in research, scholarship, and education.

Oxford   New York
Auckland   Cape Town   Dar es Salaam   Hong Kong   Karachi
Kuala Lumpur   Madrid   Melbourne   Mexico City   Nairobi
New Delhi   Shanghai   Taipei   Toronto

With offices in
Argentina   Austria   Brazil   Chile   Czech Republic   France   Greece
Guatemala   Hungary   Italy   Japan   Poland   Portugal   Singapore
South Korea   Switzerland   Thailand   Turkey   Ukraine   Vietnam

Published by Oxford University Press, Inc.
198 Madison Avenue, New York, New York 10016

www.oup.com

Oxford is a registered trademark of Oxford University Press

Library of Congress Cataloging-in-Publication Data

Murphy, G. Ronald, 1938–
Gemstone of paradise : the Holy Grail in Wolfram's Parzival /
G. Ronald Murphy.
p. cm.
Includes bibliographical references and index.
ISBN-13 978-0-19-530639-2
ISBN 0-19-530639-2
1. Wolfram, von Eschenbach, 12th cent. Parzival.   2. Grail—
Romances—History and criticism.   I. Title.
PT1688.M87 2006
831'.21—dc22   2005027731

9 8 7 6 5 4 3 2 1

Printed in the United States of America
on acid-free paper

To
Madelyn Willoughby Murphy
my mother
and
to
my four families

Acknowledgments

Researching the Grail is a quest that brings one into contact with many helping figures along the way, some who lived long ago, some who live now, some near, and some far away. I hope I can express a token of my gratitude here for the assistance I received in arriving at the goal of this quest by mentioning a few names. Let me begin in Europe. I would like to thank Bruno Koch and the personnel of the Musées Royaux in Brussels who gave me easy access to the Treasury with its priceless reliquaries and portable altars. In Bamberg, I am grateful to Walter Milutzki, Director of the Diözesan Museum, who acted as my guide and let me examine and photograph both of their portable altars, while he was at the same time attempting to direct the overflow crowd coming to view a special exhibition of Bamberg's medieval treasures. In Siegburg, at the Treasury of St. Servatius, I was given leave to examine their holdings and treated to a special showing of drawers and drawers of precious medieval cloth. A special thank you goes to the parish council of St. Servatius for arranging photography for me and for granting permission to use the results. Through all of this travel the Jesuits of the Hochschule Sankt Georgen in Frankfurt gave me a comfortable place to call home base.

In Washington, I am grateful to Georgetown University for giving me leave to finish this project, to its Jesuit Community for giving enthusiastic encouragement, and to Lauinger Library's interlibrary loan staff for doing their own successful questing on my behalf. A great deal of the research for this book was done during a sabbatical, during which time I was especially helped by Princeton University's collection of medieval German authors at the Firestone Library, as well as by the holdings in medieval art of Princeton's Marquand Library. The proximity of the two libraries to one another on one campus is a most welcome boon for the scholar. In nearby Hamilton, New Jersey, I once again made use of the Hamilton Library's quiet room to complete many chapters of this book. St. Joseph's University in Philadelphia graciously assisted me in the completion of this project by the generous award of the MacLean Chair, for which I am very grateful.

I am delighted to be able once again to acknowledge the support and encouragement of Cynthia Read of Oxford University Press. Her experience, competence, and enthusiasm are one of the most welcome parts of presenting a manuscript to her for publication. She makes it a gratifying experience for an author to work with an editor. I am deeply grateful to her now for the fourth time. I owe a special debt to her patient assistant, Julia TerMaat. I would like to thank also Oxford's anonymous readers for their suggestions, both critical and positive. Many of the suggestions have been adopted, to the enhancement of the book. I am particularly indebted to the anonymous reader who constantly, and positively, considered the manuscript from the point of view of it being a pleasure. Thank you. Two other readers volunteered to read the manuscript prior to its submission in an attempt to head off my various slips and typos. A special thank you for this selfless service goes to James Walsh, S.J., of Georgetown University, and to my former student Jennifer Niedermeyer.

It is hard to express sufficient gratitude to Bonnie Wheeler of Southern Methodist University, who at a conference of medievalists insisted on reading the whole manuscript one evening in one fell swoop. Her immediately enthusiastic reaction and her insightful discussion of the thesis the following morning was a support that the author will never forget.

I would like to thank Vintage Books, of Random House, for numerous citations of their English version of *Parzival*, translated by Helen Mustard and Charles Passage. For translations of Scripture into English, I have generally relied on the Revised Standard Version (RSV) and the New International Version (NIV). Translations of the Old Latin are mine. For illustrations and views of the Holy Sepulcher and for carefully researched information on the stone of the burial couch, I would like to thank Professor Martin Biddle of Oxford University. I am further grateful to many sources for the illustrative material found in this book. Among those to be acknowledged are the Centre des monuments nationaux, Paris; Bildarchiv-Monheim; Professor Walther K. Stoitzner and the Chorherrenstift Klosterneuburg; The Vatican Library; Michael Thuns and LVR-Rheinisches Amt für Denkmalpflege; The Pierpont Morgan Library,

New York; The Conway Library, Courtauld Institute of Art, London; The Bridgeman Art Library, New York; Könemann Verlagsgesellschaft, Cologne; and The Walters Art Museum, Baltimore. Once again, a very special word of thanks goes to the Diözesan Museum in Bamberg and to the parish council of St. Servatius in Siegburg for giving me permission for the use of reproductions and for providing me with more detailed photographs of the portable altars in their care—as well as for being so helpful to a visiting scholar.

Lastly a word of thanks to my mother, who helped me not only by providing a warm and comfortable place to work but even by volunteering to correct my manuscript, from which task she was only dissuaded by a lack of medieval German and Latin. She helped by patiently watching me go on in the quest.

Contents

Gemstone of Paradise

Prologue:
In the Beginning

Grails, the Grail, and the Stars

As I walked up the marble staircase behind the director in the cathedral museum at Bamberg, I wondered if I was about to see the object that had inspired Wolfram von Eschenbach's conception of the Grail or be subject to a disappointment. My trip to Brussels had been a five-hour driving journey each way and had ended up with no results at the Royal Museums of Art and History. The one possibility that I sought there was not on exhibit in the museum treasury but was stored in the basement—"dans les caves"—I was told, and inaccessible at the moment. I was tired as I awoke the next day in Frankfurt, and as I looked out the window, it was raining. Rain or no rain, I didn't want to remain in ignorance about the other possibility, the diocesan museum in Bamberg. I called the director, who told me that they had the object that I had described but that I was wrong about any depiction of the rivers of Paradise on it. "Only the twelve apostles," he said. I decided to go anyway and see for myself, afraid now that this whole trip was going to be a bust. My source had been an extremely reliable study done in the 1920s, but a lot of time, and wartime at that, had passed since then. When I arrived at Bamberg it was late that rainy day, and as I drove up the steep and narrow streets of the hill to the cathedral, I had a feeling I would have trouble. And indeed I did.

When I tried to park my car near the front door of the museum a friendly driver warned me that I would get a ticket for sure if I left the car there. There was really no place at all to leave the car, so I left the cathedral and castle area and drove hopelessly through the ultra-narrow streets of the medieval Old Town, finding no spot at all. Finally I left the area, went outside the town, found a Park and Ride, got rid of the car, hopped on a waiting bus, and listened to the indecipherable Franconian talk of the driver and his buddy while waiting another ten minutes for the bus to leave. Despite the short distance to the cathedral at the top of the hill on which the city is built, I had to get off and transfer to another bus. Finally I arrived, like Parzival, for a second time at my destination. It was now five o'clock, the rain had stopped, and the director had gone home for the day. I left him a note and found my way back to the Park and Ride. Now I had to look for a place for the night. There was a small hotel nearby named after its view of an old castle, and that's where I stopped. All the rooms were full, the nice lady said, but I could have the small one if I didn't mind walking down the hall to the bathroom. I didn't mind, ate supper, and went to bed.

Early the next morning I was at the cathedral, entered the portal, admired the unusual statue of Bamberg's medieval pope, Clement II (died 1047), who was depicted wearing not only papal regalia but also the breastplate of Aaron with its twelve precious stones. I admired his tomb, which had the four virtues of Paradise and the original river of Paradise depicted on its sides. My courage began to mount; surely this is the right place.

The director was waiting for me and very graciously escorted me to the stairway that led upstairs to the magnificent exhibition hall, already filled with hundreds of jostling visitors for a special exhibition dedicated to Heinrich II. As we walked up the stairs he suddenly turned to me, smiled and said, "I was mistaken about the rivers of Paradise. When I told you I only saw the twelve apostles on the sides of the object, I didn't realize that I should also look at the top. On top are not only the rivers of Paradise depicted around the stone but also the four trees of the Garden of Paradise." My heart leapt. Now, if only the stone would be green . . .

"But what is the Holy Grail?" It was the first question I was asked by a family member as soon as I said that I was working on the Grail legend. Those who are familiar with the legend realize that a question is always the right thing when approaching the Grail, and not just for the hero in the story. In the case of the Grail, the question "What is it?" is especially relevant. When dealing with the story of a legendary object, there is always a tantalizingly blurred line between fact and fiction, but normally there is little doubt about what the legendary object is supposed to be. A legendary object, we might say, consists of two parts, the object itself and the legend that tells its enchanting story. To this one must add the question of the curious: does it exist? If the legend is the medieval one, to give an example, of Longinus's lance, with its story of the gushing blood of the crucified Savior curing the blindness of the Roman soldier as he thrust his lance into Christ's side, then the legend, on the one hand, has to be interpreted in some way as a spiritual and poetic insight about blindness and the Crucifixion. The identity of the legendary artifact, on the other hand, needs no interpretation: it is a lance. Even the title of the legend is significant: "Longinus" means "long lance." Then, there will always be the question of the curious: does the lance still exist? This is another fascinating question, one that can easily become a quest.

Unfortunately, having given the legend of the lance as an archetypal example, I have to admit that it does not correspond well with the legend of the Grail. Not only are there variant legends about the Grail that have differing messages, which in itself is not too surprising, but the mysterious object called the Grail that is the focus of each story is not the same thing in each case. The question my nephew asked is a legitimate one, and it is one of the two I asked of Wolfram von Eschenbach's version of the Grail legend. His identification of the Grail decidedly differs the most from that of all the others, and on first blush seems almost unrelated to them. Neither sacred cup nor dish, Wolfram says, the Grail is a sacred stone. One must ask him "What stone could this be?" and, in paraphrase of the Passover question, "Why is this Grail different from all the other Grails?" I feel sure he would answer "Because, if you read the story, you will realize that this stone is the real one." My next question to him and his *Parzival* is "If we identify the Grail and come to see its meaning in accord with your version of the legend, can it still be found—can I find the original?" However, I am getting a bit ahead of history and of myself. Let me turn to the dawn of the Grail legend.

If we go back and start at the beginning, the earliest written identification of the nature of the Grail and a recounting of its legend is that given by Chrétien de Troyes in his final Arthurian masterpiece, *Perceval ou Le Conte du Graal* (Perceval or The Story of the Grail). In it his young hero, a rustic simpleton, after leaving home and his widowed mother in a rather brash way, comes to a wild country area where he enters a mysterious castle. At a great feast in the hall, where he is seated in a place of honor, he sees a mysterious golden serving dish shining with jewels again and again pass before his table to disappear into another room. Yet he never has enough curiosity to ask about it or whom it is serving. If he had, his question would have brought healing and happiness to all. He is thrown out of the castle the next day. At his final appearance later in the story, he resolves to find the Grail castle once more and ask, but then the story of Perceval breaks off. The story is unfinished, and so the author never provided a second chance for the hero to ask his question at the Grail castle.

Chrétien de Troyes wrote this romance late in the twelfth century, approximately between the years 1180 and 1185 AD. The reason for his never having finished it is generally presumed to have been his death. This means that Chrétien's description of the Grail, the earliest one known in European literature, which identifies it as a golden serving dish set with jewels, a platter big enough to contain a large fish, but which holds a single communion host, was never satisfactorily explained or identified. Chrétien's interpretive story or legend, which we presume would have given the function and purpose of the Grail dish, breaks off without Perceval ever having asked the critical question that would have brought the Grail story to a conclusion: "Whom does the Grail serve?" The answer would have to have contained the author's resolution to the enigma he had created.

When Wolfram von Eschenbach takes up the task of telling the story of the Grail some twenty years later, he tells his readers that he is aware that Chrétien's version failed to give the legend a purposeful ending, and this he says he intends to do. Remarkably, he also disputes Chrétien's description of the Grail as a golden serving dish and claims, as we will explore, that the real Grail is a stone, and a green one at that.

Scholars of Chrétien de Troyes's romances have long wondered where this oldest mention of the Grail in European literature came from. Chrétien himself says that he had a written source, a book given to him by Count Philip of Flanders, and that "he, Chrétien, strives by command of the count to put into rhyme the greatest story that has ever been told in royal court: it is the Story of the Grail, the book of which was given to him by the count."[1] This book, presumably in Latin, if it existed, has never been found. Thus it is not possible to say whether or not some poet before Chrétien had already created the integrating model and plot combining the Celtic and Christian motifs that are found in his sacred dish, or if he himself was the first. There is general agreement that the sources for Chrétien's concept of the Grail as a mysterious serving dish that always serves abundant food without running out are to be found in the tales of Celtic mythology, the great majority of which would have come to France through Brittany. To which, I would add, lest we forget the Communion Host that he has on the serving dish, there is also the other source,

---

1. Chrétien de Troyes, *Arthurian Romances*, trans. with intro. and notes William W. Kibler (London: Penguin, 1991), pp. 381–2.

Christian storytelling as found in the apocryphal gospels and miracle stories, and in the stories of the multiplication of food found in the Gospels themselves.

Chrétien's Grail, both as an object and as a legend, has two roots, a blend of two storytelling traditions, Celtic-Arthurian and medieval Christian. To extend the juncture of the two roots in a manner that would bring the story to a further pleasurable intertwining and to an appropriate ending was a challenge thrown down to storytellers by the unfinished state of Chrétien's *Perceval* in 1185 AD.

The gauntlet was taken up by many writers who attempted to bring the story of Chrétien's Celtic-Christian, magical-sacred serving dish to a conclusion by supplying "continuations," before, during, and after the time when Wolfram von Eschenbach was writing. The most significant of those who took up the challenge was Robert de Boron, with his very influential version, *Joseph d' Arimathie* (Joseph of Arimathea), which was written some–fifteen to twenty years after Chrétien, at the very beginning of the thirteenth century, sometime, it is thought, between 1200 and 1210 AD. In it, the author changed the Grail from a serving dish to a cup. This cup he identified with the cup from which Jesus had drunk at the Last Supper and over which Jesus had said, "This is the cup of my blood." In Robert de Boron's story, after Jesus' arrest the cup had been given to Pontius Pilate by one of the Jews. Pilate then gave it to Joseph of Arimathea, after whom Robert named his story. After Joseph and Nicodemus had taken the corpse of Jesus down from the cross, Joseph used this vessel to collect the blood seeping from Jesus' wounds. Thus it came about that during the preparation of Christ's body for burial, the cup literally came to fulfill the words Jesus had said over the cup at the Last Supper, "This is the cup of my blood." The cup was then buried with the body of Jesus in the tomb. Later, when Joseph was imprisoned, Jesus came and appeared in his cell, bringing this vessel with him.

> Joseph, you took me from the cross. And you know well that I ate the Last Supper at the house of Simon the Leper, where I said that I was to be betrayed. As I said at that table, several tables will be established in my service, to make the sacrament in my name, which will be a reminder of the cross; and the vessel of the sacrament [the chalice] will be a reminder of the stone tomb in which you laid me, and the paten [the dish] which will be placed on top will be a reminder of the lid with which you covered me, and the cloth called the corporal [shroud] will be a reminder of the winding-sheet in which you wrapped me. And so your work will be remem-

bered until the world's end. And all who see the vessel [the Grail] and remain in its presence will have lasting joy and fulfillment for their souls.[2]

Thus the Grail, which in Chrétien's fragmentary *Perceval* had a magical, if unclear, mixed identity as a precious serving dish of Celtic origin, but containing a sacramental Christian Communion Host, has been reshaped by Robert de Boron into a cup whose legendary identity is far more rooted in the Christian story of the Passion than in Celtic myth.[3] The cup returns to Celtic origins, though, in a way; Joseph brings it to Britain. The serving dish of Chrétien has now become the original chalice, containing the mystical blood of the Crucifixion promised at the Last Supper. I mention Celtic imagery because it seems clear that Chrétien was using Celtic lore, with its stories of the cauldrons of the Dagda that never go empty, and the dish with the blood and living head of Bran, and weaving them into Arthurian-Christian romances. The twin strands of the Grail and its legend, which perhaps Chrétien would have woven into a Christian allegory, or perhaps not, had he finished, were taken up by Robert de Boron, who used their style to retell the story of the Sacrament, the gospel, and their diffusion to the Celtic North. His task was analogous to that of the Saxon poet of the *Heliand,* who retold the gospel story in a blend of Germanic and Christian terms. And thus in the hands of Robert, the Celtic serving dish with the sacramental host became the Christian chalice; Perceval became Joseph of Arimathea, and the Grail's explanatory legend rested in the Passion's continuity with the Mass and the expansion of Christianity into the myths of southern Britain and Wales. Malory, Tennyson, and Wagner then served to fix Robert's image of the Grail in the imagination as the sacred cup.

Chrétien and Robert agree that the Grail is a container, whether dish or cup, for the sacramental body or blood of Christ. The effect of these two French storytellers on the image of the Grail has been decisive, especially that of Robert's cup. These were two of the three images (Wolfram's being the third) of the Grail that were there, as we might say, in the beginning. The use of French seems to have helped make these two the most widespread of the three earliest masterpieces of the Grail. This may well be the reason that of the many artifacts in the world today for which the claim is made that they are the real Grail, the majority are cups or vessels associated with the Passion of Christ. Justin Griffin in his book *The Holy Grail* lists seven different contemporary objects: the red-

2. Robert de Boron, *Merlin and the Grail: Joseph of Arimathea, Merlin, Perceval*, trans. Nigel Bryant (Cambridge: Brewer, 2001), p. 22.

3. See Roger Sherman Loomis, *The Grail: From Celtic Myth to Christian Symbol* (Princeton: Princeton University Press, 1991).

agate Santo Cáliz of Valencia, the wooden Nanteos cup from Britain, alabaster unguent cups associated with Mary Magdalene from France, the green Sacro Catino bowl in Genoa, the Chalice of Antioch at the Metropolitan Museum in New York, and even two legendary cruets supposedly containing the sweat and blood of Christ brought to Glastonbury by Joseph of Arimathea.[4] Other claimants to being the Grail on the basis of containing in some way the blood of Christ are the Shroud of Turin, the possible burial cloth of Christ, and, in currently popular fiction, the Merovingian royal blood (*sang-réal* being supposed as the correct form of *san-graal*) with Mary Magdalene as vessel and Christ as the founder of the bloodline.

As to the third poet, and his version of the Grail as a stone (the aforementioned agate and alabaster are cups), one can make a truly remarkable observation: there seem to be no artifacts that currently lay claim to being Wolfram's sacred stone Grail. Furthermore, as Wolfram's translators note: "In the poem of *Parzival*, however, the Grail is none of the things so far mentioned, but a stone, apparently a kind of super-jewel surpassing in its powers the virtues of all other gems. Whence Wolfram derived such a concept is unknown."[5]

Wolfram von Eschenbach stands by himself at the beginning with Chrétien de Troyes and Robert de Boron, with his hand raised begging an audience, writing in German—and thus it seems not read in France, England, and beyond—saying that Chrétien has led them off on the wrong poetic path. The sacred container, the Grail, was neither a dish nor a cup; it was, and is, a sacred stone. Wolfram offers to tell the story so that all will realize that the Grail should not be related in story primarily to the objects of the Last Supper nor even to relics of the Crucifixion but to those of Holy Saturday and Easter—and to the present. No one claims such a status for a stone except Wolfram. I, for one, was so moved by his magnificent and multivoiced tale in which he expresses his view of the real nature of the Grail that I became convinced that his successful version of the legend is, as just about every scholar of the Grail stories concedes, the best of all.

Having made that admission, many scholars then surprisingly return to extended discussions of notions of the Grail derived from the dish and cup of Chrétien and Robert, while suggesting that perhaps Wolfram was thinking of a meteor fallen from heaven, or the stone of humility, or even the philosopher's stone. Many more simply throw up their hands and say, with Wolfram's con-

---

4. *The Holy Grail: The Legend, the History, the Evidence* (Jefferson, N.C.: McFarland, 2001), pp. 96–141.

5. Wolfram von Eschenbach, *Parzival*, trans. with intro. Helen E. Mustard and Charles E. Passage (New York: Vintage Books, 1961), p. xliv.

temporary Gottfried, that Wolfram is being deliberately obscure and mystifying about the Grail stone, and he, and it, should be allowed to remain so. All that counts in Wolfram is the narrative. I fear this attitude may reflect the determining force of the pre-notions of the Grail taken from Chrétien and Robert rather than obscurity on Wolfram's part. He is clear enough, I think, and I would go further and say that it is not just Wolfram's narrative but also Wolfram's insight on the nature of the Grail itself as a sacred object that should take the laurels.

What do we know about Wolfram von Eschenbach? Really not very much. His hometown has been identified as the town of Ober-Eschenbach, which nowadays has been officially renamed, in his honor, "Wolframs Eschenbach." The town is in Franconia, a distinctive linguistic and cultural territory in south-central Germany. The territory borders on northern Bavaria, and thus it is not surprising that Wolfram refers to himself as a Bavarian. In Wolfram's lifetime, one of the dominant forces in his town was the Teutonic Knights, a religious order of knights, who had significant holdings in Eschenbach, and this may partly account for the important role of the "templars" in his version of the story. Ecclesiastically, the town of Eschenbach was in the territory of Eichstätt, which is a short distance to the south, and this, as we will see, may also have had a bearing on his version of the Grail as a stone. Wolfram appears to have been of the lower nobility and not well-to-do, a vassal dependent for support on neighboring lords, and this seems to have included lords secular and ecclesiastical. Though dogged by poverty, according to a contemporary source and to his own admission in *Parzival*, he expressed pride at being a knight and following "the calling of the shield," as he put it. Significantly, he uses this particular expression rather than saying what one might have expected, namely, "the calling of the sword." He intimated thereby, I think, that he saw the knight's real role, and his own, as one of protection rather than aggression.

When he began to write his version of the story of the Holy Grail in the early years of the thirteenth century, now some twenty years after Chrétien left his tale, Wolfram, like Robert, did not simply add a continuation to Chrétien's unfinished narrative but rather changed the Grail and added a completely new framework to the plot. In contrast to Robert, he reinterprets the Grail story while at the same time hewing quite closely to the structure, persons, and events of Chrétien's plot. In the highly original framework into which he placed the story, Wolfram created both a new beginning as well as an unexpected and surprising ending, during which two blindly dueling Muslim and Christian knights recognize their family relationship. Writing as he was at the height of the Crusades, such a framework for the Grail legend gave his story real punch.

Based on the number of manuscripts and fragments that have come down to us, it seems a fair judgment that no work of medieval German literature was more copied and read—it seems to have been something of a sensation.

Where Chrétien wove together Celtic and Christian motifs, Wolfram wove together Muslim and Christian, husband and wife, astronomy and medicine, the contemporary and the ancient, into an incredibly rich medieval humanistic Christian tapestry. He integrated the Grail stone motif and his day's lapidary science and love of gems; he found a harmony between the crusaders' quest to free the Holy Sepulcher and the quest to find the Holy Grail; he integrated astrological planetary lore with Kyot, the putative source of Wolfram's tale; he found a new connection between the Passion of Christ and the Grail; he wove together the worlds of Christian and Muslim learning. No literary or cultural work of the Middle Ages, with the exception of the Gothic cathedral, to which *Parzival* has more than passing kinship, surpasses this story in integrated richness, luminosity, and graciousness. Wolfram's Grail story stands on a par with the *Divine Comedy*, and with Chrétien's Arthurian romances.

It is possible to give more precise dating for Wolfram's *Parzival* based on two and possibly three interesting pieces of internal evidence, two of which are directly related to warfare and one indirectly. Wolfram mentions the trampling of the vineyards of Erfurt, which happened in 1203, and the treasures found at the sack of Constantinople, 1204; furthermore, his astrological use of Mars and Jupiter in the ending suggests to me that he witnessed the conjunction of those two planets in Leo, which occurred in 1208. I would thus say the finished work could be dated to approximately 1210 AD, which means that he was writing the epic at the time of the continuing aftershock in Europe at the loss of Jerusalem and the Holy Sepulcher to Saladin. Wolfram's work is the first epic to deal with crusader warfare as a Muslim-Christian religious tragedy, and he is the first to envision a gracious Christian theological resolution to the conflict in Grail-story form. Wolfram stands at the doorstep of the troubles of our own time.

Wolfram may have known some of Robert de Boron's work (as well as, of course, Chrétien's), and it seems evident that he disagreed with both in that they did not take issue with the Crusades. Wolfram's approach to the Crusades, without doubt the major political and cultural event of his day, is that they are fratricidal. They repeat the sin of Cain and Abel. As Wolfram was writing, Christendom was planning another crusade. After the failure of the Third Crusade to recover Jerusalem (1192), the dissolution of its German component with the drowning of the Emperor Barbarossa in 1190, and the diversion of the Fourth Crusade to the destruction of Constantinople (1204), what was in the air was a new crusade. In 1215, the emperor at his coronation in Aachen proclaimed yet another war between Christian and Muslim for the possession of the Holy Sepulcher and the restoration of Christ's land to Christ's control.

How could Wolfram oppose the Crusades in Arthurian terms as fratricide? This he did both by his significant change of the nature of the Grail and by adding the Grail as part of the resolution of fraternal conflict at the conclusion. Moreover, he implied a great deal by suggesting, in accord with Grail legend, that the Land of the Grail (the Land of Salvation in Wolfram) was suffering from a terrible and mysterious sickness, which he attributed to the baleful influence of those two planets, the gods of war and domination, Mars and Jupiter. This tragic situation of Christendom could be exposed and reversed by changing Perceval's question and having his Parzival ask the head of the Grail community with tears in his eyes, "What are you suffering from?"

Wolfram's version is so radically different from those of his two confreres that he had to give a source to authenticate his vision. If Chrétien had a special source in the book given him by Count Philip of Flanders, then Wolfram also had to name a source, a source that, he said, would be angry at what Chrétien had done to the story. He did this by naming one "Kyot" who supplied him with the true version. We will look at this later, but at this point what is significant about Wolfram's "Kyot" is that he got his information ultimately from a source who could read the Grail's message in the stars. With the help of some modern astronomical tables and a longtime friend who is a professor of astronomy, I was able to confirm that there was more to Wolfram's claim than just a parrying of Chrétien's. If we journey back a bit . . .

In the fall of the year 1208, two brilliant planets were seen shining steadily in the predawn chill of the dark medieval sky. The light of the one was blood red, and that of the other was pale yellow. Mars and Jupiter were in conjunction, so close together—about one degree apart—and of such brightness, that any observer could almost feel that they were exerting their intense, concerted celestial influence as they shone down on the events of the earth. The radiant power of the ruddy god of war and the golden glare of the god of domination would have indicated to a thoughtful observer and poet like Wolfram that their invisible and malevolent combined influence was being felt somewhere on earth in the affairs of men.

"Where?" might any latter-day Magi have asked. If the planets reveal what is happening, as for Wolfram they did, then the constellations reveal where. As this October conjunction was taking place, both planets were moving ominously in the constellation Leo, dangerously near Regulus, alpha Leonis, the star that marks the heart of the constellation of Leo the Lion. Mars and Jupiter could thus be divined as exerting their influence in the territory of the Lion of Judah, the realm of David and of Jesus, the Land of Salvation. Several times in

Parzival Wolfram writes about the retrograde motions of the planetary spheres and how the planets have such enormous strength that they hold up and check the motion of the stellar sphere itself by their power. Looking to the eastern sky before dawn in October, he would have seen the unsettling closeness of Mars and Jupiter burning together in Leo and wondered how soon they would reach the zenith of their power, their climactic point, their *endes zil*. Mars and Jupiter, in Wolfram's version, become the causes of the mysterious sickness of the Grail castle in the final episodes of the frame story. They become a celestial mirror confirming his insight on the state of affairs in which Christendom found itself.

Wolfram rewrote the story of the Holy Grail in such a way as to tell the Christian world what the passion for fighting and dominance, devotion to Mars and Jupiter, signified about the state of Christendom in his day—and, no doubt, in our day as well. To his inherited Arthurian Grail story, therefore, he prefixed a crusading-era story of a father (whom he made a fighting knight from Anjou, the land of Richard the Lion-Hearted) who had two sons, one by a Muslim wife, one by a Christian. Then, following in the classical tradition of the climactic final fight between two good men, each representing an opposing side—Achilles and Hector, Aeneas and Turnus—near the conclusion of his epic, as I mentioned, he created a hostile meeting of the two brothers, Parzival and Feirefiz, swords in hand, not realizing that they had the same father. The positive outcome is not Homeric or Virgilian tragedy, it is Wolfram's own hope-filled creation.

Wolfram assigns to women a major role in conducting men, Christian and pagan, to the Grail. In his story, women are not equal to men—they are ahead of men. In the quest, not for military superiority but in the greater quest to become real human beings, they show the way. For Wolfram it is almost as though, as one might say, women are human beings, and men, like Parzival, become human beings; Wolfram's poetry makes men into gemstones, women into radiance. Women in Wolfram's works, like Sigune, embody loyalty, the old Germanic warrior virtue of *triuwe*, which Wolfram maintains is also the form of love to be found in God. When Wolfram comes to say the famous phrase from the New Testament "God is love" (1 John 4:8), it is significant that he does not use either of the two words for love one might expect, neither *liebe* nor *minne*, but rather uses a third. He paraphrases John's letter as *"got selbe ein triuwe ist"* (God is faithfulness; 462, 196[6]). Marital fidelity is for him an

---

6. The numbers cited here indicate column and line in Wolfram von Eschenbach, *Parzival: Studienausgabe, Mittelhochdeutscher Text nach der sechsten Ausgabe von Karl Lachmann*, trans. Peter Knecht, intro. Bernd Schirok (Berlin: de Gruyter, 1998). All citations will be from this edition.

expression of his beloved *triuwe,* and this takes Wolfram far from any contemporary troubadour and notions of courtly love. Love in *Parzival* is loyal harmony, a reflection of Divinity.

In all of this, it is the nature and deeper meaning of the Grail itself in *Parzival* that remains a fascinating mystery, obscure to scholars and unclear to readers—more to readers now, I think, than, *pace* Gottfried, to readers then. In this book I hope to show that the translucent nature of the Grail, the sacred precious stone carried by a woman who is the embodiment of beatific happiness, is the key, perhaps I should say keystone, to understanding the story.

Gemstones play an enormous role, magical, medical, and spiritual, in giving meaning to *Parzival.* In medieval thought, all gemstones, and not just the Grail, have great healing powers. In Chrétien's story, the gemstones are present to create an aura of incredible and fantastic wealth—drinking cups made out of a single ruby. Wolfram's gemstones all have the high powers attributed to them by his contemporaries, Hildegard and Albert, to heal, to heat, to enable sight and life. Wolfram associates them all, above all the Grail, with the Garden of Paradise, since in the book of Genesis all gems come from Eden by being washed out by the four rivers that flow from the Garden of Paradise. The Grail being the gemstone of gemstones, it too flows with waters coming from the Garden of Paradise. This is an important clue both to identifying the function of the Grail in *Parzival* but also to finding Wolfram's actual Grail stone. Should it still exist, as I think it does, it should bear the unique signs of the rivers of Eden.

I divide my Grail quest in this book into two somewhat interwoven stages. The first is to address the question of the nature and profound meaning of the stone that Wolfram calls the Grail within *Parzival,* and the second is to approach the challenging mystery of whether or not Wolfram's actual stone Grail could still exist and be found. Unlike Wolfram, I will have to reveal very soon what I think the nature of Wolfram's Grail is so that I can write about it in the context of the world of stones, knights and ladies, and the Crusades that populate his story. Solving the mystery of finding the actual Grail, however, the stone associated with the overflowing rivers of Paradise, is something I can only hint at in the beginning. I hope the reader will be happy to take the necessary journey with me until the last chapter, just as the reader has to do in *Parzival.* If the reader just sees the Grail immediately, with no preparation of the heart and mind, as once did Parzival, then I fear he or she will do what Parzival did then, see it and keep eating.

Three last observations. First, Wolfram very deliberately created a human-religious dilemma. Finding the Grail, and becoming the Keeper of the Grail, involves the sociopolitical realm for Wolfram more than for Chrétien and for

Robert. Wolfram believes strongly in loyalty, personal fidelity, *triuwe*. He believes that his baptism requires him to have that kind of feudal loyalty to Christ and Christendom. On the other hand, family fidelity, *triuwe* in the realm of blood kinship, obliges him equally to be faithful to any member of his family, even if nonbaptized. Wolfram very carefully and deliberately creates a blood-versus-baptism dilemma for the protagonist when he is confronted by his pagan brother. The parallelism between his story and the situation of the crusader is obvious, but how is it to be resolved? Wolfram's solution, embodied in the Grail, calling on the nature of the Trinity, the waters of baptism, and human sight, is brilliant.

Second, the real nature of the Grail, in my opinion, is best identified in Wolfram's version of the legend. The Grail is indeed, as he said, a real, existing object, and it can be found. It is not unrelated to the serving dish and to the cup of the Last Supper, but it goes one crucial step further in piety, and is similar to the dish and the cup, in that it too is a container for the body and blood of Christ, and is related to the Passion events, although it is of stone. Moreover, let me dare to affirm that I believe that I have found Wolfram's Holy Grail stone, that is, both what he meant in general and the actual one that may have been his inspiration, and I will happily share that find with the patient reader in the course of the following investigation.

Finally, if Wolfram had a poetic soul brother in his age, it was surely not the crusade-preaching St. Bernard of Clairvaux but rather the Abbot Suger of Saint-Denis in Paris. It was this abbot who did more than any other person to give us the miraculously translucent walls of the stone building we call the Gothic cathedral. It was he who delighted in showing, like Wolfram, that light is sufficiently related to divinity that it can pass through stone. It was the Abbot Suger who designed the extended chapels with high vaults and arches around the sanctuary of Saint-Denis so that, as he wrote in his *De Consecratione*, "by virtue of them the whole church would shine with the wonderful and uninterrupted light of the most luminous windows, a [crown of light] pervading the interior beauty."[7] When he dedicated this foundational church of Gothic architecture, he even had the king and all the notaries present each place their own stones in the foundation walls, *propriis manibus*, with their own hands, thus identifying themselves with the light-transmitting stone walls of the building. Suger was delighted to report that some even brought their own gemstones and put them in place with their own hands while singing "Lapides Preciosi

---

7. Sumner McKnight Crosby, *The Royal Abbey of Saint-Denis from Its Beginning to the Death of Suger, 475–1151* (New Haven: Yale University Press, 1987), pp. 236–8. The dedication and consecration of the sanctuary and choir was in 1144.

The translucent walls of the thirteenth century Sainte-Chapelle in Paris. This church building carried the Abbot Suger's revolutionary, neo-platonic, light-transmitting style to a new apex. At the ceremony of the consecration of Suger's own new church of St. Denis in 1144, the king and ecclesiastical dignitaries placed gemstones in the walls while chanting "All Your walls are precious stones" (*Lapides preciosi omnes muri tui*). The Sainte-Chapelle was designed under royal patronage as a reliquary for holding the crown of thorns. *Centre des monuments nationaux, Paris. Photographer: Jean Feuillie.*

Omnes Muri Tui" (All Your Walls Are Precious Stones), identifying themselves in the language of the new church style as being the stones of a heavenly and translucent Jerusalem in the North.

News of this ceremony spread far and wide, and may have reached Wolfram in Franconia. He would have been delighted to read or hear in Suger's account of the consecration of Saint-Denis that he as abbot had covered the reliquaries of the saints "who shine like the sun at the side of the Lord" with the most precious materials, with coverings of gold and of gemstones, *iacintorum et smaragdinum,* "garnet hyacinths and emeralds."

In the pages of the following interpretation of *Parzival,* in many places I have translated many of Wolfram's lightly disguised French names and symbolic places into English according to my reading of the story. Translators generally have not done this. My purpose in translating is not to take away any of the mystery of *Parzival* nor of the Grail but to point to where it really lies. For Wolfram this is not in some imagined faraway land across the sea or even in not too faraway France—not in some fantasy land called Terre de Salvatsche, but in the "Land of Salvation," another mountaintop altogether, and hardly a long horse ride away if, as Wolfram would say, you drop the reins.

It is hard to imagine a work written in the first decade of the thirteenth century that would be so unique and diverse—spiritually at odds with Christian crusading, and so much in love with the divine spirit of gemstones. Wolfram was so profoundly in tune with the culture of his day that he was able to use its older and deeper values: loyal kinship, the Holy Trinity, the waters of baptism, to urge his own world, from the inside, to drop the reins, come down from the horse, as he had Parzival do, and to follow the Turtledove, Christendom's own prescribed path of love. In his vision, "Condwiramurs," "Love Leads," will show the way to arrive at a realization of the Christian brotherhood that extends to the Muslims and beyond and that ends at the Holy Grail stone—the stone of the Phoenix, the stone that brings mankind to the woman called "Repanse de Schoye," "Overflowing Happiness."

I

The Idea of the Holy Grail

If you look up the meaning of the word *Grail* in the dictionary, it is clear from what you will find that in the popular mind the concept of a sacred platter or cup based ultimately on Chrétien de Troyes's version (c. 1185), and perhaps even more on Robert de Boron's version (c. 1200) of the story, have indeed won the day: "Grail: [ME *graal*, fr. MF, bowl, grail, fr. ML *gradalis*] 1 *cap*: the cup or platter used according to medieval legend by Christ at the Last Supper and thereafter the object of knightly quests—called also *Holy Grail* 2: the object of an extended or difficult quest."[1] The *Encyclopedia Britannica* adds: "Robert de Boron's poem [*Joseph d' Arimathie*] recounted the Grail's early history, linking it with the cup used by Christ at the Last Supper and afterward by Joseph of Arimathea to catch the blood flowing from Christ's wounds as he hung upon the cross."[2]

The further confusion as to exactly how to envision the Grail is well described by Roger Sherman Loomis:

> Before proceeding . . . it seems desirable to define what Chrétien meant by the word *graal*. It is certain that it was not universally understood even in France, for some French miniaturists depicted it as a chalice. Others, misled by the poet's statement that the vessel contained the sacramental

---

1. *Webster's Seventh New Collegiate Dictionary* (1976).
2. *The New Encyclopedia Britannica*, 15th ed., vol. 5, Micropedia (1976), p. 409.

wafer, the Host, represented it as a ciborium, a covered goblet surmounted by a cross, the normal receptacle of the Corpus Christi.
Foreigners usually avoided the difficulty by taking over the word instead of translating it. Wolfram von Eschenbach, author of *Parzival*,
declared flatly that the Grail was a stone, much to the bewilderment
of scholars.[3]

It will be my purpose to explain Wolfram's declaration by unfolding the
nature and purpose of the stone Grail as it is found in his epic poem of *Parzival*,
and then, based on its role and characteristics in the epic, to identify, if possible,
the actual one. The problem of the origin and meaning of the word *grail* itself,
however, which does not appear in literature until Chrétien's *Conte du Graal*,
remains a challenge. Thus it is important to consider the sole definition given
by a contemporary of Chrétien, Robert, and Wolfram: Helinand of Froidmont,
Helinandus Frigidi Montis in the Latin form, a Cistercian monk in Beauvais
who lived from 1160 to around 1230. In his much-cited *Chronicon* he has the
following entry for the year 718 AD.

> At this time in Britain [possibly Brittany] a certain monk received an
> amazing vision from an angel. The vision was of Saint Joseph [of
> Arimathea], member of the council, who took down the body of
> Christ from the cross, and also of the serving dish [*de catino*] or plate
> [*de paropside*],[4] in which the Lord ate supper with his disciples. The
> same monk wrote down the story and it is called *De Gradale* (*The
> Serving Dish*) [*de gradale* literally: "Concerning the 'Gradual' or
> Grail"]. "Gradalis," in French, "gradale," is said to be a wide dish
> [*scutella*, diminutive of the Latin *scutum*, "shield," the Roman sol-
> dier's rectangular shield;[5] thus the dish was most likely rectangular
> in general shape] that is also somewhat deep. In it, precious foods
> with their sauces [the sauces explain the need for some depth to the
> dish] are customarily served to the well-to-do gradually [*gradatim*],
> one after the other, in different courses. In the popular vernacular it
> is called a "graalz." This is because it is so "agreeable" [*grata*] to the
> person eating from it. This could be because of the container itself,
> which is of pure silver or some other precious metal, or also be-
> cause of what it contains, i.e., the many courses of fine food.[6]

3. *The Grail: From Celtic Myth to Christian Symbol* (Princeton: Princeton University Press, 1991), p. 28.

4. From the Greek *paropsis*, which designated a plate for liturgical purposes.

5. The smaller Roman round shield was called by another term, *clipeus*.

6. Helinand of Froidmont (Helinandus Frigidi Montis), *Chronicon*, in *Patrologia Latina*, ed. Jacques-Paul
Migne (Paris: Migne, 1844–64; reprint, Turnhout, Belgium: Brepols, 1982), vol. 212, cols. 814–5 (under the year

This is a good contemporary approach to giving a definition and explanation of the word *grail*, and it appears from it that in Helinand's time many courses were served one after the other from the same richly appointed serving dish. Helinand offers two etymological reflections on the word *grail/graalz*. It could come from the Latin *gradalis,* because of the *gradual* serving of the courses, or it could come from the Latin *gratalis,* because of the *gratifying* nature of the dish and its contents. Between the *d* and the *t,* the voiced versus the unvoiced form of the same dental, there is hardly a great deal upon which to make a choice, and in any case, in the final form of the word, *graalz,* there is no longer a *d* or *t* present to help with determining the derivation. The first derivation would be more pleasing to Chrétien, the latter to Robert.

Helinand, however, has also suggested a possible source for the story, a source book written in Latin called *De Gradale,* which he has been unable to find. Perhaps, if there was such a book, it was the version of the tale referred to as the book given to Chrétien by Count Philip of Flanders to turn into French poetry. Perhaps also it is simply the introduction to Robert de Boron's prose *Estoire* taken a bit too literally.[7] Helinand then goes on to say that he cannot find this Latin *De Gradale* or any other Latin version of the story of the graalz.

> I have not been able to find this story written in Latin, but it can only be had in French from certain of the nobles, nor is it easy, as they say, to find the whole thing. So far I have not been able to get the story to read, even though I have been persistent in asking people for it. However, as soon as I do, I will translate the more probable and useful parts of it into a succinct Latin version.[8]

It sounds like Helinand had run into the fact that Chrétien had not finished, or that Robert de Boron's version was too long for him, on the basis of his apparent familiarity with its initial part attributing the story to a monk in Brittany who lived in the eighth century. Helinand seems also not to have been

---

entry beginning 718A). The text is as follows: "Hoc tempore in Britannia cuidam eremitae monstrata est mirabilis quaedam visio per angelum de sancto Joseph decurione, qui corpus Domini deposuit de cruce; et de catino illo sive paropside, in quo dominus coenavit cum discipulis suis; de quo ab eodem eremita descripta est historia, quae dicitur de gradale. Gradalis autem sive gradale Gallice dicitur scutella lata, et aliquantulum profunda; in qua pretiosae dapes cum suo jure divitibus solent apponi gradatim, unus morsellus post alium in diversis ordinibus; et dicitur vulgari nomine graalz, quia grata et acceptabilis est in ea comedenti: tum propter continens, quia forte argentea est, vel de alia pretiosa materia; tum propter contentum, id est ordinem multiplicem pretiosarum dapum."

7. *Sources of the Grail: An Anthology,* sel. and intro. John Mathews (Hudson, N.Y.: Lindisfarne, 1997), pp. 162–88.

8. Helinand of Froidmont (Helinandus Frigidi Montis), *Chronicon, P.L.* vol. 212, cols. 814–5.

enamored of what he expected would be the more imaginative and lengthy excursions of the text into the fantastic.

What, then, of Wolfram's notion that the Grail is a stone? Even though his *Parzival* was one of the most popular and spiritually challenging tales of medieval Germania—as Albrecht Classen notes, "this courtly romance might be one of the most intriguing literary works of its time in terms of intellectual and spiritual epistemology"[9]—still Wolfram's view on the nature of the Grail as a stone is nowadays treated by critics with mystified respect and then allowed, as if inconvenient, to disappear from discussion and gradually, as it were, slip from sight. This, while his *Parzival* paradoxically remains acknowledged as the greatest medieval telling of the story of the Grail. Roger Loomis summarizes this opinion:

> In short there breathes throughout the poem a spirit bold, realistic, generous, tender, and magnanimous. For most moderns who can either read the original German or can find a satisfactory translation ... *Parzival* is the most satisfying medieval treatment of the legend of the Grail.[10]

In the scholarly quest for the identity of the Holy Grail in Arthurian literature, Wolfram's version, namely, that it is a mysterious stone carried by Repanse de Schoye, the beautiful lady whose name in Wolfram's French signifies overflowing or spreading joy, is a stumbling block. Dutifully examined along with the other variants based on the dish or cup from Chrétien's version, and with great respect for the spirituality of Wolfram's *Parzival*, Wolfram's stone Grail is often allowed by scholars of Grail legend to disappear quietly into the waste forest of mystifying and unintelligible metaphor. Jesse Weston found that when she removed all accretions, the root of the Grail was older than Celtic and Christian conceptions and was to be found in vegetation ritual.[11] In contradistinction, Wolfram claims that his stone is both the root and branch of all the Grail's powers. Other scholars have noted as well that the Grail has parallels in the bloody dish, the *dysgl* [Welsh for "dish"] containing the head of Bran from Welsh mythology, as well as in the ciborium, the covered

9. Albrecht Classen, "Jewish-Christian Relations in the German Middle Ages," in *Amsterdamer Beiträge zur Älteren Germanistik* (Amsterdam: Editions Rodopi, 2003), 58:137.

10. *The Grail*, p. 222.

11. Jessie L. Weston, *From Ritual to Romance* (Princeton: Princeton University Press, [1920] 1993), esp. pp. 71–2, 162. Weston is aware of Burdoch's liturgical view but rejects the thesis of Byzantine ritual's influence on the Grail ceremony on the curious ground that the ritual "spear" used in cutting the bread is not a full-sized spear, and on the basis of her hypothesis that the earlier vegetation mysteries from Greece were what contributed to the mysterious nature of the Eucharistic rites of Constantinople.

vessel that contains the Body of Christ, Communion hosts, the Corpus Christi. Still others have pointed out the presence of the Orient in *Parzival*, from the elaborate processions that seem to echo the Eucharistic liturgy of Constantinople to the importance of oriental precious stones, such as the Stone of Humility, in the *Alexanderlied*, the poem of Alexander's journey to the farthest edge of the East to reach the Garden of Paradise.

Joachim Bumke put the question of the difference between the overall story of Perceval and the rest of the Arthurian corpus this way: "The story of Parzival is different from the other Arthurian tales principally in that Christian motifs play a great role in it. The theme of sin and repentance in both Chrétien and Wolfram stand[s] in a very close relationship to the Grail."[12] He summarizes the prevailing views of the Grail as being a magic-sacred container that supplies food and nourishment whose origin is debated but that bears certain Celtic, Christian, and oriental features, when it first appears in writing in French Arthurian literature near the end of the twelfth century.

The question for us thus becomes, in reference to Wolfram's concept of the Grail, what stone is there that could be associated with being a magic provider of food, a precious stone, and, above all, a stone that holds the blood and body of Christ?

It is possible that two of the lines written by Robert de Boron, not on the Grail but on the burial of Christ, might have influenced Wolfram in his change from cup to stone. In the verse version, around 1200, which is the earlier version, of his *Joseph d' Arimathie*, Robert has two lines concerning the Entombment of Christ that have given his editor, and myself, pause.[13] The Gospels of Mark and Matthew both mention that the corpse of Christ was placed in a tomb that "had been cut out of rock"—"quod [Joseph] exciderat in petra" (Mt 27:60), erat excisum de petra" (Mk 15:46). The Gospels both make mention of the act of cutting the cavity out of rock. This is not the case in Robert's verse. Jesus is described simply and starkly as being placed "in a stone," *en une pierre*, with no distractive comment. The second line is concerned with the stone that is used in the Gospels as a block to seal the entrance opening—in the Gospels, *saxum magnum* (Mt) and *lapidem* (Mk).

Robert in his poem first describes Joseph as having wrapped the body of Christ in the *syndoine*, the shroud that he had bought, and then: *Et en une pierre le mist* (and placed the body in a stone, 577). Then he adds *Et d'une pierre le*

---

12. Joachim Bumke, *Wolfram von Eschenbach*, 5th ed. (Stuttgart: Metzler, 1981), pp. 52–3.

13. This discussion is based on Richard O'Gorman's critical edition of the verse and prose versions: Robert de Boron, *Joseph d'Arimathie* (Toronto: Pontifical Institute of Medieval Studies, 1995), pp. 80, 357–8. The verse version is earlier, and I have remained with it for my analysis.

couvri, Que nous apelons tumbe ci (and covered him with a rock, which we call a "tomb" here, 579–80). The first line (577) is suggestive enough to have influenced Wolfram, and the second line (579) as well. *Pierre* in the second line has to mean the stone lid over the burial couch rather than the "rolling stone" at the entrance. This corresponds very well with crusader-era illustrations of the Resurrection, for example, the depiction of Nicholas of Verdun, in which the lid is shown tossed off in the background, usually canted at an angle.

This image of the Body of Christ resting "in a stone" also corresponds well with the practice of placing particles of the Host, the Body of Christ, on a cloth in a small recess in the altar table for "burial" during the liturgical consecration of an altar, as was done in the Middle Ages. One can only speculate over such things, but rather than thinking of Wolfram's nonuse of Robert's image of the Grail as chalice, it is more interesting to think of Wolfram's possible fascination with Robert's unusual verses—if he knew them—of Christ being "placed in a stone," *en une pierre*, and being "covered with a stone," *couvri d'une pierre*, as an initial poetic suggestion of the correspondence that could be found between the Holy Sepulcher, the altar, and the Grail. Wolfram's image of the stone Grail may also, of course, be entirely his own insight. In any case, his use of a stone containing the body of Christ evokes both the Holy Sepulcher in Jerusalem and the ceremony of the consecration of an altar in medieval times.

Another challenge regarding the nature and function of the Grail in the story is not to look backward too much for many and various possible sources that Wolfram might have used, because, as Sidney Johnson observed, "In doing so, we may be losing sight of the creative genius that is apparent in Wolfram's well-developed concept of the grail and how it fits into his monumental work as a whole." In other words, a pressing methodological concern is to see "how the grail is to be understood in the light of the entire work."[14] This is true especially if one maintains that the Grail stone is a gemstone related in some way to the Sepulcher and to the consecrated altar, and this is a task I will undertake.

Before examining how such an analogous concept of the Grail would fit into an overall interpretation of *Parzival*, I would like to comment on the work of two investigators who have suggested that the origin of the Grail idea lies in the burial cloth of Jesus, Noel Currer-Briggs and Daniel C. Scavone, as well as the work of three scholars who have dealt directly with the meaning of the stone Grail, A. D. Horgan, Sidney Johnson, and Bodo Mergell.

---

14. Sidney Johnson, "Doing His Own Thing: Wolfram's Grail," in *A Companion to Wolfram's Parzival*, ed. Will Hasty (Columbia, S.C.: Camden House, 1999), p. 88.

The entombment or burial of Christ in the box-like rectangular stone sepulcher. Joseph of Arimathea is at one end and Nicodemus at the other, the stone lid ready in the background, in what became standard iconography for this scene. This depiction is from the masterpiece of Nicholas of Verdun at Klosterneuburg in Austria, the *Verduner Altar* which was dedicated in 1181. The three distinctive "portholes" in the protective stone cladding allow the crusader pilgrim to kiss the actual burial stone of the tomb. The Holy Sepulcher is thus represented by Nicholas of Verdun as it appeared in his time. The palm tree stands as quiet witness to the place, the Holy Land, and to the "palmers," the pilgrims and crusaders for whom the site of the Holy Sepulcher was the goal of their journey. *Chorherrenstift Klosterneuburg. Photo: Prof. Walther K. Stoitzner, Vienna.*

Both Currer-Briggs and Scavone are impressed by the presence of Joseph of Arimathea in the Grail legends.[15] It is Joseph who is said to bring the Holy Grail to England, seen here as the cup of the Last Supper or as a vessel he held under the cross to catch the blood of the Savior. The fact that the Grail is connected to Joseph they see as suggested by his role in the Bible. It is he who bought the linen cloth, the shroud, in which to wrap the corpse of Jesus. It was he who had asked Pilate for permission to remove the body of Jesus from the cross late on Good Friday afternoon, and who then took down the body, wrapped it in a shroud, which must have absorbed much of the blood on the body, and then placed it in his own tomb that had recently been hewn out of rock. In Matthew's Gospel, the incident is described as follows.

> As evening approached, there came a rich man from Arimathea, named Joseph, who had himself become a disciple of Jesus. Going to Pilate he asked for Jesus' body, and Pilate ordered that it be given to him. Joseph took the body, wrapped it in a clean linen cloth and placed it in his own new tomb that he had cut out of the rock. He rolled a big stone in front of the entrance to the tomb and went away. (Mt 27:57–60)

Both authors feel the shroud cloth was the original container of the blood of Christ and is thus the basis for all later legends about the blood of Christ contained in a dish or cup held under the cross by Joseph, or the cup of the Last Supper. To this one could add that the legends of shed blood being collected under the cross, which could be attributed in any case to pious Jewish practice, are the expression in story form of the words Christ spoke at the Last Supper: "this is the cup of my blood which will be shed for you." The combination of "is" and "will be" in the sentence point to a present cup and a future event that will not come to pass until the next day. Thus a storyteller needs to weave a way to have the cup of Thursday's supper also be present on Friday afternoon so that it can contain the "blood which will be shed for you."

If the shroud is the absorbent container, at least on the Christian side of the Grail story, then I would suggest that through Joseph of Arimathea the connection has also been established to the stone tomb into which Joseph placed Jesus. We now have two elements that we find in Wolfram's Grail image: cloth and a sacred stone. A connection to the Mass is also not far away, in that during the Eucharist the sacramental Body of Christ is placed on a white cloth

15. See Currer-Briggs, *The Shroud and the Grail: A Modern Quest for the True Grail* (London: Weidenfeld and Nicholson, 1987), and Scavone, "Joseph of Arimathea, the Holy Grail, and the Shroud," available at www .shroud.com/scavone2.htm.

called the corporal (lit.: "body cloth," "shroud"), which is always placed on an altar, thus reproducing the situation Joseph of Arimathea created when he took down the body of Christ from the cross, wrapped it in a cloth, and placed it in the box-like stone container within his own tomb.

A. D. Horgan sees the Grail stone in *Parzival* as a metaphor for God and for Christ himself. He begins his comments by identifying the area of difficulty: "The fundamental difficulty about the Grail, as it is described to us by Wolfram von Eschenbach, is that whilst in certain particulars it strongly recalls the blessed Sacrament, in others this identification seems to be ruled out as a possibility. It is a stone."[16] Horgan points out many references in the Old Testament to God in which he is referred to metaphorically as Israel's rock, such as those in Deuteronomy 32: "The Rock, his work is perfect, and all his ways are just . . . [he] scoffed at the Rock of his salvation . . . you were unmindful of the Rock that bore you . . . indeed their rock is not like our Rock, our enemies are fools." In Psalm 18:2, "the Lord is my rock, my fortress," and in Isaiah 17:10, "you have forgotten the God of your salvation, and not remembered the Rock of your refuge." There is a ring of truth here, but there is also a ring of military defense being the function of God that seems not quite in accord with the lavish munificence of the Grail stone in *Parzival*.

When Horgan refers to the New Testament, I think he is much closer to the mark, especially when he cites 1 Corinthians 10:1–13, where St. Paul alludes to the rock in the desert from which water came when Moses struck it with his rod: "all ate the same spiritual food and all drank the same spiritual drink from the spiritual rock that followed them as they went, and that rock was Christ."[17] This is indeed similar to the flow of water from the font in book 16, the final chapter of *Parzival*. My concern here is that such a view reduces the Grail to a metaphor referring to Christ, whereas in the poetry of Wolfram he says clearly that the Grail is an object, and though a symbolic object also more than a symbolic object, since it actually has the power to bring about what it signifies: baptismal water, the resurrection of the Phoenix, feeding the multitudes with the food that satisfies each and all. What we must seek here, then, in my opinion, is a rock, a stone object that is related to Christ himself and to Christ's liturgical and sacramental presence in the Christian community. Sidney Johnson comments on Horgan's thesis:

[Horgan's] argument appeals because it allows us to view Wolfram's grail as a stone on a biblical basis without resorting to the Joseph of

16. A. D. Horgan, "The Grail in Wolfram's *Parzival*," *Mediaeval Studies* 36 (1974): 354.
17. Horgan, "The Grail in Wolfram's *Parzival*," pp. 356, 360, 365.

Arimathea-Longinus legend which Wolfram undoubtedly knew, but did not follow in his grail conception.[18] It also does not rely on Irish-Welsh folklore about which we know only second or third hand, the original being something we must attempt to recreate. It eliminates the non-Christian, Arabic and Iranian sources, which may have been based on a stone, and concomitantly reveals Wolfram's Kyot as a delightfully enjoyable spoof by default. We can say that, in a sense, Wolfram has taken the basic idea of a stone or rock quite literally, has given it concrete form, which is imbued with Christian charac-teristics, and has completed Chrétien's romance in a coherent, meaningful, and imaginative way.[19]

Actually, there may be a spoof here, and of course it is Kyot-related, since the great work of Guiot of Provins, satirical though it may be, is *La Bible*. Is Wolfram here hinting at the Bible as his real source?

Johnson is quite right to say that Wolfram has given the rock "concrete form," but he seems to wish also to leave it here as a biblical metaphor. There is a problem with this, though, since Parzival genuflects three times in the direction of the Grail when he finally realizes what it is and where he is, before he asks the saving question. A triple genuflection is something that is clearly and solely reserved for the blessed Sacrament, and it would be idolatrous for a stone, real or metaphoric, and thus we are back at Horgan's initial observation that in certain particulars, the Grail strongly resembles the blessed Sacrament; in others, it does not. Stone and Communion Host he finds irreconcilably different, except as metaphor.

In his insightful essay, Johnson attempts to deal with the stone of humility found in the *Alexanderlied* and its possible relationship to the stone Grail of *Parzival*. I can only agree with him as he comments that Friedrich Ranke's interpretation of the Grail stone's proper name, *lapis exilis*, "thin stone," as an echo from the well-named *Iter ad Paradisum* (Journey to Paradise), seems to fit well, but not in respect to its signification. Wolfram's Grail stone signifies far more than human transitoriness, and it appeals to fidelity, *triuwe*, as much as to humility. Johnson comments that Wolfram's Grail underlines the "sac-

18. I cannot concur, however, with this remark, since Wolfram uses the bleeding spear/lance in the Grail procession, and it is accompanied by great lamentation. Wolfram's audience, in view of the famous "recovery" of the lance head in the First Crusade, could scarcely have thought of anything else but the Longinus legend at that point in the story. Wolfram does use the lance, if not the legendary name of the Roman soldier who thrust it, Longinus ("long lance"). The lance is the lance from the Crucifixion.

19. Johnson, "Doing His Own Thing," p. 91.

erdotal mission" of royalty and is "the center of a divinely ordained community which emphasizes spirituality in a world that otherwise is absorbed with personal ambition."[20] This is indeed the case, but the statement fails to mention the contemporary medieval absorption of the whole Western world with ethnic and religious warfare, in particular with warfare over the possession of a sacred and life-giving stone, the Holy Sepulcher in Jerusalem.

May I push the discussion one step further and say that I believe both Horgan and Johnson have brought research on Wolfram's concept of the Grail to the point where we can now say that it is a rock, a rock directly related to Christ, and that what remains to be seen is just what rock fulfills the multiple functions of the Grail in Wolfram's poem in a meaningful and satisfying way. Just what was the author's poetic intent in changing the concept of the Grail from that of serving dish or sacred cup to that of a sacred stone? If we examine the Grail stone as described in *Parzival*, we find that it is both real and metaphorical, that it bears some of the characteristics of the blessed Sacrament, some of the Holy Sepulcher in Jerusalem, and some of the altar stone.

This last suggestion, that Wolfram's Grail might be an altar stone, was made by Bodo Mergell in 1952, but seems not to have found acceptance or to have been taken up seriously. Some of the reasons for this may lie in his adjoined remarks on the name of the stone, *lapsit exillis*, in which he comments that all the echoes in the name are deliberate, and thus "thin stone," "it fell to the exiles," and so on should be conjoined to form a sort of deliberate multiplicity of intended meanings, thus "the thin stone," "the stone of humility," "the stone which fell from the stars," "the stone which fell to the exiles."[21] These multiple meanings, all of which have been proposed in the past, Mergell joins and illustrates in an imaginative cruciform diagram. This imaginative and demandingly fanciful reading of the two Latin words in the text that name the stone may have distracted readers from his thesis that Wolfram's Grail stone is an altar stone.

Mergell notes how Wolfram's notion sharply deviates from that of Chrétien and of Robert de Boron:

> Wolfram's concept of the Grail as a miraculous *pure* stone is a considerable deviation from the traditional notion of the Grail as the vessel from the Last Supper and the vessel containing the blood as

---

20. Johnson, "Doing His Own Thing," p. 93.

21. Mergell seems to be confusing the many manuscript variants of both Latin words with diversity of authorial intent. Different copyists' variants are important but should not be seen as expressing a diversity of meaning deliberately intended by the author.

in Robert de Boron, and from Chrétien's notion of the Grail as the
Host carrier and container.[22]

He goes on to point out that whether Wolfram's point of departure for his
concept of the Grail comes more from Old Testament or New Testament stone
symbolism, what is of decisive importance is that the foundation of Wolfram's
Grail idea does not come from theological speculation *but* from [his] living
knowledge of the fullness of meaning in the liturgical symbolism of the
church's altar, the *mensa Domini* [table of the Lord] and of the consecrated altar
stone placed in it. He goes on to add that these small altar stones were called
lapides itinerarii [stones for travel]. He then points to the presence of the bare
altar stone on Good Friday in book 9, and the miraculous distribution of bread
from the Grail stone—additions to the story made by Wolfram.[23] While I wholly
agree with Mergell's insight on the Grail, I feel that he may not have gotten a
satisfactory hearing because of his failure to integrate this notion adequately
with the overall elements of the plot and with the gemstone symbolism in the
tale. The gemstones can appear to go against the notion of a stone related to
the celebration of the Eucharist, and their distinguished and context-providing
role in *Parzival* needs to be explained; nor does Mergell attempt to divine the
author's intent in using the stone.

A further error on Mergell's part seems to be that he is unaware of the
vast numbers of medieval portable altars in existence then and still in existence
in Germany, France, and the Low Countries.[24] They give evidence to this day
of the extreme popularity and use of portable altars both of the flat and of the
box or reliquary type (the latter became extremely popular in the time of the
Crusades), which could have then given him a reason for Wolfram's inclusion
of the altar stone: its ubiquity and its relationship to the crusaders' goal, the
Holy Sepulcher. Mergell insists and argues that his candidate for Wolfram's
Grail, the small palm-sized altar stone, just managed to survive into the twelfth
century. Though this may be true for the small palm-sized model, the idea that
the portable altar itself just barely survived into Wolfram's time is very much
mistaken. Just the opposite is the case—it flourished.

Mergell was mistaken to remain with the very small model. Actually, there
was an enormous output of exquisitely made, approximately book-sized, port-

22. "Nun weicht Wolframs Auffassung vom Gral als einem wundersamen *reinen* Stein erheblich ab von
den überkommenen Gralvorstellungen des Abendmahls- und Blutgefäßes bei Robert von Boron, des Hostien-
trägers und -behälters bei Chrestien von Troyes." Bodo Mergell, *Der Gral in Wolframs Parzival: Entstehung und
Ausbildung der Gralsage im Hochmittelalter* (Halle: Max Niemeyer Verlag, 1952), p. 1.

23. Mergell, *Der Gral in Wolframs Parzival*, pp. 43–5.

24. Numerous and strikingly beautiful examples can be found very well reproduced in Peter Lasko, *Ars
Sacra 800–1200*, 2nd ed. (New Haven: Yale Univesity Press, 1994).

able altars designed as reliquaries with a small rectangular chamber covered by a flat stone that was firmly fixed to the top surface. The output of such consecrated portable altars continued throughout the eleventh, twelfth, thirteenth, and fourteenth centuries and was, I believe, directly connected to the popularity of pilgrimage and of military pilgrimage: the crusade. There is hardly a cathedral or civil museum in Germany that does not have one or several examples of them adorned with enamel, gold, and jewels on display in their treasuries. Though wrong, perhaps, about the type, and inadequate in interpretation of the function of the Grail in the narrative, Mergell's suggestion was, in my opinion, fundamentally correct.

A summary review of the numerous characteristics Wolfram gives to his Grail stone in *Parzival* is called for at this point.

1. It is a stone and an object *der stein ist ouch genant der grâl* (469, 28); *daz was ein dinc, daz hiez der grâl* (235, 23); the Grail should not be seen as an abstract ideal in Wolfram.

2. It is portable but is carried only, with its permission, by a beautiful lady with the significant name Repanse de Schoy ("Overflowing Happiness"), the radiant queen without falsehood; she holds it on an oriental green silken cloth, *ûf einem grüenen achmardî* (235, 20–1).

3. It is the bliss of Paradise, both the source and perfection of that bliss; and it is earthly happiness in overflow that she is carrying, "truoc si den wunsch von pardîs, / bêde wurzeln unde rîs. Daz was ein dinc, daz hiez der Grâl, / erden wunsches überwal" (235, 21–4).

4. When carried in procession, it is preceded by candles and balsam-incense: *vorem grâle kômen lieht—die dâ truogen balsemvaz* (236, 1–11).

5. It is placed solemnly before the host, Anfortas, upon a thinly cut, lightweight, blood-red stone tabletop; the tabletop was cut so thin that sunlight shone through it. "Sine trüegen einen tiuren stein, / dâ tages de sunne lieht durch schein . . . ez was ein grânât jâchant (a blood-red stone), / beide lanc unde breit. / durch die lîhte in dünne sneit / swer in zeime tische maz" (233, 17–23). The Grail is thus associated with two colors: the green of silken cloth on which it is borne, and the red of the table on which it is placed. It is conjoined with translucent stone. In accord with the liturgical usage of placing reliquaries containing the Host and relics of the saints on a nonconsecrated tabletop in order to consecrate it for the celebration of Mass or one of the sacraments, the Grail is placed on the translucent portable stone table.

From the thirteenth century "Crusaders Bible" of the Pierpont Morgan Library. David dances before the Ark of the Covenant as his wife scolds him from the window above. The Ark as it is borne into Jerusalem is imagined by the medieval illustrator to be something familiar to his world: a portable altar or reliquary. It is thus seen, lower left panel, placed on the altar table. *Photograph: The Pierpont Morgan Library, New York. MS M.638, f.39v.*

6. The stone Grail is called *lapsit exillîs* (or possibly *lapis exilis*, or *iaspis*, or *lapsit exillis*, or even *exillix* and *exilix*, according to the manuscripts). Wolfram's Latin name for the Grail was not immediately intelligible to the copyists (as sometimes with his French names) and he may have used this device to suggest the mystery of something both concrete and transcendent and therefore not quite intelligible (469, 7–8).

7. The Grail is the stone of the Phoenix, the fabled stone by whose power the Phoenix of classical mythology rises in rebirth from its ashes "von des steines kraft der fênîs verbrinnet, daz er zaschen wirt: / diu asche im aber leben birt" (469, 8–10). The stone, therefore, is the place where the dead body is placed, the place of death and resurrection, and the stone contains the power to turn death into life. The living death of Anfortas is also described in terms of classical mythology: he is suffering under the power of Saturn, Mars, and Jupiter. The description of the Resurrection in Greek terms should be a clue to the reader that the ceremony being described in the Grail feast might not be a standard description (of the Eucharistic liturgy) in biblical images, but rather a symbolic description done in alternate heroic images, based partly on chivalric and courtly imagery, partly on Eastern and Western Christian imagery.

8. A white dove shining with brilliant light comes down every Good Friday with a Communion Host and places it on the Grail stone to renew its powers. "Ez ist hiute der karfrîtac, / daz man für wâr dâ warten mac, / ein tûb von himel swinget: / ûf den stein diu bringet / ein kleine wîze oblat. Ûf dem steine si die lât: diu tûbe ist durchliuhtec blanc . . . immer alle karfrîtage / bringet se ûf den" (470, 1–10). The resurrective powers of the phoenix stone come from a Communion Host that comes from Heaven brought by the Dove and placed the bare stone on Good Friday. From the Dove the Grail receives all of its powers to bestow a largesse like that of Paradise. The coat of arms of the knights of the Grail, the *templeisen*, is the turtledove. The coming of the heavenly Dove brings the Grail into the realm of the Eucharist and suggests the Epiclesis of the Mass. In the liturgy of Good Friday, the altar is indeed bare. Altering the emblem of the Grail knights from dove to turtledove adds the connotation of love.

9. Only the baptized can see the Grail. Feirefiz: "ich ensehe niht wan ein achmardî" (810, 7–13). Parzival's half-brother, Feirefiz, cannot see the Grail until he is baptized. This suggests that the eyes of faith

From the "Crusaders Bible" of the Pierpont Morgan Library. King David prays before the Ark. The illustrator depicts the Ark as what would have been a familiar sight to thirteenth century crusaders: a portable altar stone or reliquary placed on an altar table to consecrate it for Mass. *Photograph: The Pierpont Morgan Library, New York. MS M.638, f.40.*

are required to see the presence of the Dove, which is *durchliuhtec* (his radiance shines through things), and the Communion Host, as well as the Grail itself. Otherwise one sees, as Feirefiz does, only the exterior covering, the "green *achmardi*" of the stone.[25]

10. The neutral angels were sent to it when the fighting began between Lucifer and the Trinity *di newederhalp gestuonden, / dô strîten beguon-*

---

25. This is, of course, very close to the nearly contemporaneous Thomistic theological explanation of the real presence of Christ in the Eucharist as being a change in the substance of the bread and wine, but not the accidents—transubstantiation. The substance is changed, but cannot be seen, while the perceivable accidents of the bread and wine, taste, color, weight, etc., remain. Feirefiz's situation seems almost a story-type exemplification of the theory of transubstantiation, a neologism of the twelfth and thirteenth centuries. For discussion see Miri Rubin, *Corpus Christi: The Eucharist in Late Medieval Culture* (Cambridge: Cambridge University Press, 1991), pp. 12–35.

den Lucifer unt Trinitas (471, 15–7). Like Parzival, these angels are a mythic exemplification of those who do not commit themselves to feeling any concern to speak up—for God (or for Lucifer). Though the possible salvation of these angels is later retracted, Wolfram's pedagogic use of their lack of commitment and lack of overflow of feeling is not. They are a cautionary tale for the early Parzival. This would imply that one of the mythic purposes of the Grail, and the suffering around it, is to arouse feelings of compassion and loyalty among the indifferent. The faith of the neutral angels, a faith that could indeed "see" the conflict of the Trinity with Lucifer but was without sufficient ardor or loyalty to move them to take part, is a warning to Parzival and to Christianity-on-crusade that faith without love and concern is reprehensible.

11. The Grail is the source of the water that overflows into the baptismal font, and also provides the priest. "Der toufnapf wart geneiget / ein wênec geinme grâl. / vol wazzers an dem mâle / wart er, ze warm noch ze kalt. / dâ stuont ein grâwer priester alt" (817, 4–7). The baptismal font is a ruby, red as the table stone in the Grail procession, on a green jasper base—the two gem colors associated with the Grail; water flowing from the Grail into the ruby font would suddenly appear blood-red (816, 20–1). Many authors have noted the allusion to the blood and water that flowed from the wound of the lance in the side of the crucified Christ. From early times, the flow of blood and water was seen as the mystical origin of the sacraments of the Eucharist and of baptism.

12. The country in which the Grail can be found is Terre de Salvaesche, the Land of Salvation.[26] The Grail provides the sustenance, food and drink, for all the people living on Mount Salvation, Munsalvaesche, in the Land of Salvation, Terre de Salvaesche.

13. The Grail is wide enough to have writing on it, and the writing gives the names of those who are called to be keepers of the Grail. This is a characteristic of many of the reliquary-style, or box-style, altar stones. The names of apostles, prophets, saints, and kings are engraved in enamel on the portable altars' sides and tops.

---

26. Herbert Kolb believes that not only Wolfram understood Munsalvaesche as *mons salvationis* (Mount Salvation), citing Wolfram's parallels in the *Jüngerer Titurel* as *der behalten berc* ("the saved mountain" or "the mountain of the saved") but that even Chrétien may have intended such a meaning, deriving *munt salvage* from *salvaige* ("rescue"), rather than from *sauvage, silvaticum* ("wooded," "wild"). For his discussion, see Kolb, *Munsalvaesche: Studien zum Kyotproblem* (Munich: Eidos Verlag, 1963), pp. 129–36.

14. The Grail is defended militarily by an order of knights whose insignia is, paradoxically, the turtledove.
15. The Grail has the power to keep the sinful and wounded alive (Anfortas) but does not keep them beautiful.
16. The Grail can be found in the stars by the nonbaptized (Flegetânîs), and Christian and non-Christian can be called to its banquet (Parzival and Feirefiz) in the Land of Salvation.

It can be seen from this brief consideration of the characteristics Wolfram assigns to the Grail that it has the characteristics of not one but three entities considered as united in a spiritual whole. (1) Many characteristics fit the blessed Sacrament of the altar: the Communion Host descending every year from above on Good Friday by the power of the Spirit, the Dove; it can only be seen by the baptized—others see just the cloth beneath it; the balsam incense is carried in procession before it. (2) Other characteristics fit more the Holy Sepulcher in Jerusalem: that Christian and Muslim fight in its vicinity, and especially that there is an order of military knights to defend it, the Knights Templar, the *templeisen*—and this would not be true of the blessed Sacrament in general and throughout the world. Moreover, it is the altar stone whereon the Phoenix rose or rises from its ashes. (3) Many characteristics fit with identifying the Grail simply as a metaphor for Christ: the Grail is the rock cleft for the pouring of water, it sustains the sinner in life, it provides for the miraculous feeding of the multitudes in the Land of Salvation.

What all three have in common, however, is that, whether physical or metaphorical, liturgical or mythological, miraculous or poetic, or a mixture of these (such as Wolfram's description of the Grail as a portable object, but one so heavy that it can only be carried by Repanse de Schoye, "Overflowing Happiness," or his simultaneous description of the Grail as both "a thing" and the "complete bliss of Paradise"), all are depicted by Wolfram as a rock. The only rock I can think of that can fulfill all these requirements, including that of being the Holy Sepulcher in a sense both metaphoric and yet real, is the altar stone. The creation and blessing of a portable altar stone, or any altar, required, and requires, the excavation of a small rectangular cavity in the top surface into which relics are placed. As mentioned, this chamber is then sealed with a small rectangular stone fitted over the opening. Imagine my surprise when I learned that the word in liturgical Latin for this little chamber, sealed with its thin slab of stone, was then, and is still, *sepulchrum*, the Sepulcher.

> By the seventh-eighth century the dismemberment of the bodies of the saints led to the custom of inserting such relics in the top of the altar slab in a cavity or opening known as the *sepulchrum* or sepul-

cher. In this were entombed the bones of the saints, together with three grains of incense representing the spices connected with the rites of burial [especially the anointing of Christ's body before his burial] and three fragments of a consecrated host.[27]

It seems that to consecrate an altar for the Mass, it was felt necessary not only to "bury" the relics of saints in a small cavity in the altar, as is done to this day, but also and foremost, to "bury" the Body of Christ in the stone cavity, which then indeed became a poetic, sacramental union with the Holy Sepulcher. Thus Horgan's fear that "stone" and "Sacrament" are an irreconcilable, either-or choice, in the case of the Grail, can be eliminated. Placing the Body of Christ, a consecrated Host, inside a small stone box may seem a curious practice, but St. Thomas Aquinas later in the thirteenth century defended it: "When a spiritual entity exists fully and completely in something, it contains that thing and is not contained by it."[28] Since the celebration of the Eucharist is a celebration of the death and Resurrection of Christ from the Sepulcher, priests would have felt the re-creation of such a tomb would have been an extremely appropriate way to consecrate the altar table. The Council of Chelsea declared as early as 816 AD that if suitable relics were not available to place in the altar cavity, then the Sacrament of the Eucharist was sufficient. This was repeated in 1433 AD by the English canonist Lynwood: *Ubi tamen non habentes reliquas, solent aliqui apponere Corpus Christi* (Where they do not have relics, some customarily just place the Body of Christ there).[29]

The obligation of having a standard consecrated altar for Mass was something of a problem for crusaders and other travelers. To carry a large, extremely heavy consecrated altar was out of the question, especially on shipboard, so priests as early as the time of St. Cuthbert had recourse to bringing a small consecrated *super-altare* (lit. "on top of the altar"), which was a small stone or

---

27. Cyril E. Pocknee, *The Christian Altar* (London: Mowbray, 1963), p. 39. See also Joseph Braun, *Der christliche Altar in seiner geschichtlichen Entwicklung* (Munich: Guenther Koch, 1924), 1:656 ff., and M. Andrieu, *Ordines Romani du haut Moyen-Âge* (Louvain: Spicilegium sacrum lovaniense, 1931), 4:389, 400. Modern sentiments about interring the Communion Host in the altar stone may be somewhat ambivalent about the appropriateness of the action, but in the Middle Ages the poetic equivalency of the altar stone to the Easter tomb attracted positive emotions. The Host was considered something that had the power to effect actions, including, above all, consecratory ones, and was not perceived of as being "inconvenienced" by the situation in a stone. We might compare it to placing the Host in a pyx or a monstrance in more recent times. By the beginning of the fourteenth century, however, some voices were heard, such as that of John Andrea (died 1348), opposing the practice. See Rubin, *Corpus Christi*, pp. 36–7.

28. *Summa Theologiae*, On Sacraments, 3a pars, quest. 62, art. 3 ad 3. He adds that in any case, the divine grace that is in a sacrament is in it as something flowing, *esse fluens*, in the sense of passing through it. This is curiously similar to Wolfram's concept of gemstone as a stone that does not contain light, except for the carbuncle, but silently permits light's passage through it.

29. Pocknee, *The Christian Altar* p. 40.

wooden rectangle containing relics of the saints and particles of the Host, the Body of Christ, which could be used as a substitute for a large consecrated altar. It was usually an insert, requiring a cavity to be cut into an unconsecrated table.[30] It is clear that this might not be convenient if the table to be thereby consecrated was of stone or of heavy wood. And so an alternate practice seems to have existed of pacing the small stone rectangle on top of the table, with the chalice and paten at least partially upon it for the celebration of Mass on a journey.

The latter method must have been awkward, not to say unstable, and soon the preferred method seems to have been to use a small reliquary chest, or *kefse*, which would have a rectangular cavity already cut into its own top, thereby eliminating the need to cut into a table.[31] Into this cavity in the reliquary the bishop could easily place the three particles of a consecrated host, putting them with three grains of incense into the "sepulcher" and then placing a small altar stone above it to seal the "tomb." When this reliquary with its small consecrated altar stone was placed on an unconsecrated table, the table was then considered consecrated and appropriate for the chalice and paten of the Mass. This is the depiction that can be seen in *Parzival*.

Many medieval bishops were buried with such portable altars with them, for the journey, and with a very small chalice and paten in their hands. These small chalices and patens were designed to be used directly on the altar stone atop the reliquary box when there was no table at all present. Such reliquary-style altars were small, lightweight, entirely self-contained, held the Body of Christ, and were consecrated and very portable altars. In Latin, such reliquaries with an altar stone, and all portable altars, were most often referred to simply as *lapides*, "stones," since it was the stone alone that was of liturgical interest. It is these portable altars, *Tragaltärchen*, or *lapides itinerarii*, that are still to be found in every museum in Germany, and are such brilliant works of art in gold and gems that it is hard to describe them adequately.

Often enough they were made of oak and covered with gold and enamel work, with the small rectangular altar stone covering the sepulcher worked into the top, with precious and semiprecious stones adorning them to make them

---

30. See Braun, *Der christliche Altar in seiner geschichtlichen Entwicklung*, 1:444–517, and Pocknee, *The Christian Altar*, p. 43.

31. The term *kefse* comes from the Latin *capsa* (we are more familiar with its diminutive in the English *capsule*), which simply means a box or container. Braun gives *kefse* credit for being the oldest word used in German for "reliquary." See his *Die Reliquiare des christlichen Kultes und ihre Entwicklung* (Freiburg im Breisgau: Herder, 1940), p. 40. He gives other terms then occasionally in use for such reliquaries as: *sarcophagus, sepulchrum, tumba, feretrum, capsa, capsella,* and *capsula*. After approximately 1480, the German *Kefse, Kapse* comes to mean more a pyx.

a worthy container for the Body of Christ and a worthy place for the offering of the sacrifice of the death and Resurrection of Christ. Stones mentioned in the Bible were especially favored;[32] paradisial green and red stones (serpentine and porphyry) were used most often for the altar stone itself. Jasper and other stones were worked into the sides, since thereby there were then references to heaven glistening in the very stonework of the portable altar: "And in the spirit he carried me away to a great high mountain and showed me the holy city of Jerusalem coming down out of heaven from God. It had the glory of God and a radiance like a very rare jewel, like jasper, clear as crystal" (Rev 21:10–11).

The effect of the Crusades on the liturgy was becoming very apparent at the time of Wolfram's decision to make the Grail a stone in his version of the legend. Altars in Christian churches up to this time had often been of wood, based on the poetic reasoning that Christ had made his sacrifice on the cross, and the wooden cross was the altar upon which he died and said, "Into Your hands I commend my spirit." Under the influence of the returning crusaders, however, who had prayed at the Holy Sepulcher in Jerusalem, and had fought to free it from the Saracens, arguments arose over the possibly greater appropriateness of using stone rather than wood as the material for the altar. When Christ had offered Himself, his body was placed in a sepulcher, one could argue, and therefore the "altar" upon which the Victim's body had been laid by Joseph of Arimathea and Nicodemus had been of stone. All over Europe and especially in Germany, representations of the Deposition from the cross and of the placing of the Body of Christ in the tomb were being painted, sculpted, and even built. One of the finest is still in Eichstätt, where Wolfram may well have visited it. Reproductions in stone of the Holy Sepulcher were used in the liturgy, especially in England and in Germany, during Holy Week.

No less a worthy than Thomas Aquinas was asked to give an opinion as to what material he thought more appropriate for the altar: the traditional wood or the new stone. Writing in about 1265, some fifty-five or so years after *Parzival*, and, who knows, perhaps under its influence, he joins the majority of his contemporaries and opts for stone:

Quod quidem competit significationi hujus sacramenti, tum quia altare significat Christum; dicitur autem I Corinth., X,4; Petra autem erat Christus; tum etiam quia corpus Christi in sepulchro lapideo fuit reconditum. Competit etiam quoad usum sacramenti.

32. See Daniel Rock, *The Church of Our Fathers: As Seen in St. Osmund's Rite for the Cathedral of Salisbury*, London: Hodges, 1903–4), 1:201–2.

Now, with regard to what is appropriate for the symbolism of this sacrament: both because the altar signifies Christ, as it says in 1 Corinthians, 10:4, "The stone was Christ," and also because the body of Christ was put to rest in a stone sepulcher, therefore stone is also what is appropriate for use with this sacrament.[33]

With this, we now turn to a consideration of the world of stone, a world where gems and precious stones had delighted the eye and had enjoyed unquestioned magical powers and spiritual meaning for far more than a thousand years. At the dawn of the thirteenth century, Wolfram von Eschenbach was so fascinated by them, as were his contemporaries, that he let them shine in every part of his story, and then identified one of them as the most powerful gemstone of all: the true Grail.

---

33. *Summa Theologiae*, 3a pars, quest. 83, art. 3. See also Nicholas Bliley, *Altars According to the Code of Canon Law* (Washington, D.C.: Catholic University of America, 1927), p. 23.

2

The World of Precious Stones

The importance of the gemstone is to be found everywhere in Wolfram. He not only identifies the Grail as a precious stone but also uses stones to mark the inner structure of his work by identifying its two foci: first, the progress of his hero toward feeling the compassion necessary for 'owning' the Grail, and second, the suffering of the community on Mount Salvation as they faithfully await the healing of Anfortas. Wolfram has not only supplied two new chapters/books to be the ending of the tale that Chrétien did not finish but also added two new books to be the beginning of the story whose function it is to give Parzival a pagan brother and thereby to raise the thematic question of the waters of baptism in the context of the Grail stone. The two books at the beginning stand in parallel to the two that Wolfram has placed at the end. These four books form a distinctive framework, marked by the roles of precious stones, that guides the reader to a new interpretation of the traditional Grail material received from Chrétien. Wolfram's creation is a masterful new reading of the Grail legend based on water and stone, baptism and Passion, indifference and love. And it is filled with the glow of gems.

The precious stones first appear in the new beginning of the epic at the grave of Gahmuret, Parzival's father, at the end of book 2, the baptismal font having been pointedly absent at the end of book 1. The precious stones are then to be found at the critical times of Parzival's first sight of the Grail, book 5, and at the time of his repentance in the hermit's cave, book 9. Finally, the gems mark both books of the ending: in the book 15, the gems are associated with the valor of Feirefiz and Parzival, and are wasted in fighting; in book 16, the world of gems with all their medicinal potency are not able to cure Anfortas of his illness, but they set the stage for the arrival of Parzival. Parzival comes with the cure; having chosen to be accompanied by his chivalrous pagan brother and having become a person at home with the spontaneous overflow of human feelings, he arrives at the Grail stone itself.

Whereas Chrétien uses gemstones to denote a magical and almost fabulous sense of decorative beauty and wealth, surreal to the point of fairy tale—think of the feast in which each guest's drinking cup consists of a single hollowed-out ruby—in Wolfram the gemstones not only serve this fantastic function but also and primarily are present as mysteriously translucent stones whose serene paradisial beauty and prelapsarian powers of radiation are still intact. They evoke Eden. Moreover, though they are matter in its hard and dense form, in their ability to permit the soundless passage of light through their material density, they are both astounding things in themselves and metaphors for the beautiful potential of being a creature of God. They enjoy a status not quite as high as a sacrament, since they were not instituted by Christ during his lifetime on earth, but not quite as low as a sacramental, such as a medal, a cross, or rosary beads, since they come from the world of the Creator before the Fall, and thus for their effectiveness they require neither human fashioning nor priestly blessing. They enjoy a status almost as a natural sacrament, a gift instituted by the Creator "in the beginning" to do good, capable of bringing about what their color signifies to the poetic mind.

The very special nature of gems is something that has withstood the passage of time. Though today far fewer might still hold to the effectiveness of gemstones as a healing remedy, none would doubt the fascination aroused by their unique beauty and value. In the thirteenth century, the belief in their effectiveness was a point accepted by scholars and priests, abbesses and monks, lay men and women of all classes, learned and unlearned alike. Medieval Christianity had the testimony not only of pagan antiquity but also of enthusiastic and competent Christian contemporaries, such as Bishop Marbode and Abbess Hildegard of Bingen—teste David cum Sybilla—to support its belief in the powers of gems. The two wrote extensively on the specific "virtues" of each type of gem, and when an occasional unimaginative rationalist voice had the temerity to object, there was trouble.

Peter Abelard was one of those voices. When he suggested that the belief in the medical effectiveness of gemstones for healing was the product of a deluded mind under the probable influence of diabolic suggestion, it prompted a council of the church to issue a summary condemnation, a condemnation that threw in for good measure a defense of the medical use and effectiveness of herbs. From the Council of Sens in France, in 1140 AD: "Errores Petri Abelard: 16. Quod diabolus immittat suggestiones per appositionem lapidum vel herbarum." (The Errors of Peter Abelard: No. 16: That the devil puts suggestions in the mind when stones or herbs are used [in medical practice].[1] Why would the medieval church so unequivocally embrace and defend what appears to be merely the secular natural science and traditional folk medicine of its day? The answer is that the premier theologian of late antiquity and the theologian most influential in the Middle Ages, St. Augustine of Hippo (354–430 AD), had located gems in the theological world as a very exceptional gift of God, as resident in the overflow of the rivers of Eden, pure and untainted holdovers from the Garden of Paradise. Augustine had thereby, in addition to his own very considerable authority, given a powerful and memorable scriptural and theological basis for honoring the powers of gemstones and herbs: they are from Paradise.

Augustine's view is to be found in his commentary on the book of Genesis. In it he first makes a curious and seemingly almost unconscious parallel between the composition of human beings and that of gemstones.[2] In attacking the Manichees, Augustine takes advantage of the statement of Scripture that God, despite the possibility open to him of using any more celestial material, made human beings from the clay of the earth, *de limo terrae*.[3] Augustine finds the material appropriate in that clay is not simple dust but rather a mixture of water and earth, *limus enim aquae ac terrae commixtio est*. He then makes the comparison between the nature of human beings and clay. In commenting on the text *finxit deus hominem de limo terrae* (God made man from the clay of the earth), Augustine first proposes that clay is the mixture of water and earth. The

---

1. *Enchiridion Symbolorum Definitionum et Declarationum de Rebus Fidei et Morum*, 1st ed. ed. Henricus Denzinger, rev. Adolfus Schönmetzer, S.J. (Freiburg im Bresgau: Herder, 1967), p. 237.

2. Augustine's focus here was actually on a different matter, one in which he used clay as an example. He was attempting to refute the Manichaean tenet that God was good and evil. God's breath, the Spirit, they argued, is the life-giving component of Adam in the Genesis story, and therefore when Adam sinned, God sinned. And, if God is capable of being sinful, then God is Himself good and evil. To avoid giving evil such divine status, Augustine argued that Adam's life-spirit, his breath of life, described in Genesis as coming from God, was part of Adam's animal nature. He then used clay as a comparison: like water in clay (Adam's divine spiritual nature would not come to him until the Spirit of Christ descended).

3. St. Augustine is using the Vetus Latina (Old Latin) version of the Bible. St. Jerome's Vulgate was not yet available to him, nor was it the accepted version at the time—nor, one might add, did the two saints have an especially amicable relationship to one another. In the Middle Ages, Jerome's Vulgate had replaced the Old Latin version, but not entirely, especially when readers delved into Augustine. In this case, however, both versions agree on Adam, mankind, being made *de limo*, i.e., "from clay." Modern versions often use "from the dust," and in that case, of course, Augustine's poetic argument about human composition from water and earth would not hold.

text then goes on to imply that a human being has an "animal soul" that holds him together, and thus the comparison with clay made by Scripture is apt. Augustine says:

> Sicut enim aqua terram colligit et conglutinat et continet, quando eius commixtione limus efficitur, sic anima corporis materiam vivificando in unitatem concordem conformat et non permittit labi et re-solvi.[4]

> Just as water collects, gels and holds the earth together in a mixture of water and earth, thus creating clay, in the same way the living-spirit [anima] of the body gives life to the material of the body, thus holding it together in harmonious unity and not permitting the body to fall into dissolution.

This comparison will make it possible for medieval authors, treating gems as water mixed with earth, to make further associations between gems and human beings, as we will see in Marbode and Albert the Great, and will even make it necessary to refute any theory that gems might be living beings. Of foundational importance, however, for the Middle Ages, is Augustine's reading of the origin of precious stones as he saw it in Genesis.

In the book of Genesis, chapter 2, before the familiar account of Adam and Eve eating from the tree of knowledge of good and evil, there is a brief and perhaps less familiar description of the Garden of Paradise, Eden, as the location of the single source, the spring or font, of all the flowing water that subsequently subdivides into the four headwaters that become the four rivers that irrigate the surface of the earth.

> In the day that the Lord God made the earth and the heavens, when no plant of the field was yet in the earth and no herb of the field had yet sprung up—for the Lord God had not yet rained[5] upon the earth, and there was no one to till the ground; but a stream would rise from the ground, and water the whole face of the ground—then the Lord God formed man from the clay[6] of the ground and breathed into his nostrils the breath of life; and the man became a

---

4. *Sancti Augustini Opera: De Genesi Contra Manichaeos*, ed. Dorothea Weber (Vienna: Österreichische Akademie der Wissenschaften, 1998), p. 128. This and the following discussion is based on this edition of Augustine's commentary on Genesis, pp. 127–37.

5. This is literally what the Old Latin has, instead of "caused it to rain."

6. As noted earlier, the Revised Standard Version (RSV), for example, has "dust" here, but I have used "clay" as the English for the Old Latin version as Augustine would have known it.

living being. And the Lord God planted a paradise ["pleasure garden"] in Eden, in the East; and there he put the man whom he had
formed. Out of the ground the Lord God made to grow every tree
that is pleasant to the sight and good for food, the tree of life also in
the midst of the garden and the tree of knowledge of good and evil.

    A river flows out of Eden to water the garden, and from there it
divides into four headwaters. The name of the first is Pishon; it is
the one that flows around the whole land of Havilah, where there is
gold, and the gold of that land is good; carbuncle[7] and the leek-
green stone[8] are there. The name of the second river is Gihon; it is
the one that flows around the whole land of Cush. The name of the
third river is Tigris which flows toward Assyria, and the fourth river
is the Euphrates. (My translations based on the Old Latin)

Thus, regardless of contemporary wrestling with the exact identity of the gems
referred to here, Augustine would have clearly had at least two categories of
precious stones, one red and one green, that he could regard as coming from
the Garden of Paradise, and as being related to the flow of Eden's rivers. Wolfram too seems to have known and followed this tradition of the red stone and
the green coming from the rivers of Paradise.[9]

    Augustine interpreted the meaning of the Garden of Paradise, its trees,
and its rivers in a way that would be decisive for iconography for a thousand
years, and would be felt most strongly in depictions of shrines, altars, or grave
markers, where the artist wished to make the statement, or the prayer, that the

7. The RSV, in effect following Jerome literally, has *bdellium* here, the meaning of which is not entirely
clear, though it may mean incense sap. Augustine understood the word from the Old Latin text as *carbunculus*,
which means the red stone, lit. a "small glowing coal." *Carbo, carbonis* is coal in Latin, here accompanied by a
diminutive ending. He was also familiar with the Greek Septuagint version of the word, which is *anthrax*, also
meaning a glowing coal, or live ember, and that would have corroborated his understanding. Carbuncle in
antiquity referred to the red stones, primarily to the ruby, but also to the garnet and the spinel in their dark red
forms. Wolfram lets the reader know in his text that he is quite aware of the Greek source and gives *anthrax* as
an alternate name for ruby.

8. The RSV has *onyx stone*, following Jerome, who translated the word as *lapis onychinus*. Augustine's Old
Latin, however, had something very different, *lapis prasinus*, which is very close to the Greek Septuagint, which
has *ho lithos ho prasinos*, "leek-colored stone" or "green grass–colored stone." The ancients thought of onyx as
"fingernail"-colored, meaning flesh-colored; sardonyx was used if there was also a dark bar or streak (unwashed
fingernails, I presume). The problem of differing translations of precious stones is caused by the changing
meaning of the words for gemstones over the course of time, and by the fact that one stone type, beryl, for
example, can come in very different and confusing colors.

9. The references in the Bible to precious stones coming from rivers should not surprise us. To this day,
much of the mining of precious stones in countries like Myanmar (Burma), and in the past, for example in India
and in Egypt's Red Sea area, was done by sifting through river deposits, much as gold prospectors did in the
American Old West. The stones are often washed out of volcanic and other deposits of rock by the flowing water
and then carried downstream. See Walter Schumann, *Gemstones of the World* (New York: Sterling, 1977), pp. 52–7.
The biblical author seems to have been aware of this way of mining.

person interred in a sarcophagus, for example, had been restored by Christ to being back in the Garden of Paradise—"ut recreati et vivificati restituamur in paradisum, ubi latro ille ipso die meruit esse" (that we being recreated and given life by him may be returned to Paradise, where the good thief merited to be on that very day).[10]

Augustine comments on the four trees of the garden of Eden, first saying that Eden itself signifies immortal and intelligible delights, for "delights, pleasure and feasting are what the word *Eden* means if translated from the Hebrew." Spiritual joys are signified by the trees that are beautiful to look at; the trees that produce edible fruit refer to the ineffable food of the soul that never spoils. The tree of life is planted in the middle of the Garden of Delight because wisdom is always in the middle, and the tree of the knowledge of good and evil is in the middle since it is up to the soul to go back to its source, God, rather than attempting to find its pleasure in itself without God. Then, most important for our study, in his commentary on Genesis 2:10–14, Augustine gives his interpretation of the river that flows from Paradise.[11]

> Now, the river that was flowing from Eden, that is to say, flowing
> from delights, and pleasure and feasting, is the river referred to by
> the prophet when he says in the Psalms: *you will give them to drink of
> your pleasure*—that is, of your Eden, which means "pleasure" in our
> language—this river is divided into four branches which signify four
> virtues: prudence, fortitude, temperance, justice. The Phison is said
> to be the Ganges, the Geon is the Nile . . . and the Tigris and the
> Euphrates still have the same names.

> Flumen autem, quod procedebat ex Eden, id est ex deliciis et volup-
> tate et epulis, quod flumen a propheta significatur in Psalmis cum
> dicit: torrente voluptatis tuae potabis eos—hoc est enim Eden, quod
> Latine voluptas dicitur—, dividitur in quattuor partes et quattuor vir-
> tutes significat, prudentiam, fortitudinem, temperantiam, iustitiam.
> Dicitur autem Phison ipse Ganges, Geon autem Nilus . . . Tigris
> vero et Euphrates etiam nunc eadem nomina tenent.

Augustine's reading of the four rivers as constituting the Creator's divine pleasure overflowing from Paradise into human life invites, he says, interpretation linking spiritual and poetic meaning to the four rivers. In justification,

---

10. Augustine, *Sancti Augustini Opera*, p. 130.
11. Augustine, *Liber Secundus* chaps. 10 and 11, *Sancti Augustini Opera*, pp. 133–7.

he notes, Mount Zion, no matter how much it might be an actual geographically sited mountain, calls for the allegorical and spiritual reinterpretation that has often been given to it.

Prudence, which for Augustine means the contemplation of ineffable truth, is something that flows around the whole circuit of the earth. In other words, in every time and place throughout the world, those who have the prudence to turn to the eternal truth can be found. For Augustine, this then suggests identification with the first river, Phison, since such contemplation circles the whole world, and in its water and on its shores can be found the gold and precious jewels of human contemplation:

> Prudentia ergo, quae significat ipsam contemplationem veritatis ab omni ore humano alienam, quia est ineffablilis. . . . haec ergo prudentia terram circuit, quae habet aurum et carbunculum et lapidem prasinum, id est disciplinam vivendi, quae ab omnibus terrenis sordibus quasi decocta enitescit sicut aurum optimum, et veritatem, quam nulla falsitas vincit, sicut carbunculi fulgor nocte non vincitur, et vitam aeternam, quae viriditate lapidis prasini significatur propter vigorem qui non arescit.

> Prudence, therefore, which means the very contemplation of the truth that is foreign to human oral expression, because it is ineffable. . . . This prudence encircles the land that has gold, the ruby, and the emerald: that is, this river land has the knowledge of how to live life, knowledge that if purified of all earthly contaminants shines like the best quality gold. This river land has the truth that no falsity overcomes like the flashing light of the ruby which is not overcome by nightfall. [One thinks of Sigune's loyalty and the red gem glowing in her hut.] This river land has eternal life which is what is meant by the greenness of the emerald, a greenness of such robust vitality that it never dries up and dies.

St. Augustine goes on to explain his associations with the other three rivers: the Geon with the heated action of fortitude, because it, the Nile, is the river that goes through a land of fervent heat; the Tigris with temperance, because it goes against (*vadit contra*) the imprudence of acting like the Assyrians; the fourth river, since it is not stated that it is connected with any one country, is associated with the fairness and impartiality that is required in the practice of the virtue of justice.

Most important for *Parzival* is Augustine's acceptance of gemstones' primeval association with the Garden of Eden: his acceptance of the garnet or ruby (the carbuncle) as the embodiment of the persistent truthfulness (loyalty, *triuwe*, in Wolfram) that will not allow itself to be overcome by the darkness of falsity, and his acceptance of the emerald as possessing the greenness of life within it that is not subject to withering on the vine and drying up. In accepting the ancient belief that the ruby can be seen to glow at night, just like an ember of a fire that refuses to go out, an *anthrax* carbuncle, Augustine gives Wolfram a theological symbol for the true fidelity without falsity that Wolfram expects of the keepers of the Grail and above all of the woman who carries the Grail and of all the women associated with it. In the emerald, Wolfram has the color for the stone and for the *achmardi*, the cloth that covers the Grail, and for the hope that life that cannot be overcome by the desiccation of death—he has the stone for the grave of Gahmuret, Parzival's father.

Three of Wolfram's near contemporaries, the Swabian Albertus Magnus (1206–1280), Hildegard of Bingen (1098–1179) in the Rhineland, and the earlier bishop Marbode of Rennes (1035–1123), can give us more help in entering the intellectual and spiritual world of precious stones of the twelfth and thirteenth centuries. St. Albert the Great, or Albertus Magnus, was in many ways the outstanding scientist-scholar of his age. Interested in everything, including magic and mineralology as well as things more directly spiritual, he was the teacher of St. Thomas Aquinas, and an early advocate of scientific method through appeal to observation and verification. His *Book of Minerals* draws on all the writers known to him and is not without a good leavening of his own observations either confirming or questioning the transmitted wisdom of the ages regarding the properties of precious stones. His description of the origins of gems echoes the language of Augustine on the origin of Adam.

> To begin, then, with our treatment of the nature of stones: we say in general that the material of all stone is either some form of Earth or some form of Water.[12] For one or the other of these elements predominates in stones; and even in stones in which some form of Water seems to predominate, something of Earth is also important. Evidence of this is that nearly all kinds of stones sink in water. . . . Furthermore, if in transparent stones there were not something earthy mixed with the Water and imposing a boundary on the mois-

12. The editor capitalizes *Earth, Air, Fire,* and *Water* when any of these terms are being used to designate one of the four elements. I have generally followed her helpful example.

The chemist of the Middle Ages has to explain the composition of an object in terms of an analysis that can only use four elements: Earth, Air, Fire, and Water. Granted that this was the case, and that no more elaborate chart of chemical elements was available, Albert's treatment is both reasonable and ingenious.

ture, they would not sink in water, as rock crystal and beryl do; for ice and the other things that are entirely or chiefly made up of Water, do not sink.

In speaking in particular of those stones which are made of Earth, it is perfectly clear that in these Earth is not the only material, for this would not cohere into solid stone. For we say that the cause of coherence and mixing is moisture[13] . . . if this moisture were not soaked all through the earthly parts, holding them fast, but evaporated when the stone solidified, then there would be left only loose, earthy dust . . . then the earthy dryness holds fast to the moisture, and the watery moisture existing within the dryness gives it coherence.[14]

One can see the basis here for the homeopathic use of gemstones in therapy. Both the human being and the gemstone have similar natures: the one made of clay, earth held together by water, combined with an animal spirit; the other, too, made of earth held together by water, and it will be debated whether or not gemstones as well have a living spirit abiding in them. (Albert says no, since precious stones do not, except for the "peranites" stone, reproduce as do all animate beings.)[15] In any case, the obvious and self-evident was not debated, namely, that gemstones were powerful as well as beautiful and mysterious things.

Albert was fascinated by the transparency and translucency of many stones, and like a modern investigator, he analyzes their composition and reaches the conclusion that their transparency comes from an internal preponderance of the element Water—which he believes lost its wetness through some process of intense heat or cold, quick freezing or heating—but that their color demonstrates that there must also be some of the element Earth present in them. The solidity of the gemstone coming from intense "fiery heat" ("geothermal process" is the more current language) is accounted for by the simple model of the *lapis coctus*, the brick, which was loose mud or clay and then after

13. Albert uses the same word and concept for "coherence" or "holding together" as did Augustine in discussing the nature of clay as dust held together by water: *conglutinatio*, "gluing together."

14. Albertus Magnus, *Book of Minerals*, trans. Dorothy Wyckoff (Oxford: Clarendon, 1967), pp. 12–3. This fine translation, by a geology professor, is accompanied by an excellent commentary. All following references are to its pages.

15. It is not clear to me what stone peranites could be. A student of mine, Matt Stoller, however, suggested that it could be a geode. A geode is a stone nodule, often of good size. It is shaped like a ball and is hollow inside. When broken open, the hollow space is seen to contain little stone crystals, such as quartz or amethyst. Perhaps this is the reason for the ancient belief that this stone is feminine and maternal, and thus able to help women in childbirth.

heating becomes a "cooked stone" and solid. Modern gemologists say something quite similar in different language when they say gems are formed by hydrothermal processes deep in the earth, and when they attribute color in sapphires or emeralds to the presence of some metal such as chrome.

Albert also notes, in more scientific style but still in parallel to the Genesis story of gems being associated with the rivers of Paradise:

> Now we see that many stones are found on the banks of perennial streams; and from this we know that the banks of certain waters are places that produce stones . . . in certain places along the banks of the river called Gion [here he uses the biblical name for the Nile. He is not speaking here from experience but is citing Avicenna and recalling the Bible story], stones are produced. Moreover, we shall frequently find that mountains are stony . . . yet sometimes we find mountains without stones [dormant volcanic mountains are indeed a gem source—Albert seems almost to be on the trail of this fact; he may also know of the remarkable passage in the Book of Ezekiel that gives an alternate description of Eden as having been a gem-filled mountain.][16]

> Let us say, therefore, that all transparent stones are caused by a large amount of the material of Air and Water which is hardened and compacted by the attack of earthly material; and if the transparency is not of any particular color, but remains like the transparency of Air or Water, then this is evidence that extreme cold alone has attacked the material. And this is like the transparency of rock crystal and beryl and *adamas* [probably here diamond] and the stone called *iris*. [Albert suggests that rock crystal is predominantly Air, since it is so very transparent and almost perfectly clear.] But beryl approaches nearer to Water, for when it is turned big drops of water, as it were, are seen [possibly aquamarine].[17]

The powers that lie in each stone are carefully noted by Albert; fifty-nine of these are also used by Wolfram, especially the red and green stones in

---

16. Albertus Magnus, *Book of Minerals*, p. 27.

The passage he may have known of is Ez 28:13–15: "You were in Eden, the garden of God, every precious stone adorned you: ruby, topaz and emerald, chrysolite, onyx and jasper, sapphire, turquoise and beryl. Your settings and mountings were made of gold; on the day you were created they were prepared. . . . You were on the holy mount of God; you walked among the fiery stones. You were blameless in your ways from the day you were created till wickedness was found in you."

17. Albertus Magnus, *Book of Minerals*, pp. 39–40.

connection with the Grail, and the diamond (*adamas*) in connection with the helmet of Parzival's father Gahmuret and his demise.

> *Adamas* . . . is an extremely hard stone, a little darker colored than rock crystal, but nevertheless of a bright, shining color, and so solid that neither fire nor iron can soften or destroy it. But it is destroyed and softened by the blood and flesh of a goat, especially if the goat has for a considerable time beforehand drunk wine with wild parsley or eaten mountain fenugreek; for the blood of such a goat is strong enough even to break up a stone in the bladder.[18]

Thus we see that Wolfram knew his gem lore, since he wrote his account of the death of Gahmuret, despite his diamond helmet, well before Albert the Great finished his summary description of the diamond and the contrary power of he-goat's blood. Concerning red stones, or carbuncles, Albert has the following to say.

> Carbuncle, which is *anthrax* in Greek, and is called *rubinus* (ruby) by some, is a stone that is extremely clear, red and hard. It is to other stones as gold is to the other metals. It is said to have more powers than all other stones. . . . But its special effect is to disperse poison in air or vapor. When it is really good, it shines in the dark like a live coal, and I myself have seen such a one.[19] When it is less good, though genuine, it shines in the dark if clear limpid water is poured over it in a clean, polished black vessel [Wolfram's *Parzival*, as noted, in the case of Sigune and Anfortas also has a ruby shining in the darkness]. . . . [Aristotle says that:] there are three kinds [of carbuncle]: *belagius* [spinel, balas ruby; *paleise* in Wolfram], *granatus* [garnet] and *rubinus* [ruby]. And—what surprises many people—he says that garnet is the most excellent of these; but jewelers consider it less valuable.

This brief description by Albertus Magnus suggests many reasons for Wolfram's use of the red stones, and I will go into them later in my discussion of the text of *Parzival*. Here it is interesting to note that the belief held by Augustine eight hundred years before the turn of the thirteenth century was still

---

18. Albertus Magnus, *Book of Minerals*, p. 70. Due to their extreme hardness, diamonds could not be given a very high polish in medieval times, and were often thus not as valued as other gems.

19. The translator, Dorothy Wyckoff, comments here that "of course some minerals do exhibit luminescence or phosphorescence after being rubbed, heated or exposed to sunlight; and it is possible that Albert had seen 'such a one'; but it is also possible that he was deceived by some trick of coating a stone with phosphorescent material from fish or fungi." Albertus Magnus, *Book of Minerals*, p. 77.

intact: the carbuncle stone, the "live coal" stone, cannot be extinguished by night. There is a difference in emphasis, however. Whereas Augustine uses the accepted fact of the live-coal glow of the ruby allegorically as an embodiment of truth that can never be overcome by night, Albert is looking at the glowing gem as an unusual natural phenomenon. Wolfram too knows of the eternal glow of the ruby, the garnet, and the spinel, the latter known in German as the *paleise*. He seems to have expressed his hope for the salvation of the Templars, for whom he and Guiot de Provins both seem to have had sympathy, and also wished that they would overcome their present darkness in the unhealthy situation of defeat. Wolfram expresses his hope in a way very much his own, by the creation of a new word for a Knight Templar: *templeise*.[20] This word did not exist in German before Wolfram invented it, and it is always interesting to attempt to get behind Wolfram's word creation. The word seems to be a symbolic conflation of *tem[pel]*, the temple, and *paleise*, the spinel or balas ruby, the red gem described earlier, the carbuncle, that has the ability to *shine* on in the darkness, and, as Augustine would say, not to be vanquished by night: a "Temple Ruby." One could expect then that Anfortas, as head of the Grail Templars, should be associated with the balas ruby, and indeed this is so. When he is first introduced in book 5, he is depicted as a sick man suffering from the cold, but on his head he is wearing a sable fur hat whose brim is edged in the Arabian style. In the midst of this headdress, there is a glowing translucent ruby, *ein durchliuchtic rubîn*.[21] If this understanding is correct, then Wolfram's word for the Knights Templar suggested a confident hope that even in the darkness of their current state of defeat, suffering the loss of Jerusalem, they would find the way to radiate an inextinguishable fidelity to the temple and the Sepulcher.

The association of gem and person was not at all as foreign to the gemologist of the Middle Ages or of antiquity as such an association might seem to be today.[22] The new word is a profound wish for the survival of the ideal of the knight, and the curing and the restoration of the beauty of Anfortas and of all those who eat in the Grail castle on Mount Salvation. The *paleise* (and its virtue) is, unsurprisingly, one of the stones present in Wolfram's list of those

20. The standard word in Middle High German for a Knight Templar was *tempelære*, based on the Latin *templarius*. The adjectival noun form, *templensis*, is, I think, too distant. Wolfram may have taken the French *templois* and altered the final vowel sound to arrive at his possible compound of temple and gem.

21. The fur hat itself, as Wolfram comments, being sable, is of two colors, *zwivalt*, a word that suggests the two-ness of doubt, *zwîvel*, as does the presence of Arabian edging around the Templar hat. The fact that the ruby is shining in the edging calls all the more attention to its presence. Book 5; 231, 7–14.

22. Except, of course, for the rock-like persistence, aided by jewelers, of the idea of the birthstone.

being used by the Grail company to help sustain Anfortas, helping "to disperse poison in air or vapor."[23]

When he deals with the subject of garnet a bit later, Albert attributes to it the power to "gladden the heart and dispel sorrow; and according to Aristotle," he says, "it is hot and dry. But as to the statement of some people—that it is a kind of hyacinth—that is not true."[24] Interesting indeed, since one of those "some people" was certainly Wolfram von Eschenbach, whose Grail king feasts from a thin-cut table of garnet hyacinth and who could indeed use help from a stone that can gladden the heart and dispel sorrow.

Before coming to the emerald, a quick look at the powers of several other stones according to Albert:

Carnelian is a stone the color of flesh, that is, red; when broken it is like the juice of meat, it is very often found near the River Rhine. . . . It has been found by experience that it reduces bleeding, especially from menstruation or hemorrhoids. It is even said to calm anger.

Draconites [mythological?] is a stone extracted from the head of a large snake. Its power . . . is only effective if it extracted while the snake is alive and quivering. . . . it is said to dispel poisons . . . and they say it also bestows victory.

Jet is said to benefit those who suffer from dropsy, and it tightens loose teeth they say . . . if ignited it burns like incense . . . if water and scrapings of it are given to a virgin . . . she does not urinate, but if she is not a virgin she urinates at once. And this is the way virginity should be tested.

Jasper, the best is translucent green . . . it keeps the wearer from licentiousness. In books on magic we read that if incantations are recited over it, it makes one pleasing and powerful and safe. [This might be modern peridot.]

Sapphire (also lapis lazuli). I have observed the power of one that cured two abscesses. They say too that this stone makes a man chaste and cools internal heat, checks sweating and cures headache and pain in the tongue. I myself have seen one put into the eye to

---

23. Book 16; 791, 26, "paleise unt sardîne."
24. Albertus Magnus, *Book of Minerals*, p. 96.

remove dirt from the eyes, but it should be placed in cold water beforehand and likewise afterwards . . . it invigorates the body, and
brings about peaceful agreements, and makes one pious and devoted to God, and confirms the mind in goodness.[25]

Sarcophagus. Sarcophagus is a stone that devours dead bodies, for
in Greek *sarkos* means "flesh" and *phago* "eat." Some of the ancients
first made coffins for the dead of this stone because in the space of
thirty days it consumed the dead body. For this reason our stone
monuments are called *sarcophagi*.

Though the stone being referred to here is probably being confused with
the marble used for the sarcophagi of the wealthy from ancient times, Albert
treats it as a special gemstone, with special characteristics—in this case the
rapid removal of flesh from the bones of the dead. This peculiar "stone" is
present in the burial of Gahmuret's father, in which scene it is clear that its
powers are being prevailed against by the ruby and emerald, exerting their
powers of preservation of light against the night and preservation of the greenness of life against death. A parallel scene is also present in Wolfram's *Willehalm*.

The emerald or smaragdus was a category that also included other green
stones such as the peridot and serpentine, the latter being one of the preferred
stones for use in the top surface of a portable altar. Albertus reports the old
story that the emerald is robbed from the "nests of griffins who defend them
with great ferocity." This he has from Pliny, and Albert smoothly blends this
mythological approach to the origins of emeralds with more scientific observation:

Some varieties are named from their places of origin—those of
Scythia, or of Britain and of the Nile. . . . It has been found by experience in our own time that this stone, if it is good and genuine, will
not endure sexual intercourse: because the present King of Hungary
wore this stone on his finger when he had intercourse with his wife,
and as a result it was broken into three pieces. And therefore what
they say is probable—that this stone inclines the wearer to chastity
. . . it increases wealth, and confers persuasive speech in [pleading]
cases . . . [it helps memory] and it has been found by experience to
strengthen weak sight and to preserve the eyes.[26]

25. Albertus Magnus, *Book of Minerals*, pp. 81–116.
26. Albertus Magnus, *Book of Minerals*, pp. 119–20.

These two characteristics, the stone that can only tolerate chastity, the absence of falsity in love, and the ability to give and strengthen eyesight both come alive in the characters of Repanse de Schoye, the queen free of all falsity who alone is permitted to carry the Grail, and of Feirefiz, who at the end becomes able to see.

Coming now to St. Hildegard of Bingen, whose lifetime may have just overlapped that of Wolfram, we find that she knows much of the theory of origins and even goes beyond her predecessors in giving confident detail both about what happened in Heaven before the Fall and on the geothermal processes that generate jewels. Confidence she was not lacking. In her preface to her book on stones, she associates gems with the fall of Lucifer rather than that of Adam and Eve. She organizes the preface to her work on precious stones in a framework: Lucifer on both sides and the more scientific discussion in the middle, thus forcing the reader both to do science and to think of the moral and religious dimension of what was presented scientifically.

> All stones have fire and wetness within them. But the devil finds precious stones abhorrent, he hates and despises them because they are a reminder—their beauty shone forth before he corrupted the glory given to him by God. He also hates them because precious stones are born of fire, the thing in which he has his punishment.[27]

Hildegard then theorizes that the shock of contact between hot volcanic rock and the sea creates spuming foam, the spume adheres to rock and subsequently dries out and hardens to a gemstone under the heat of the sun in about three to four days (*per tres aut per quatuor dies in lapidem durescit*), and the rivers then take the gems to all the parts of the world. Thus, having ingeniously combined Water with Air (foam) under the influence of hot Earth and the sun's Fire, and not neglecting the role of the rivers from Genesis, Hildegard has given an ingenious synthesis for how gems are formed from Water and the other three elements. The colors, however, in her view, do not come from some admixture of Earth, as Albert the Great theorizes, but from the time of day of the stone's formation into a solid. Because precious stones are formed from Fire and Water and have heat and moisture locked within them, they possess the created world's great primordial matter and energy. Contained in "nuclear" form, we might say, to use more contemporary language, each gem has the ability to radiate power for change. Energy condensed in solid material

---

27. *S. Hildegardis Abbatissae Subtilitatem Diversarum Naturarum Creaturarum Libri Novem. Liber Tertius (Quartus), "De Lapidibus,"* in *Patrologia Latina*, ed. Jacques-Paul Migne (Paris: Migne, 1844), vol. 197, col. 1247. The following citations are taken from the same source, cols. 1248–9.

form constitutes the nature of the gem. Thus many operations can be carried out with them by those who have mastered the secret knowledge of releasing the energy of their nuclear radiation. Hildegard says, however, in her preface:

> the operations which gemstones perform are good and honest and useful for mankind—not things like seduction, fornication, adultery, hostility, homicide, and suchlike, which tend toward the vicious and are against what is human, for it is the nature of precious stones to seek whatever is honest and useful, and it is their nature to reject whatever is depraved and bad for human beings, just as virtues reject vices and as vices are unable to cooperate with virtues.

She continues with a biblical explanation:

> God, you see, decorated the First Angel as it were with precious stones, and when Lucifer saw them shining in the mirror of the Divinity, and in contemplating those gems came to an awareness of the many wonderful things God wanted to do, his mind began to soar because of the beauty of the stones that were on him and were shining in God. He began to think that he was capable of things equal to those of God, or even more than equal—and, at that, his bright radiance was extinguished. But just as God favored Adam and wanted him to recuperate, so God did not permit either the beauty or the powers of these precious stones to pass away, but willed them to be on the earth in honor and blessing, and for medicine.

Hildegard sees gems as possessing tremendous elemental force and power for healing. Stones contain the basic element Water above all, and then greater degrees of hot and cold, which for her are very important for judging a stone's most appropriate use in healing. The story about Lucifer is interesting, since it parallels other traditions about the origin of the Grail and the gemstone as being in Heaven, in Paradise, rather than in the Garden of Paradise. The story also sounds remarkably like Aesop's old fable about the dog with the bone in his mouth who looked into a river and became jealous of the bone he saw in the mouth of the dog in the water. When he opened his mouth to bark and scare the dog in the river, the bone in his mouth fell into the water and was lost. Lucifer forgets that it is only in the mirror of God's luminosity that the stones, and he himself, have their brilliance.

Hildegard's preface puts its knowledge of the geothermal origins of gems in the framework of the tale of Lucifer, thus not falling into his temptation of forgetting where brilliance comes from. The knowledge of stones needs to be seen in the framework of the mirror of their divine Creator. The comparison of people and gems or, here, of angels and gems is maintained by Hildegard, but the glory of them both is seen as shining in God, *quia decor lapidum qui in ipso erat in Deo fulgebat*—because the beauty of the stones that were on him were dependent on divine radiance, shining in God—and because they both should be useful on earth, held in honor and benediction and, as she insists, for medicine to cure the sick. This is what Parzival will be for Anfortas, once Parzival comes to be radiant with tears of compassion.

Several examples of Hildegard's lithotherapy:

The carnelian is composed more of hot air than of cold, and it is found in sand. If someone is suffering from a nosebleed, heat up some wine, and place a warmed carnelian in it and then give it to him to drink and the blood flow will stop.

Rock crystal is born from frigid water . . . and so if someone is suffering from his eyes' feeling hot, take a rock crystal and warm it in the sun, then, once it is warmed have him place it often over his eyes. Now, since rock crystal is by nature made of Water it will draw bad humors from the eyes and the person will be able to see better. . . . Rock Crystal: now if there is someone who is suffering pain in the heart area, in the stomach, or in the womb, have the person warm a crystal by sunlight, and then when it has been warmed, pour hot water over it. Then have the patient put the rock crystal in the same hot water for a little less than an hour and then remove the crystal, and then drink the water frequently, and the patient will feel better in the heart, in the stomach or in the womb.

The Sapphire: the sapphire is hot. It augments its power at around noon time . . . it is turbid even if it is primarily of Fire rather than of Air or Water, and it is full of the love of wisdom. Now if someone has *vell* [a German word inserted here, meaning "fur" or perhaps here a "film"—conjunctivitis?] in his eyes, let him hold a sapphire in his hands, and let him warm the gem in his hand or in fire, then let him touch the moistened stone to his eye, and do this morning and evening for three days. The *vell* will diminish and gradually disappear.

Hyacinth [garnet] is useful if held in the hand for warding off bad dreams, and especially so if someone feels that they are being made mentally ill [*amens*, "out of their minds"] by phantasms or if they have been *bezaubert* [put under a spell] by magic words. In this case, take a loaf of warm, wheaten bread dough and make a cut in the upper crust in the form of a cross, but don't cut all the way through, then pass the garnet stone through the cut, holding it from above, while saying, "May God who removed all precious stones from the devil when he went beyond his proper realm, remove from you, N. _____, all phantasms and magic words, and take away from you the pain of this mental illness." . . . [The garnet hyacinth is then to be drawn a second time through the cross cut in the same loaf of bread, and a parallel prayer recited, when the bread has been baked and is still warm.] Then, give the patient the bread which is around the cross area to eat. If due to physical or bodily weakness he is un-able to eat leavened bread, then give him some unleavened bread, that is, *brot* ["bread"] to eat, first blessing it with the garnet hyacinth and the above prayer.

The garnet hyacinth is, of course, the stone of which the thin table placed before the Grail king is made. In Wolfram's use, though, the garnet is able to sustain the Grail community but is not powerful enough to dispel the depres-sion or sickness that trouble Anfortas and his kingdom. God is holding back its powers, which normally would sustain a faithfulness and joy that cannot be extinguished. The presence of the garnet hyacinth suggests to the reader that the problem of the Grail community might be sadness and failure of loyalty. The curative question that must be asked of the suffering Grail king should properly be related to recognition of the very type of illness that the garnet can normally cure: sadness, disloyalty caused by being under a spell. One day the rescuer will come and ask the very question that frustrates the garnet and troubles the reader: *Œheim, waz wirret dier?* (Uncle, what are you suffering from?)

The two stones that play the greatest role, though—the emerald and the "carbuncle"—now follow in Hildegard's treatment of their therapeutic virtues.

Smaragdus. The emerald increases in power in the morning of the day and at sunrise, when the sun is powerfully placed in its orbit to begin its journey, and thus the greenness of the earth and field grains are at maximum vitality because the air has been cold up to this point and the sun is already hot, and the grasses are sucking greenness as powerfully as a lamb sucking milk. This is because the heat of the day is scarcely enough to heat up the greenness of the day and to nourish it so that the grasses and grains will become fertile and bear fruit. Therefore the emerald is strong against all human weakness and illnesses [and keeps An-fortas, "not-strong," alive]. . . . And so it follows that anyone suffering in the heart, in the stomach, or in the side should have the emerald with them so that one's body heat will be increased by it, and he will then feel better. But if the patient becomes overwhelmed by the flood of these sicknesses . . . then the person should quickly put the emerald in his mouth so that it will become wet because of his saliva. This is done so that the saliva becomes warm because of the stone, and then the saliva can be frequently brought into the body and frequently spit out. This done, without any doubt the flood of these illnesses will immediately cease.

Carbuncle [ruby, garnet, spinel]. The carbuncle grows in power during a lunar eclipse. When the moon is exhausted to the point of failure, at the very time when it is even showing how failing it is because at God's behest it has been showing what famines, plagues, and changing of kingdoms are coming to pass, at that very point the sun pulls together all the strength in the firmament that it has, and warms the moon with its heat and resuscitates it with its fire and lifts it up and makes it shine again (like putting the tongue into the mouth of another in order to rouse the dead tongue to life). It is at that moment that the carbuncle [ruby, garnet, spinel] is born. For this reason the ruby gets its brilliance from the sun during the waxing of the moon—so much so that it gives off light more at night than in the daytime—and it continues to strengthen until the heat of the sun displaces it. Now, just as eclipses of the moon are rare, so this stone is rare. Its power [virtus] is a rare thing and to be held in great awe, and there should be great fear and caution shown in using it.

If a sickness [sucht] or chills or shaking [riddo], fever, or gout [gicht], or any other infirmity should attack a person during a change in his humors, put a ruby on his belly button [super umbilicum] at midnight, since that is the time when its force is particularly strong. Do not, however, leave it on there any longer than it takes for the patient to feel a bit warmed by it, and then quickly remove it, because the power of the ruby will pass through the person and penetrate his internal organs to a greater extent than any medical ointment is able to do. Therefore remove the ruby immediately [*statim*], the moment the patient detects even a slight effect on his body. If you let the gemstone remain on his belly button even a little bit longer than that, the virtue of the ruby will completely penetrate his whole body and he will begin to dry up. And that is how the ruby stone holds any disease whatsoever in check and removes it from a person.

As with Augustine, even though she is speaking far more medically and adds the astrological example of the resuscitation of the eclipsed moon (and her own CPR, the lingual method of oral resuscitation), for Hildegard the ruby continues to stand for the nonextinguishabilty of life even when its light is exhausted to the point of almost being eclipsed—vanquished, in Augustine's words, "by night."

Wolfram uses all four threads of the Christian tradition on gems: he uses Augustine's gem-laden rivers of Eden for the Grail and for Gahmuret; Hildegard's for the medical maintenance of keeping Anfortas alive; Bishop Marbode's (1035–1123) for the analogy of person and gem, for Parzival and Condwiramurs. He uses the more scientific tradition found in Albert the Great, in Arnoldus Saxo, and even in the later Thomas Aquinas to establish the nature of all gems as water, water that will culminate in the ruby and jasper gems of the flowing baptismal font, and in the tears of repentance, compassion, and happiness.

Wolfram's poetic use of gems echoes or even predates those of his contemporary Arnold the Saxon (fl. 1220). Most of Arnold's information on gems is from Aristotle, and it serves to confirm that what to us in *Parzival* seems to be a bit recondite is actually knowledge shared by many. The jasper (in the green transparent form), Arnold relates, clears up human vision (*jaspis visum clarificat hominis*);[28] he also says of the emerald that it heals sight, *visum sanat*, thus hewing to the ancient tradition going back to the real or alleged example of Nero using glasses of precious green stone to watch the games. Further, Arnold adds, *lapis antrax, id est carbunculus . . . lucebit nocte:* the anthrax stone, that is, the carbuncle [the ruby, or the garnet or spinel], will shine at nighttime.[29] He insists, as do all the authors, medieval as well as their classical sources,

---

28. *Die Encyklopedie des Arnoldus Saxo, zum ersten Mal nach einem Erfurter Codex*, ed. Emil Stange (Erfurt, Germany: Fr. Bartholomäus, 1905), p. 85 (hereafter: Saxo).

29. Not without a bit of humor, Arnold mentions that the carbuncle will shine at night if it is placed in the presence of a *horicy*. I am not sure of the meaning of this word. The nearest equivalent in Medieval latin seems to be *hursacrum* from Hebrew *hur* (?) or Greek *pyr* (fire) plus "sacred." It was a small fire used in pediatric medicine. Saxo, p. 85.

that gemstones have an energy or power within them to do things. Interestingly, he demonstrates this by calling on the example of magnetite. Following Aristotle's treatment of stones (as translated by Gerrardi), Arnold points to the stone that had the power to enable the exploration of the world. "Lapis magnes trahit ferrum, et obediens est huic lapidi per virtutem occultam, que inest ei." ("The magnet stone attracts iron, which is obedient to this stone because of invisible power intrinsic to the stone.")[30] Magnetite is the perfect example to show how it is possible to assert that a stone has a commonly accepted power to perform an action, even though the eyes cannot see the invisible force that is acting in attraction or repulsion. Arnold adds immediately that magnetite attracts iron from one corner and from the other repels it;[31] and thus, one could add by analogy, a green stone, used skillfully and from the right end, should have the power to repel or disperse green poison in the air (as in book 16) or to draw it out, or even to draw out better vision from the eye. Magnetite is probably the best and for us most intelligible example, or prime analogue, for the "attraction and repulsion" energy accepted by the classical and medieval world as the way the innate virtue in the gemstone functioned.

Arnold has several other comments that are not at all from his sources in the classical world. When he comments on the emerald, he repeats that the best are stolen from the nests of griffins and that the emerald assists sight and grants eloquence in legal cases, but when he comments on the sapphire, he repeats that it is of celestial hue and has the capacity to restrict sweating and interior ardors but also adds: it placates God and restores peace (*Placat Deum, et pacem reconciliat*).[32] If you find a precious stone with the image of a bear engraved on it, this will render a person astute, strong, long-lasting, and pleasing to God and to everyone (*Deo et omnibus placentem*). If you find an engraved stone with Mercury carrying a staff with the serpent entwined on it, you will enjoy good health, and you will be *persona grata* to God and to all people. Finally, and the most interesting stone of all:

> If you should find one in which there is a *sacrarium*, that is to say,
> one designed like a small reliquary [*capsula*] for carrying holy things,
> this stone will grant to those carrying it the honor of perpetual vir-
> ginity, and will make them pleasing to God and human beings.

30. Saxo, p. 86.
31. Arnold is also completely aware of the hidden power of magnetite to perform its most famous navigational function. He says "magnetite has the property to point to the north with the end of the stone that attracts iron, and at the same time the opposite end of the stone will point to the south." Saxo, p. 86.
32. Saxo, p. 74.

Si inveneris, in quo sacraryum, id est, in modum capsule ferentis
sacra, hic lapis reddit ferentes se perpetua virginitate ornatos, et facit
eos gratos deo et hominibus.[33]

If the date of Arnold's *Encyclopedia* can be relied on, and his editor, Emil
Stange, based on internal evidence, places it at around the year 1220, we may
have here a hitherto unrecognized contemporary reaction to, and interpretation
of, Wolfram's Grail stone. When I read this passage for the first time, I was
quite taken aback; I had expected no such reference to a *capsula* in Arnold's
otherwise traditional list. The foregoing passage on the powers of a portable
reliquary stone certainly appears to be a liturgical Christian insertion, being
strikingly out of place in an otherwise quite classical and Aristotelian text. It
is the last sentence in a section that is devoted to the powers of stones with
images of centaurs on them; having nothing to do with centaurs whatsoever,
nor anything to do with the following passage, which is concerned with stones
with engraved *ceti* (whales), this passage certainly could reasonably be judged
to have been put in later after a reading or hearing of the powers of Wolfram's
Grail stone. Even the editor, Emil Stange, seems aware of the unusual presence
of Arnold's remarks on the portable reliquary stone and thus separates the
passage from the rest of the text with long dashes.

In any case, the passage is a surprisingly clear instance of how the sacred
reliquary stones of portable altars were understood in the context of (other)
powerful gemstones. Moreover, Arnold's reliquary stone has the same characteristics as Wolfram's Grail stone, in that it is carried by someone to whom
the stone grants two familiar attributes from *Parzival* (and an initial clerical
one that he might not want!): perpetual virginity, and grace and favor before
God and man.[34] Indeed, grace and favor before God and man points directly
to the final thought in *Parzival*'s concluding lines, "a life so concluded that
God is not robbed of the soul through fault of the body, and which can obtain
the world's favor with dignity, that is a worthy work."[35] We know that *Parzival*

33. Saxo, p. 76. With what seems to be his quiet sense of humor, Arnold adds that in addition to these
good things there may also be a little sting as well (*licet sequator cauda scorpionis*).

34. I disagree with the suggestion that Wolfram used Arnold. Aside from the chronological difficulty with
the suggestion, the supposition that Wolfram based his sequence of stones in book 16 on Arnold's lapidary is
hard to sustain. The sequence in Arnold's description of plain gemstones [*De Gemmarum Virtutibus*, Saxo, p. 69]
is alphabetical, beginning with *abeston* and ending with *zimech* and *zignetes*. Wolfram's list is far from alphabetical.
Arnold's briefer description of stones, *De Lapidibus* (Saxo, p. 85), begins with *onix*, *corallis*, and *galactidis*, which
is not related to the sequence in book 16 of Wolfram, which begins with his beloved carbuncle and then moonstone. The real possibility from the foregoing passage is that Arnoldus Saxo was an attentive reader of Wolfram.

35. Wolfram von Eschenbach, *Parzival*, trans. with intro. Helen M. Mustard and Charles E. Passage (New
York: Vintage Books, 1961), p. 431. Unless noted, translations are from this version. Other translations are mine.

was the most popularly read epic of the Middle Ages in German-speaking lands. From this passage it looks as if Arnold was one of its readers, and as a lapidarist, saw the meaning of the *kefse*, the reliquary stone that Wolfram used for the Grail, and decided to include it, perhaps with humor and at the last minute, in his list of stones containing great powers. If this is indeed a reference to Wolfram's Grail stone, Arnold's description is an important confirmation as to its nature, and confirmation that Wolfram was understood and appreciated, if occasionally with humor, in the language of his contemporaries, again *pace* Gottfried.

Bishop Marbode of Rennes lived from 1035 to 1123, and is thus much earlier than Wolfram. His authoritative treatment on stones, *De Lapidibus*, is the great authority whose influence also came down to Wolfram. Like Arnold, he is very concerned to name the invisible powers possessed by each gemstone, but he also goes beyond naming the stones' medical "virtues"; he, too, insists on identifying the source of their invisible power and on bringing this source into harmony with biblical tradition. In this, he followed Augustine, who named the prelapsarian stream of Paradise as their origin, and Hildegard, who identified them with the splendor Lucifer had before he saw them in the mirror of the Godhead. Marbode more radically identifies the stones' power and color with the divine power, divinity, resident within them, and sets them far above herbal medicine. No one should doubt or fail to see, he says, that "the potency of gems comes from the divine power within them. The potency given to herbs is enormous, but the very greatest power is that of gems." ("Quin sua sit gemmis divinitas insita virtus. Ingens est herbis virtus data, maxima gemmis.")[36]

To give an example of Marbode's medical treatment, one need only look at his account of the capabilities of the emerald. He mentions that there are twelve types, and gives the geographic origins of several of the species, including the Nile. He mentions that the emerald helped Nero with his eyesight at the games, and repeats that the emeralds of best quality are robbed from griffins' nests. The emerald can act as sunglasses or as an aid to discerning the future; it can give the orator persuasive words or help people who have the falling sickness; it can even avert storms from their courses. Much of this is repeated from the ancients, but then Bishop Marbode recalls the stones of the heavenly Jerusalem from Revelation 21:18–21. The twelve courses of stones that

---

36. *Marbode of Rennes' (1035–1123) De Lapidibus, Considered as a Medical Treatise with Text, Commentary and C. W. King's Translation, Together with Text and Translation of Marbode's Minor Works on Stones*, ed. with comm. John M. Riddle (Wiesbaden: Franz Steiner Verlag, 1977), p. 34, from the prologue. King's translation into verse is ingenious, but here it perhaps does not quite feel at ease with the full power of the word *divinitas* in the text: "for sages tell that by creative heaven / distinctive potency to gems is given . . . though in the herb a potent virtue lurks / greatest of all that which in jewels works." The "distinctive potency" within the gem is divinity.

constitute the walls are described in terms of the type of stone that will be used for each course. The number 12 suggests that the stones stand for people: the twelve tribes of Israel, the new and the old; the twelve pearly gates, each made of a single pearl, are the twelve apostles. The streets will be translucent gold sheets. The twelve stones named for the walls are jasper, sapphire, chalcedony, emerald, sardonyx, sard, chrysolite, beryl, topaz, chrysoprase, hyacinth, and amethyst. This is the beginning of his identifying of specific stones with types of religious attitudes and persons.

Taking the twelve stones of the heavenly Jerusalem, he explains each one not as a divine source of medical properties but of divine virtue in human beings.

> Jasper of green color
> reveals the greenness of faith
> which in all perfect men
> never grows weak deep within
> by its strong protection
> the devil is resisted. ("Twelve Stones," 119)[37]

Jasper is the primary foundation of God's Church and it is green in color. Whosoever has it on himself will not be harmed by a phantom. It signifies those who hold always their faith of God and never depart from it or wither away [numquam arescunt], but always remain fresh and green [semper virent] in it nor do they fear the devil's craftiness. ("Prose Lapidary," 125)

It is quite clear that the typical virtues associated with the green stone from Augustine's lapis prasinus, through Hildegard and Albert, are still present: remaining fresh, not withering or, as Augustine would say, drying up. But here, however, they are now associated with the Church and its foundation. In Wolfram's use the stones are a sustaining help to a Church very much in need of divine virtue and very sick indeed, for while living on Mount Salvation its personnel had strayed away from the very powers of these stones, rendering their paradisial help less effective. The base of Wolfram's baptismal font (bk. 16) is jasper.

---

37. This and the following texts can be found in Marbode of Rennes, Marbode of Rennes' (1035–1123) De Lapidibus, ed. Riddle, pp. 119–29, under the titles "Lapidary of Twelve Stones in Verse," "Marbode's Medical Prose Lapidary," and "Marbode's Christian Symbolic Lapidary in Prose," which are cited accordingly in the text. Both the first and third of these can be found in the Patrologia Latina, vol. 171, cols. 1771–4. The English translation here is King's as occasionally amended by me.

Sapphire has an appearance
similar to the heavenly throne
It depicts the heart of simple men
waiting with sure hope
Whose life and moral ways
are a delight to the Most High. ("Twelve Stones," 119)

Sapphire has the sky's color. It signifies those who placed on earth
aspire to heavenly things, and who despise all worldly matters just
as if they were not on the earth, as "Our commonwealth is in
heaven." ("Prose Lapidary," 125)

Beryl, one of the stones associated with seeing and eyeglasses, may be our
aquamarine or a pale emerald. In his description of beryl, Marbode associates
it with incoming light, with the translucency that he then associates with being
a wise and tranquil human being.

Beryl is clear
like the bright sun in water;
It stands for the prayers of minds
that are naturally wise.
What is better to please the mysterious
Leisure of the Highest repose? ("Twelve Stones," 120)

Beryl shines just as water struck by the sun
and it warms the hand of the holder. It marks those who are fragile
but struck by the radiance and grace of the true sun, that is Christ,
they shine [*lucent*] with good works and they warm those who
    associate with them
by the heat of charity and by the example of a good life. ("Prose
    Lapidary," 127)

The stones thus express the different forms of spirituality, of divinity, that exist
in the different hues of human personality. Marbode even goes so far as to say
that St. Paul was an opal. St. Paul asserted that he had become "all things to
all people to save all" (1 Cor 9:22), thereby showing that he was an opal, since
the opal "changes its color according to the condition of the sky" (*Amutat
colorem suum cum facie celi*).[38] For Marbode, the world's precious stones possess

---

38. Actually Marbode calls Paul a *jacintus*, which to him must have meant a stone that can change its hue
with its environment; therefore, I have called it an opal. The words for stones do not remain very constant over
time, as many lapidarists have remarked. This is on p. 128.

their own innate divine power from Creation, and in their spectrum of diverse colors, they call attention to the diverse manners in which the Creator's divine light is resident in the spectrum of human beings: in the diversity of human virtues. Marbode connects the virtues' identity with specific gems: jasper, the greenness of faith; sapphire, the heavenly color of hope; chalcedony (his carbuncle?), the flame of internal love; emerald, persistent faith in adversity; sardonyx, humility despite virtuousness; sard, the blood of martyrs; beryl, perfect preaching; topaz, ardent contemplation, and so on; and thus each of the foundation stones of the heavenly Jerusalem is able to contribute to raise a perfect city of God on his holy mountain, and the gemstones of these spiritual graces are able to make the city shine *luce fulgentes*, with their gleaming light. Even more directly, he says: "These precious stones signify actual living human beings: diversity of colors, multiplicity of virtues." ("Hi pretiosi lapides / carnales signant homines / colorum et varietas / virtutum multiplicatas"; "Twelve Stones," 121). This view of gems, which lends itself easily both to a Christian and an ecumenical view of human virtue, may be the spirit that underlies the creation and appreciation not only of all the therapeutic jewels on the holy mountain of Munsalvaesche but also of the virtuous character of the noble Baruch, who places the gems on Gahmuret's grave, and the gem-like inner nobility of Feirefiz.

Before leaving this topic it is good to look at what the great and sober thinker of the age, St. Thomas Aquinas (1225–1274), the student of Albert the Great, had to say, several decades after the time of Wolfram. In his own way, that is, not referring to the rivers of Eden, nor to the fall of Lucifer, nor even to innate divinity, but in the scientific thought of his day, Thomas too acknowledges that gemstones are somehow beyond normal, that they are "supercelestial," that is, they are from the cosmic realm beyond the heavens. At first, with his customary serene trust in reason, Thomas says simply "it is obvious that gems are water" (*patet naturam lapidum esse aquam*).[39] With this cool observation, it would seem that any romantic analogy as to their nature and function must have disappeared by his time—but far from it. Aquinas adds that one must also consider that there is the undoubted question of the hidden effects invisibly performed by certain stones. Then comes the old evaluation in a new form:

> there is no doubt that gemstones have something of the hidden
> power [*aliquid de virtute occulta*] of the bodies that are above the vault

---

39. *Tractatus de lapide philosophico*, chap. 2, available on the Internet at www.uan.it/alim; ALIM, Archivo della latinità italiana del Medioevo, pp. 31–4.

of heaven . . . they have something in them that is beyond the powers of the four basic elements of nature . . . it appears evident that
some stones have something of the fifth essence . . . some stones
have something in them of the nature of the stars.

To a world that thinks of gemstones in such exalted terms, Wolfram can
say that the Grail is a gemstone, a stone that comes from beyond the stars and
contains within itself the hidden power of divinity.

3

The Crusaders' Quest

The Holy Sepulcher

Wolfram lived and wrote in a world filled with the sound and spirit of the Crusades, especially with echoes of Richard and the Third Crusade, and of the Fourth Crusade, whose storming and looting of Constantinople was happening as he wrote and is alluded to in *Parzival*. In his era, though before his lifetime, on Friday, July 15, 1099, Jerusalem had been successfully taken from the Muslims in the First Crusade and had been secured as a Christian city by the slaughter or expulsion of all non-Christian inhabitants. When Chrétien ceased work on his version of the legend of the Grail, around the year 1187, Jerusalem with all its sacred places had been more or less securely in Christian hands for over eighty years. Constantinople, with all its treasures and sacred Christian relics, was in the hands of Eastern Christianity, as it had been for almost a millennium since Constantine, and no one would have thought its walls were anything but impregnable, nor, in any case, would any Christian army, at least, ever dream of breaching them, or of stealing the relics within. The Christian city of Zara on the Adriatic was under the protection of the king of Hungary, a kingdom now Christian—who would have thought that it would ever be overwhelmed by a Venetian-led army of crusaders? In short, there was perhaps no situation facing Chrétien de Troyes in his time that would have elicited from him a passionate plea for his Perceval to avoid fratricide, the sin of Cain. There was no real need to give space to both Muslim and Christian chivalry, and no compelling reason for him to associate Muslim-Christian brotherhood with the attaining of the Holy Grail.

All this had changed by the time Wolfram surveyed the knightly world he portrayed in his epic in the first decade of the thirteenth century. At the Battle of the Horns of Hattin, the surrounded Christian army, having placed itself foolishly in an arid desert place without access to water, blinded by the smoke of grass and brush fires set at the orders of Saladin, and within sight of the water of the Sea of Galilee on the horizon, was forced to surrender, completely defeated.

> In the last desperate moments of the fighting, Balian of Ibelin and a few others hacked their way free but King Guy and most of his knights were so exhausted that they simply sat on the ground and threw their swords away. So utterly overcome were they physically and emotionally that they scarcely noticed the Saracens who came to make them prisoners. . . . In his tent, after the battle, Saladin treated his captives well. He personally served King Guy a goblet of iced water to quench his thirst, a sign among the Muslims that his life was safe.[1]

The flower of Christian knighthood in the Holy Land had thrown away their swords and sat on the ground in order to give themselves up in surrender to the Muslims—a posture of "physical and emotional" defeat clearly repeated by Parzival and Feirefiz at the end of their battle, in which the sword of the Christian was broken and the gallant pagan Feirefiz cast his own sword away. Saladin sat the defeated leaders before him and treated with them (with one understandable exception) in chivalrous courtesy, as did Feirefiz with his brother. Before the end of the same year, 1187, had come, Jerusalem was once more in Muslim hands. Between the time when Chrétien wrote of the Grail and the time when Wolfram wrote his version of the Story, all had changed in the land of Christ's Last Supper. What Chrétien could write about calmly, the search for the serving dish, the Holy Grail in the savage land, if written by Wolfram after the fall of Jerusalem in the same tenor, could have been read as an encouragement to the German and European princes to return to their military quest for repossession of Christ's Grail.

Chrétien never finished his story; he never gave it an ending—either happy or tragic. Often it is suggested that this lack of an ending was caused by his death. Perhaps so, but perhaps also it was caused by an insuperable futility

---

1. Geoffrey Regan, *Saladin and the Fall of Jerusalem* (London: Croom Helm, 1987), pp. 128–9.

that he had built into his story: Perceval is searching for his mother from whom he rode away rather callously as she fainted at the bridge, a mother who is now dead. Perhaps one should also consider that the lack of a satisfying ending for Chrétien's version of the story could have been caused by another kind of death as well, the terminal shock of Hattin and its inevitable consequence, the final fall of Christian Jerusalem to Saladin.[2] Traces of the psychological effect of the loss at Hattin and the loss of possession of Jerusalem, the Lord's property, show up, I believe, in the enigmatic prologue to Wolfram's *Parzival*, where the disturbing and bitter effects of doubt, *zwîvel*, lack of confidence—lack of faith, perhaps, in the crusading belief that God is with us—are taken into full consideration before Wolfram begins. Chrétien's chivalrous prologue, on the other hand, is in praise of selfless generosity and clearly comes from the former time.

Wolfram's two great epics, *Parzival* and *Willehalm*, are a poet's protest against the whole notion of religious crusade and in particular against Christian-Muslim enmity. In both works he attempts to make his contemporaries realize that a Christian crusade aimed at killing Muslims in order to secure possession of Christ's grave and restore his feudal territory to him is a mistake of literalness concerning the whereabouts of the Lord Christ's rock grave and the location of his "territory." He suggests that the literalness is a sign of profound sickness causing both suffering and ugliness among the baptized who live on Mount Salvation. Wolfram's unexpected poetic weapon in his attempt at enlightenment is the gemstone. In a world of legend, where the asking of the right question is so important for a happy ending, Wolfram in his *Willehalm* epic asks a simple question through the mouth of the pagan king Terramer, the wise king and faithful father of a daughter who has become a Christian. In the context of the marriage between his daughter, whom he compares to sunlight, and her former fiancé, a Muslim whom he compares to a gem, Terramer asks "How does sunlight pass though a precious gem without causing any splinters or the least damage?" (*Wie vert sunn durch edelen stein, / daz er doch scharten gar verbirt?*)[3]

---

2. At the time of the much-delayed Sixth Crusade, there was a brief and *mirabile dictu* peaceful return of the city, except for its Muslim shrines, to crusader administration. This transfer was negotiated by the German emperor Frederick II in 1229. Frederick was a very learned man and an assiduous reader, the *stupor mundi*, an intellectual who was quite ecumenically inclined and who dealt with the Muslims with admiration and respect, and in Arabic. It is quite possible, I would like to suggest, that Wolfram's two epic works may have had an influence on Frederick and thus helped inspire his remarkable, if brief, achievement of peace in Jerusalem.

3. Wolfram von Eschenbach, *The Middle High German Poem of Willehalm*, trans. Charles E. Passage (New York: Ungar, 1977), p. 199, cited hereafter as *Willehalm*, trans. Passage. Translations are from this version, or modified from this version. Wolfram von Eschenbach, *Willehalm, nach der 6. Ausgabe von Karl Lachmann*, trans. and commentary by Dieter Kartschoke (Berlin: de Gruyter, 1968), 354, 28–9, p. 196.

It is not primarily the curative value of the stones that interests Wolfram in his two epics so much as the amazing way that so many gemstones are translucent, the property they have of permitting light to shine through them. Imagine the amazement concealed in this insightful observation made in a hostile military world of sword and armor, a world where every puncture, slash, or shattering of a soldier is caused by a spear, a lance, or a speeding crossbow bolt as it penetrates metal armor, where every metallic ringing cut or shower of wooden splinters is because of the fearsome movement through space of a war axe or a two-handed sword as it meets wooden shields. There must always have been, in that pregunfire world of steel armor and weapons, a constant and tremendous din of endlessly repeated hitting, cutting, and denting; the hacking and crashing sound of hardened metal receiving the impact of sharpened, speeding iron everywhere on the battlefield as a war club, mace, the edge of a heavy sword, the point of knight's lance made its grinding way through chain mail or armor plate to the flesh and bone of the enemy.

And yet, says Wolfram, there is a greater wonder. How quietly light makes its way easily and gently through the hardest objects in the material world. It passes with the greatest of ease through the diamond, which is so hard it can even scratch the steel of weapons, and it does so in total silence. Light passes just as well through the ruby and the emerald, without any disturbance, creating no noise or fracture of any type, causing no splinters to fly. Light passes through a gemstone without, as Wolfram says through Terramer, causing any damage whatsoever. Light and gems are similar to those in happily married love. They go together, he says, as did the love of his daughter, which was the sunlight that passed though Tibalt, her former fiancé, a gem of a human being, a man loyal without falsity. Light and gems intermingle quietly, without causing any damage, like wife and husband.

Gems in their trans-*luce*-ncy are thus a symbol of the possibility of faithful and noninjuring love. For Wolfram, even more radically, translucency is the function of the gravestone, the sepulcher, of Gahmuret's grave and of the dead of Alischanz in their sarcophagi. Because of the translucency of Christ's own tomb, through which his light penetrated, passing through the very hardest of stones, death itself, the Christian gravestone is revealed to be a gem. The Holy Sepulcher is the gemstone that is the sign without parallel that there is ultimate hope, that the love of God, the divine light, is faithful even to the end and beyond. This fidelity, like the inextinguishable fire of the ruby, shines through the dense and dark stone of the valley of the shadow of death. This was the reason that the crusades could have their appeal to the ordinary foot soldier as well as to the noble and king, and why the real battle cry of the crusaders in the Holy Land was not *Deus vult* but *Sanctum Sepulchrum*. The stone enclosure

The Resurrection as depicted by Nicholas of Verdun. The soldiers are sleeping with their shields in front of the roundels as Jesus rises from the stone Sepulcher. The covering stone of the Sepulcher is dramatically pushed off. In the corner of the sarcophagus is the burial cloth, reminder of the moment of death, to add poignancy to this moment when Jesus passed through the stone. *Chorherrenstift Klosterneuburg. Photo: Prof. Walther K. Stoitzner, Vienna.*

of Christ's grave was their hope of heaven, their phoenix stone, hope for the forgiveness of sins, the goal of their quest, of their penitential pilgrimage, and ultimate assurance of arrival at the gate to Paradise. They came to render their feudal service in loyalty to their Lord, they came to stand and worship at the stone through which the Light, and they with it, passed on Easter.

When the Crusade was first preached at Clermont in the year 1095, Pope Urban II was responding to an appeal from the Byzantine emperor, Alexius I, for help. He called on the French nobility to take up the cross, and he called on them to remember the valor of their ancestors and go to the rescue and liberation of the Eastern Christians. He cites a list of depredations done by the infidels to the people and churches of the Christian East, and then begs his listeners most of all to think of the Holy Sepulcher:

> Let the Holy Sepulcher of our Lord and Savior, which is possessed by the unclean nations, especially arouse you, and the holy places which are now treated with ignominy and irreverently polluted with the filth of the unclean. Oh most valiant soldiers and descendants of invincible ancestors, do not degenerate, but recall the valor of your ancestors. . . . Let hatred, therefore, depart from among you; let your quarrels end; let wars cease; and let all dissensions and controversies slumber. Enter upon the road of the Holy Sepulcher. Wrest that land from the wicked race. . . . Jerusalem is the center of the earth; the land is fruitful above all others, like another Paradise of delights. This spot the Redeemer of mankind has made illustrious by His advent, has beautified by His sojourn, has consecrated by His passion, has redeemed by His death, has glorified by His burial.[4]

The Sepulcher and the Eastern Church were not the only motives for ecclesiastical advocacy of a crusade to the East. Violence had become so endemic in the West that the Western church had been attempting to stem it through its own councils and decrees. Feudal society was a military society, and so the church could only attempt to brake but not stop the way of fighting. The Peace of God (*Pax Dei*) restricted warlords' attacks on church property, the clergy, and the cattle of the poor. The Truce of God (*Treuga Dei*) restricted the days of warfare with some success by prohibiting fighting from Thursday to Monday morning of the week, and during the holy seasons, such as Lent and Holy Week. It is noteworthy that Good Friday then was one of the most important days on which fighting was obviously forbidden—something of which Parzival, in ignorance, is in striking violation as he rides along in full armor on that day. The Council of Narbonne, in August 1054, had passed a decree giving an explicit theological basis for the prohibition of feud and fighting, basing it on St. Paul's doctrine of the Mystical Body of Christ: "We do hereby decree and command as a command of God and of Ourselves, that no Christian may kill any another Christian whatsoever, because: whoever kills a Christian, without any doubt sheds the blood of Christ [qui Christianum occidit, sine dubio Christi sanguinem fundit]."[5]

---

4. Taken from the account of the monk Robert of Reims; translation from Morris Bishop, *The Horizon Book of the Middle Ages*, ed. Norman Kotker (New York: American Heritage, 1968), p. 210.

5. *Sacrorum conciliorum Nova et Amplissima Collectio*, ed. Joannes Dominicus Mansi (Venice: Antonius

This very important decree is one to which Wolfram directs himself in his work. The decree says nothing about the nonbaptized. Does one shed the blood of Christ when one strikes down a nonbaptized person? Or are there more ways than by the flow of baptismal water that one can be baptized? Is it perhaps possible that in the tears of a good and compassionate human being, another form of baptismal water is flowing up from the heart? Wolfram spends his whole epic raising this question, often indirectly, but persistently. If tears of compassion are also a kind of baptism, then for him, killing the compassionate pagan is not different from killing a baptized person. The attacks on Zara and Constantinople by the crusaders in 1204, undeterred by Innocent III's threat and subsequent imposition of excommunication, must have shown Wolfram, and those who had the courage to look, that the leaders and preachers of crusades were not essentially concerned with baptismal status at all—of any variety.

I believe the events during Wolfram's lifetime, the Fourth Crusade most explicitly, removed the veil of Christian legitimacy from the crusaders' attempts to help Christ regain his territorial patrimony. The destruction of Constantinople in 1204, despite the crosses and icons of Mary and Jesus raised over the walls in the sight of the crusaders, may have opened Wolfram's eyes to the realization that the killing in a crusade was fratricide, an open defiance of the Council of Narbonne, a shedding of the blood of Christ, and that no grail-vessel for containing the Body and Blood of Christ, whether plate, cup, or even stone, would be obtained in his story without his Parzival going for it in concord and mutual respect with his nonbaptized brother.

Pope Urban's appeal to the Franks was not the first time that defensive or offensive violence in the East was thought of not only as useful channel into which to direct feudal military energy but also as an act of piety and devotion. Jonathan Riley-Smith has described how Pope Gregory VII (reigned 1073–1085) had also advocated military help for the Eastern Church:

> Gregory's advice to warriors was generally couched in conventionally pastoral terms, but early in his pontificate he came up with a scheme to lend military assistance to the Byzantine empire. As the plan evolved it became more and more heady. He hoped to lead himself an army of 50,000 men, which after helping the Greeks against the Turks would march on to the Holy Sepulcher. . . . He

---

Zatta, 1767; reproduction, Paris: H. Welter, 1902), see *Concilium Narbonense*, viii kalend Sept. Anno MLIV. Indict vii. See also *Dizionario dei Concili*, dir. Pietro Palazzini (Rome: Città nuova editrice, 1963–1968), 3:158.

stressed, in terms which created the necessary conditions for meritorious violence and were to be used constantly by crusade apologists, that aid to the Christians in the East—which he compared to laying down one's life for one's brother—was an expression of compassion and love of neighbor.[6]

One can simply imagine how appalling these statements would appear to anyone who had heard, as surely Wolfram did, of the slaughter of the inhabitants of Jerusalem after the conquest, of Richard the Lion-Hearted's slaughter of the hostages at Acre, and of the attack on the Christian city of Zara, and, as we have said, the Fourth Crusade's attack and sack of Constantinople. The expedition to save the holy churches of the East had vitiated Urban II's appeal at Clermont to help Byzantium, and destroyed what no pagan army had been able to do: it overwhelmed and looted the capital of the Christian East. The date, 1204, is important, for it indicates that at the time of Wolfram's writing of *Parzival* he was fully aware of the tragedy of the city's fall, as he notes the great wealth taken from the Greeks.

The reality of what happened can be glimpsed over the centuries from the testimony of Robert de Clari. His account is that of an ordinary soldier, unlike that of Villehardouin, who participated at a much higher level, and it is of interest to us because it may be closer to the oral accounts that would have made their way back to Europe and to Wolfram. It looks first of all as though the crusaders were well aware of the threat of papal excommunication for any attack on Zara, and knew that the doge disregarded it.

> When they were armed, the doge spoke to all the high men of the
> host and said to them: "Lords, this city has done much harm to me
> and to my people, and I would gladly avenge myself on it. So I pray
> you to help me." And the barons and the high men answered that
> they would help him. Now the people of Zara knew that the Vene-
> tians hated them and so they had secured a letter from Rome, say-
> ing that anyone who should make war on them or do them any
> harm would be excommunicated. And they sent this letter by good
> messengers to the doge and the pilgrims [the crusaders, non-
> Venetians] who had landed there. When the messengers came to the
> camp, the letter was read before the doge and the pilgrims, and
> when the letter was read and the doge had heard it, he said that he
> would not give up having his revenge on those of the city, not even

---

6. Jonathan Riley-Smith, chapter entitled "Holy Sepulcher; Holy War," in *The First Crusaders, 1095–1131* (Cambridge: Cambridge University Press, 1997), p. 50.

for the excommunication of the apostolic [i.e., by the pope]. And he prayed the barons to help him. The barons all answered that they would gladly help him, save only count Simon de Montfort and my lord Enguerrand of Boves.[7]

The two who refused to stay continued into Hungary and then proceeded to fulfil their vows to go to the Holy Land. The excommunication was later lifted for the pilgrim-crusaders on appeal to Rome, but not for the doge and the Venetians. Robert de Clari is also quite frank about the nonlegitimacy of the public motive for going to Constantinople, namely, to restore the young Alexius, at that time in Germany, to the throne.

> The doge of Venice saw right well that the pilgrims were in sore [financial and logistic] straits, and he spoke to them and said, "Lords, in Greece there is a land that is very rich and plenteous in all good things. If we could have a reasonable excuse for going there and taking provisions and other things in the land until we were well restored, it would seem to me a good plan."[8]

The youth Alexius was soon sent for, and then the excuse was present.

When the city of Constantinople fell to the Venetians and the pilgrims, Robert complains, the common people who had done so much of the fighting were ignored, and the "high men" took all the best houses in the city without the common people or the poor knights knowing a thing about it. He accuses them, again, of bad faith. When it comes to the wealth found in the city, Robert de Clari may have written the account that most resembles the remark of Wolfram. Robert says:

> Not since the world was made, was there ever seen or won so great a treasure . . . not in the time of Alexander nor in the time of Charlemagne. . . . Nor do I think, myself, that in the forty richest cities of the world there had been so much wealth as was found in Constantinople.[9]

Most interesting for my purposes is to find what of all this treasure he finds the most excitingly valuable. He talks of all the wealth of the city in gold and marble, but his greatest awe is reserved for treasures of the chapels and churches, the same treasures the pilgrims sought to venerate in the Holy Land,

---

7. Robert of Clari, *The Conquest of Constantinople*, trans. Edgar Holmes McNeal (New York: Columbia University Press, 1936), pp. 43–4.

8. Robert de Clari, *The Conquest of Constantinople*, p. 45.

9. Robert de Clari, *The Conquest of Constantinople*, p. 101.

the objects connected with the gospel story of the Passion, the Deposition from the cross, and the Resurrection. In the chapel of the Boukoleon Palace (the Chapel of Our Lady of the Pharos [the lighthouse])

> were found many rich relics. One found there two pieces of the True Cross as large as the leg of a man and as long as half a *toise*, and one found there also the iron of the lance with which Our Lord had His side pierced and two of the nails which were driven through His hands and feet, and one found there in a crystal phial quite a little of His blood, and one found there the tunic which He wore and which was taken from Him when they led Him to the Mount of Calvary, and one found there the blessed crown with which He was crowned, which was made of reeds with thorns as sharp as the points of daggers.
>
> There were two rich vessels of gold hanging in the midst of the chapel by two heavy silver chains. In one of these was a tile and in the other a cloth [Robert de Clari then tells the story of a roofer who was putting tiles on a poor woman's roof as an act of charity. A man appeared to him and asked for a cloth, wiped the sweat from his face, returned the cloth, and disappeared; when the roofer looked at the cloth, it had the face of Jesus on it] . . . and there was kept the *syndoine* in which Our Lord had been wrapped, which stood up straight every Friday so that the features of Our Lord could be plainly seen there. And no one, either Greek or French, ever knew what became of this *syndoine* after the city was taken. . . . In this abbey there was the marble slab on which Our Lord was laid when He was taken down from the cross, and there could still be seen there the tears which Our Lady had let fall on it.[10]

It is touching to see that even in the midst of all of the secular wealth of Constantinople, news of which came to Wolfram, a poor knight is still thinking in terms of the fundamental story of the West, of the value of the wood of the cross, the crown of thorns, the nails, the lance, and the shroud that eased the way into the tomb, the Holy Sepulcher. It may be for this reason that Western Christianity felt some sense of shame in taking the relics of the Passion without having gone to the land of the Passion. In any case, these are the reports that also came to Wolfram as he wrote that the French Grail was the wrong thing. The true Grail was still the stone.

10. Robert de Clari, *The Conquest of Constantinople*, pp. 103–4, 112–3.

A knight and a priest from the portal (inside) of Reims cathedral. The "hands of the priest" administer, in the words of Trevrizent, "the greatest pledge ever given," the Body and Blood of Christ, to the attentively loyal knight. Behind the priest is the cloth covered altar. The knight is wearing a full suit of chain-mail armor, bespeaking the danger that lies ahead. He has his spurs on his feet and his pilgrim's staff under his arm, ready to go on crusade to liberate his Sovereign's Holy Sepulcher. Wolfram would have noticed the irony of the muted presence of the covered altar stone. *The Bridgeman Art Library, New York.*

The other aim of the crusaders, however, if unrealized, was still there—to liberate Christ's grave from hostile control, to pray at the Holy Sepulcher in Jerusalem—and this seemed to require further warfare. Wolfram adopts an interesting view that is quite explicit in his *Willehalm*, about Christian-Muslim warfare if hostilities are simply unavoidable. His chivalrous view might be summarized as follows: *if you win, if you overcome the pagans, behave toward them in such a way that you don't commit sin.* I believe he has heard all the tales about how Richard treated the captives at Acre and the slaughter of the non-Christian inhabitants of Jerusalem. He reminds his fellow Christian knights that pagans are not different from them, that everyone is born pagan, and that many biblical heroes, like Noah and Job, to say nothing of the Wise Men who followed the star, were good souls and surely saved—without the waters of baptism. He puts these thoughts into the mouth of Gyburc, a Christian wife and convert to Christianity whose pagan father, Terramer, is waging war to bring her back, and against whom the Christian knights are fighting:

> The toll of death that has occurred on both sides and for which I
> bear the resentment of baptized and heathen alike, may God make it
> up to them both if I am to blame for it. If you defeat the pagans, do
> it in such a way that you don't hurt your salvation. Listen to a sim-
> ple woman's advice, respect her as the work of God's hands. The
> first man that God made was a heathen. Believe me that Elias and
> Enoch, though they were heathens, are still alive. Noah too was a
> heathen, who was saved in the ark. A heathen likewise was Job,
> whom God did not for that reason reject. Note also the Three Kings:
> one's name was Caspar, the others' Melchior and Balthasar, and we
> must admit they were heathens, but they are not marked for damna-
> tion. God himself at his mother's breast, with His own hand ac-
> cepted His first gifts from them. Not all heathens are marked for
> perdition. We know that all the children to whom mothers have
> given birth since Eve's time have incontestably been heathens, even
> if their mothers had baptism. Every baptized woman gives birth to
> heathens, even if the womb enclosing them is baptized. (The bap-
> tism of Jews is different, they do it by cutting with the knife.) We
> were all heathens once. A good person is greatly grieved when the
> Father has to mark His own children for damnation—however, He
> who always had real mercy may well have mercy on them.[11]

---

11. Taken, with some modifications based on the original, from *Willehalm*, trans. Passage, pp. 174–5.

The argument is very persuasive, and this not least because all the examples of saved pagans are biblical examples, and also because the speaker is a woman, source of light for Wolfram, a guide for men toward human behavior, and she is a convert from paganism. Especially provocative for those who would kill pagans is the thought that not just Gyburc, who is a convert, but every Christian, and every Christian knight, was born pagan and remained so until they were baptized; they are all converts.

In his introductory prayer to the *Willehalm*, Wolfram elaborates on the fatherhood of God and the consequences for his spirituality, and gives a beautiful guidepost for reading both of his epics: we are (all) God's relatives. In an era of very strong kinship bonds, where kinship and blood determined royal, baronial, and even farmers' rights to hold land and office and right of succession, Wolfram composes an extremely touching prayer of invocation as he begins to write.

> Pure, foreign to falsity, You, God, Trinity, Creator over all creation, your changeless power has no beginning and has no end. If in your power you drive away sinful thoughts from me, You are the father and I am the child. You who are noble beyond all nobility, let your virtue rest, be merciful instead, Lord, toward whatever wrong I do to You.
>
> Lord, do not let me overlook what has been given to me: salvation and endless happiness. I am aware that I am your child and your family relative, poor though I may be and You so very rich and strong. By becoming a man, You made me a kinsman. Without any doubt, the *Our Father* gives me the name and recognition of being a child of your divinity.
>
> And so baptism gives me the consoling reassurance that has freed me from doubt: I realize through my faith that I have been named after You: You are Christ—Wisdom above all knowledge— and I am Christian.
>
> Your height and depth and your broad extent have never been fathomed to their end. Moreover, You hold the orbits of the seven planets in your hand so that their retrograde motion supports the heavenly sphere. Earth, Air, Fire, Water exist completely under your sway. Wherever animals, wild or tame, walk about, everything functions at your command. Your divine power has separated bright day from dark night and set limits to both by the movement of the sun. There never was, nor ever will be, anything like You. You know the

powers of each and every gemstone, and the properties of all the herbs, down to the last detail.

The right way to write and the right words have come forcefully from your holy Spirit. I am deeply aware of You. Of all the things that are written down in books, none of it has given me talent or knowledge. The only thing that has educated me and given me some-sense of artistry, comes from realizing meaning. (translation mine)[12]

Wolfram has a very strongly Trinitarian spirituality, which is made almost mystical by his sense that the Incarnation has made him a relative of God, and that baptism has given him the name Christian and reinforced his divine child-hood, implied so clearly by the first words of the Lord's Prayer. Baptism has given him confidence in his having been named after Christ, but it is the Incarnation, the "Becoming a Human Being" of the Second Person of the Trinity that is the prior basis for calling God Father, and for feeling that he belongs to the Trinity as a poor relative. This leaves room for non-Christians to feel that they are God's children, since it was both Creation and the Incarnation, rather than baptism, that first made human beings relatives of God.

The Second Person of the Trinity is referred to in patristic style as Wisdom, ironic in that the church of Holy Wisdom, Hagia Sophia in Constantinople, was besieged in the Fourth Crusade in Wolfram's lifetime. Wolfram names among the important things of which God is the perfect and expert knower the movements of the heavens and the virtues and powers of stones and herbs—both of which, of course, are in the last chapter of *Parzival*, and are thus not to be dismissed as Wolfram showing off his erudition.

Finally, Wolfram openly says how aware he is of God: "of You," he says with the force of simple directness. It should be crucial for the interpretation of Wolfram's authorial intent that he maintains that his talent for writing, in both form and content, is inspired by the Spirit of God. He does not feel indebted to books for what he writes but owes it much more to getting at the sense of the matter through insight and realization. If this is the case, and I believe it is quite clear that he is here praying in a sincere manner, then he believes that his insight into the real nature of the Grail as a stone is something which he arrived at as an inspiration from the Spirit of the Triune God.

He even goes so far as to put the greatest of respect and awe for the Christian stone sarcophagi, the rectangular box-like coffins, the *sarcsteine*, that bestrew the battlefield at Alischanz, into the mouth of the good but nonbap-tized pagan king, Terramer. There seems to be an implicit reprimand here to

---

12. *Willehalm*, 1, 1 to 2, 27, pp. 1–2. Passage, pp. 25–26.

the Christian reader; no Christian has expressed such reverence or even been in awe at the presence of these stones containing the dead waiting for resurrection. Terramer ("Land and Sea"), in full armor, says:

> How shall we perform knightly deeds in front of the tombs of the baptized men? My furious onsets cannot manage to conquer Louis the Roman [emperor] or force him back, because the baptized men have the advantage that Jesus the sorcerer has bestrewn the field with many stone coffins [sarcsteine, lit. "coffin stones"]. Their flesh and bones lie inside them, but are whole! He who on the cross wore the thorny wreath upon His head as a harsh helmet performs such wonders for them.[13]

Once more it is the heathens who show proper amazement and ask the right questions—the baptized simply take things for granted. Pagan respect for the Christian hope of resurrection—and for the stones of Alischanz—is the basis for the Baruch's providing of Christian burial of Gahmuret. Wolfram is unable to distance himself from the many passages in which the stone of the sepulcher or sarcophagus plays a role—nor should he do so. But let us leave the *Willehalm* and return to the sacred *sarcstein* of the crusaders in Jerusalem.

Theoderich was a German, possibly a Rhinelander, who visited Jerusalem and wrote what is now called his *Guide to the Holy Land* (*Libellus de Locis Sanctis*). His account is datable to approximately 1172–1173, and is an important source for descriptions of the Holy Sepulcher from this time to the fall of Jerusalem in 1187 to Saladin. Wolfram could have had access to this book and to some of the stories described in it as well. Theoderich is completely focused on the Sepulcher as the center of Jerusalem and the world, and is much taken with the ceremony of the holy fire or holy light.

> It only remains then, that we should tell of the holy places, on account of which the city itself is called holy. We have thought, therefore, that it would be right to begin with the Holy of Holies; that is, with the sepulcher of our Lord. The Church of the Holy Sepulcher, of marvelous skill, is known to have been founded by the empress Helena. Its outer wall being carried, as it were round the circumference of a circle, makes the church itself round. The place of our Lord's sepulcher occupies the central point in the church, and its form is that of a chapel built above the sepulcher itself and beau-

---

13. *Willehalm*, 357, 16–30, transl. Passage, pp. 200–1. This passage comes immediately after Terramer's wonderful question "How does light pass through gemstone without causing any damage?"

tifully ornamented with a casing of marble. . . . The entrance is by the northern door and the exit by the southern door. The eastern door is set apart for the use of the guardians of the sepulcher. Between these three small doors and the fourth door—by which one goes into the sepulcher itself—is an altar which, though small, is of great sanctity. On it our Lord's body is said to have been laid by Joseph and Nicodemus before it was placed in the sepulcher. Above the actual mouth of the sepulcher, which stands behind the altar, these same men are shown in a picture of mosaic work placing our Lord's body in the tomb, with our Lady, his mother standing by, and the three Marys, whom we know well from the gospel, with pots of perfume, and with the angel also sitting above the sepulcher and rolling away the stone, saying, "Behold the place where they laid him" (Mark 16:6). Between the opening and the sepulcher itself a line is drawn in a semicircular form, which contains these verses: "The place and guardian testify to Christ's resurrection, / Also the linen cloths, the angel, and redemption." . . . No one can enter the mouth of the sepulcher itself except by crawling upon one's knees, and having crossed it, one finds that most-wished-for treasure—I mean the sepulcher in which our most gracious Lord Jesus Christ lay for three days—which is wondrously adorned with white marble, gold and precious stones. In the side it has three holes, through which the pilgrims give their long-wished-for kisses to the very stone on which our Lord lay.'[14]

Theoderich also adds, as have others who saw the edicule, or "little building" within the church that encloses the Holy Sepulcher, that

the roof of the structure itself is formed of slabs of gilt copper with a round opening in the middle, around which stand small pillars in a circle, carrying small arches above them, which support a cup shaped roof. Above the roof itself [in other words, atop the Holy Sepulcher's edicule] is a gilded cross, and above the cross is a dove, likewise gilded.[15]

The sign Wolfram chose to use for his *templeisen*, knights guardian of the Holy Grail, was, of course, the dove. In Jerusalem, Jesus' Sepulcher was the

14. Theoderich of Würzburg, *Guide to the Holy Land*, trans. Aubrey Stuart, 2nd ed. with new intro., notes, and bib. Ronald G. Musto (New York: Italica Press, 1986), pp. 8–9.

15. Theoderich, *Guide to the Holy Land*, p. 10.

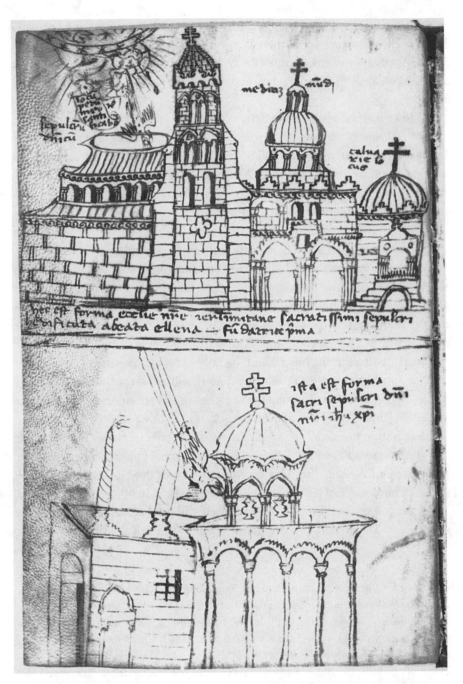

Two anonymous sketches from the fourteenth century, showing a dynamic and sacramental view of the Church of the Holy Sepulcher. The upper sketch in the top left corner shows Christ in the heavens, with cruciform halo and wounds visible in his hands, sending the Holy Spirit as a Dove down upon the (*continued on pg 86*)

revered stone over which the golden dove hovered and over which the Templars kept watch, the source of all their life and purpose, just as at the Grail castle on Mount Salvation the Temple Knights revered the stone upon which the Dove descended on Good Friday, and which is the source of their life and purpose.

The crusaders' visits to the actual Sepulcher of Christ had an enormous effect on Western religious art. From this point on, in paintings and mosaics of the Resurrection, the rectangular burial couch will be depicted, and not just a generic entrance to a rock cave. Nicholas of Verdun at this time produced masterpieces that clearly depict the actual Sepulcher, even with its three "portholes" to receive the devotional kisses of the pilgrim to Jerusalem. The Resurrection is shown as Christ rising out of the rectangular stone box that so many crusaders had made it their main purpose to see and honor in Jerusalem. Perhaps most startling of all in its clarity is a drawing from the period showing the Church of the Holy Sepulcher as being rebuilt by the crusaders. In the sky above, emerging from a heavenly cloud, Christ appears, wounds visible in his hands. With the one hand, he is sending the Holy Spirit as a shining Dove down upon his gravestone through the oculus, the central hole in the roof of the outer basilica. In the other hand, he is holding an open scroll on which is written *Locum peduum meorum santificabo* (I will consecrate the place where my feet trod). The drawing contains sketches of the crusader churches on the sites of Mount Calvary and above the rock of the Holy Sepulcher.

In addition to kissing the stone through the three portholes in the marble cladding, there was another ritual, equally emotional but far more wondrous: the miracle of the holy fire. This ceremony involves the Holy Sepulcher itself in the same passage of light that Wolfram so admired in other precious stones. The light passes through the stone by itself without causing any disturbance whatsoever. Theoderich and the abbot Daniel were not the only pilgrims to

(*continued from pg 85*) Church of the Holy Sepulcher through the oculus in the dome. In the lower sketch the Holy Spirit is within the Church and is descending further through the hole on top of the "edicule" the little building that houses the Holy Sepulcher, down to the stone Sepulcher itself from which Christ rose, perhaps initiating the ceremony of the Resurrection's Holy Light. The image echoes the liturgical epiclesis, the ritual and prayer asking that the Holy Spirit descend upon the stone of the altar to consecrate the Body and Blood of Christ. The descent of the Dove to the phoenix stone described by Wolfram in book 9 seems curiously similar. Christ in the upper sketch is holding a scroll in one hand on which is written, "I will sanctify the place where my feet trod" (*Locum peduum meorum santificabo* [sic]). *Biblioteca Apostolica Vaticana, Città del Vaticano. Cod. Urb. lat. 1362.f.1v*

crowd the church to observe the miracle of the light-through-stone, but the following are their words. Theoderich wrote:

> It is customary in the church of the Holy Sepulcher, both in the church itself and in all the other churches in the city, at daybreak on the morning of Easter Eve, to put out the earthly lights, and to await the coming of light from heaven for the reception of which light one of the silver lamps, seven of which hang there, is prepared. Then all the clergy and the people stand waiting with great and anxious expectation, until God shall send his hand down from on high. Among other prayers, they often shout loudly and with tears, "God help us!" and "Holy Sepulcher!" Meanwhile, the patriarch or some of the other bishops who have assembled to receive the holy fire, and also the rest of the clergy, bearing a cross in which a large piece of our Lord's cross is inserted, and with other relics of the saints, frequently visit the Holy Sepulcher to pray there; watching also whether God has sent his gracious light into the vessel prepared to receive it. The fire has the habit of appearing at certain hours and in certain places . . . it comes to the sepulcher itself, sometimes to the Temple of the Lord. . . . However, on the day when our humble selves, with the other pilgrims, were awaiting the sacred fire, immediately after the ninth hour that sacred fire came, upon which, behold, the ringing of church bells, the service of the Mass was said throughout the whole city, the baptismal and other services having been previously celebrated.[16]

The whole point of the appearance of the holy fire was that it was completely spontaneous. The tomb entrance was closed, no one was allowed in. Suddenly, without any form of human intervention (or at least so it was believed), one of the seven lamps in the tomb would be seen to be burning. The Light had come miraculously through the stone and into the burial chamber. Then the light, after the priests had entered the tomb, was spread to all present through openings and through the low doorway of the Sepulcher. Light of Resurrection passing through the stone of matter. Apparently when the Western clergy took over from the Easterners, they did not quite know how to bring the miracle about, and after a very few years the Greeks were given charge of this ceremony again—and once more light passed through stone. The abbot Daniel reports observing the same phenomenon of the translucency of the

16. Theoderich, *Guide to the Holy Land*, pp. 14–5.

grave of Christ on Easter, and takes more than a little glee in the fact that the holy light came to the tomb under the Eastern Christians but not under the Franks.[17] However, whether Eastern or Western liturgy was involved, the message is the same: the rock of the Holy Sepulcher of Christ is a gem, the gem of all gemstones, because of its translucency to the light of Christ in his Resurrection. This light passed through the stone tomb without damaging it in any way, or as Wolfram's Terramer might have said, without causing dent or splinter.

There is no wonder that the crusaders wanted somehow to bring this sacred stone *monumentum* back home with them, so that in some way on the Eve of Easter they could light their candles from the Light that came from Christ's own tomb. One of the finest crusader-era replicas of the Holy Sepulcher in Germany is at Eichstätt in Bavaria, a short distance from Wolfram's Eschenbach.[18] As I drove there early on a morning in late September, the cold misty rain that had been falling in Eschenbach gradually changed into intermittent snow flurries, and by the time I reached Eichstätt I noticed that it had become much colder. There was a thin coating of snow on the grass; it had snowed there during the night. Wolfram would have been happy over the thin coating of snow on the ground, but at the time I was too preoccupied with roads and parking places to enjoy the serendipitous snowfall.

The folks I ran into at the end of the parking lot were very friendly and solicitous, and after I had figured out with their help how to work the parking automat, I asked the question. "Can you tell me where I can find the grave of Christ?" I expected them to look at me as if I were some kind of religious nut, but I could think of no other way to phrase the question. They were not fazed in the slightest. This is after all a very Catholic part of Germany. They began chattering happily as if I had just asked where the main square of the town was, and agreed finally among themselves that what I was looking for was in the Capuchin church. One gentle lady offered to walk me halfway to the spot. After she left me, I walked four more blocks and found the Capuchin church. There was a woman walking in front of the church, and I couldn't resist asking my question again. "Is this where I can find the grave of Christ?" With similar aplomb, as if I had just asked for the nearest bakery, she said that I only had to go in the entrance and then turn to the right and then I would find the grave of Christ on my right. The down-to-earth nature of all the answers to the ques-

---

17. The abbot Daniel's report (1107 AD) can be read in C. W. Wilson's translation (1888) on the Internet at www.holyfire.org, under "Orthodox Christian" and "Daniil." The ceremony of the passage of light continues to this day in Jerusalem, and analogous ceremonies using candles or the Paschal Candle are celebrated at Easter in Orthodox and Catholic churches.

18. Wolfram's Eschenbach was in the ecclesiastical province of Eichstätt.

The Holy Fire, the Holy Light, emerging from the edicule of the Holy
Sepulcher into the Church of the Holy Sepulcher. Easter Saturday, 1990.
Photograph: Prof. Martin Biddle. Copyright.

tion still gives me a chuckle. I wondered what would happen if I were to ask
the same question in Washington, D.C., where the Franciscans also house a
reproduction of the Holy Sepulcher

I went in and found the sepulcher. It seemed to be almost as large as the
real one in Jerusalem, which I had visited two years before—just a little bit
smaller. Because it was built in 1166, it is used by scholars such as Martin
Biddle to determine the shape and condition of the Sepulcher in Jerusalem at
that time.[19] It has the three entrance–ways that have been described since very

19. Martin Biddle, *The Tomb of Christ* (Phoenix Mill, England: Sutton, 2000). For a photograph and discussion of the replica in Eichstätt, see pp. 29, 31, and 84. This work has two chapters on the appearance of the
tomb in Jerusalem at the time of Wolfram, and a final illustration, on p. 139, of the Easter celebration of the Holy
Light in the Church of the Holy Sepulcher in 1990. Biddle verifies the accuracy of the 1166 copy (dedicated
1194) of the Holy Sepulcher in Eichstätt, and uses it to help establish the condition and shape of Christ's tomb

The west end of the Eichstätt replica of Jerusalem's holiest shrine. The approximately three-fourths scale building was begun in 1166 at the time of the crusaders' control of Jerusalem, and consecrated, together with a hospital for wounded returning crusaders, in 1194 when Jerusalem had been lost. The architects faithfully followed the lines of the edicule as it was in the twelfth century. *Bildarchiv-Monheim, Germany. Photographer: Roman von Goetz.*

early times for visitors to the outer portion of the tomb. It is necessary then to stoop over and almost crawl to go into the fourth entrance–way, which brings the visitor into the burial chamber itself, and there at the visitor's right hand, as in Jerusalem, is the stone rectangular burial couch that contained the body

---

in Jerusalem at that time. He is very helpful and patient in answering questions from scholars outside his field, I can say gratefully.

of the Savior. The front panel of the stone coffin in Eichstätt still exhibits the three twelfth–century roundels, or "portholes," eight inches in diameter, cut into the protective stone panel so that the visitor (in Jerusalem, at least) can reach through and touch or kiss the original stone of the sarcophagus of Christ—without removing any stone chips from it as relics or pious souvenirs (something the abbot Daniel found a way to circumvent). There is no statue of Christ in the burial couch at the present time because, as a sign informs the visitor, the "image of Christ is being renovated." That there should be a statue of Christ in, or on, the sarcophagus is completely consistent with the crusader-era liturgical rites of Good Friday and Easter.

Of very great interest to me is the possibility that Wolfram may have been here for the consecration of this sepulcher in 1194 by Bishop Otto. As I stood inside the tomb replica and looked at the rectangular stone couch that represented the stone box that once contained the body of Christ, I wondered if Wolfram had once stood on the same spot where I was now standing. Had he been inspired by what he saw to realize what the words "container" or "vessel" in Chrétien's version of the Grail really meant? Was it perhaps here that he was inspired to make the connection between the Holy Sepulcher and the Grail as the real container of the Body of Christ in two stone forms: the original nonportable form of Good Friday evening and Easter, and the transportable altar-stone form of the sacramental liturgy?

Dieter Kühn's detailed research has led him to believe that Hartwig, count of Sulzbach, the twenty-seventh bishop of Eichstätt (from 1196 to 1223), may have been a donor and benefactor of Wolfram. Wolfram acknowledges Count Boppe II of Wertheim as his feudal lord, and Count Boppe was a vassal of Bishop Hartwig. Count Boppe, who was regent during the old age of his father, was the benefactor of the then newly founded order of the Teutonic Knights. Among his many generous donations to them, he gave the knights many revenue-yielding possessions in the town of Eschenbach, including the Eschenbach family as vassals. Clearly this establishes a relationship to the order of knights and to the bishop of Eichstätt. Kühn feels that Bishop Hartwig may even have been the donor who supported Wolfram during the time that he was not in Thuringia. If this is the case, and I think it ties many threads together, it would not be surprising to find Wolfram standing among the attendants at the blessing of the reproduction of the Holy Sepulcher in Eichstätt in 1194, at the time when Hartwig was the chief administrator of the diocese.[20] Ecclesi-

20. For a very interesting discussion of the historical details supporting the idea that Bishop Hartwig and the chancery of Eichstätt were among the benefactors who supported the work of Wolfram, see Dieter Kühn, *Der Parzival des Wolfram von Eschenbach* (Frankfurt am Main: Insel Verlag, 1986), pp. 160–73.

The interior of Eichstätt's replica of the Holy Sepulcher, with light
streaming through the grate that is above the burial couch, the sepulcher
itself. The view is from the inside of the vestibule looking toward the
western end. The small doorway leads to the Holy Sepulcher itself on the
right hand side. Looking beyond the doorway below the grate, one can see
two of the three roundels or "portholes" in the protective cladding on the
side of the Sepulcher, just as in Jerusalem. Their purpose, according to
Theoderich, was to enable the pilgrim to kiss "the stone that held the body
of Christ for three days." The lid above the burial couch can be seen edge-
on, just above the roundels. It is about seven inches thick and very heavy.
Bildarchiv-Monheim, Germany. Photographer: Roman von Goetz.

astically Wolfram's Eschenbach was at the time under Eichstätt, and he might have been required, at least by propriety, and I think by piety, to attend. If so, then indeed, the impressive reality of the stone grave may have made the impression on him that helped inspire the stone Grail and the sarcophagi of *Parzival*.

The construction of replicas of the Holy Sepulcher was not uncommon in northern Europe, especially in England and Germany, and goes back as early as the ninth century to the crypt at Fulda. Other sites in Germany were at Externsteine and at Augsburg, and in England it seems as though almost every parish church had to have one for the liturgy of Holy Week.[21] In Eichstätt, the Holy Sepulcher reproduction not only served for devotional use but also was connected with a hospital founded by Irish Benedictines for the care of returning injured or sick crusaders. The connection of these reproductions not only to the crusaders but also to the liturgy of Good Friday and Holy Saturday (Easter Eve) is made clear by Bishop Ulrich of Augsburg, who in his description of the Easter ceremony notes that in his ritual he is following standard practice. In speaking of his then new chapel of the Holy Sepulcher, he reports that he, "according to custom, buried particles of the Host under a stone, and then on Easter Morning [raised them up] and brought them to the church."[22] Thus the placing of the sacramental Body of Christ under a stone was used both to consecrate altars, as we have seen, and to provide a living visual connection to the original Resurrection of Jesus from the Sepulcher in Jerusalem. The altar stone and replicas of Christ's tomb in Germany and in England served as poetic phoenix stones, as devotional Easter phenomena that would have been familiar to many, if not all, of Wolfram's readers, whether they had actually been to Mount Zion in Jerusalem or had never left their home parishes.

What those who were present at the services would see seems somehow marvelously echoed in Wolfram's description of the Grail. Pamela Sheingorn's research concentrates more on England than Germany but is still very useful for looking at the spirit of the liturgy in the light of *Parzival*. First she considers the term used, *sepulchrum Domini* (the grave of the Lord) and the occasional use of *Anastasis* (Resurrection), which is generally restricted to the church of

21. See Pamela Sheingorn, *The Easter Sepulcher in England* (Kalamazoo, Mich.: Medieval Institute, 1987). This remarkable book contains a catalogue of Easter Sepulchers that runs from p. 77 to p. 368, using liturgical texts and records of wills and donations to substantiate her findings. Of special interest to us is her text for Durham (pp. 129–30) and her record of the synod of Worms and its attempt to exclude the laity from observing the removal of the cross and the sacramental Body of Christ from the sepulcher on Easter Eve—because of the superstition that anyone who witnessed it could not die that year. Shades of Anfortas.

22. Gustaf Dalman, *Das Grab Christi in Deutschland* (Leipzig: Dietrich'sche Verlagsbuchhandlung, 1922), p. 56.

A closer view of the side panel of Eichstätt's Holy Sepulcher shows the "portholes" cut in the stone cladding for the devotion of the pilgrim; their presence indicates the intention of having an extremely close copy of the Holy Sepulcher in Jerusalem. They are about eight inches in diameter. The heft of the lid stone is also apparent. *Author's photograph.*

the Sepulcher in Jerusalem. That the two echo one another is the point of building such replicas in Europe.

> The specific type of *sepulchrum Domini* that began to appear in Germany in the thirteenth century and gave the monument symbolizing Christ's tomb the form of a canopied sarcophagus is called the "Holy Grave" (*heiliges Grab*). . . . As well as referring to the Easter Sepulcher, the terms *"sepulchrum"* and "sepulchre" have the related meanings of an individual place of burial and of a small box [!] such as a reliquary.[23]

This is the same trio of meanings that Wolfram depends on in his evoking the nature of the Grail. Sheingorn divides the liturgy into three parts: the *depositio* (the taking down from the cross and burial), the *visitatio* (the coming of the women to the tomb on Easter morning), and the *elevatio* (the raising up of Christ). Often on Good Friday, both the cross and the Host were placed in the grave. Both were removed secretly on Saturday night, so that on Sunday morn-

---

23. Sheingorn, *The Easter Sepulcher in England*, p. 4.

A view from above of the lid stone of the Holy Sepulcher replica at Eichstätt. A Greek cross is carved at its midpoint with two six-petaled rosettes one on either side. On Good Friday a statue of the body of Christ was placed in or on such stone replicas, often with a communion Host inserted in them, thus making the whole replica analogous to the actual burial of Christ in the tomb, as well as making it a non-portable analogue to the portable altar. When used liturgically in this manner, on Easter morning the body of Christ would not be found in the Sepulcher, the statue having been removed and Host taken to the altar in the early morning by the priests. *Author's photograph.*

ing the "risen" Host could be seen on the main altar. As we have seen from Sheingorn's work, the effective poetry of the event required that lay people were not supposed to see the secret transfer of the Host from the sepulcher to the main altar: "A synod held at Worms firmly excluded the laity because of a superstition that had arisen that anyone witnessing the raising of the cross on

Easter morning would not die that year."[24] The burial cloth, however, was left in the sepulcher so that it could be seen on Easter morning to give witness that Christ had risen, and so that it could be a part of the ritual reenactment of the *visitatio*. What about churches that did not possess a sepulcher reproduction? Sheingorn's answer is significant: "many continental churches which never possessed Holy Sepulchres performed the rites at altars, drawing both on the equation altar = *sepulchrum* and on the fact that there was an altar in the Holy Sepulchre in Jerusalem."[25] This equation is one that fits well with the altar and the altar stone as well. Now it remains to examine a description of the service, in this case from Durham, England, and to think of the service of the Grail.

> There was in the abbye church of duresme [Durham] very solemne service uppon easter day between 3 and 4 of the clocke in the morninge in honour of the resurrection where 2 of the oldest monkes of the quire came to the sepulchre, beinge sett upp upon good Friday after the passion all covered with redd velvett and embrodered with gold, and then did incense it either monk before the sepulchre, then they both rising came to the sepulchre, out of the which with great reverence they tooke a marvelous beautifull Image of our savior representinge the resurrection with a crosse in his hand in the breast whereof was inclosed in bright Christall the holy sacrament of the altar, through the which christall the blessed host was conspicuous, to the behoulders, then after the elevation of the said picture carryed by the saide monkes uppon a fair velvett cushion all embroidered singinge the anthem of christus resurgens they brought it to the high altar setting that on the midst thereof whereon it stood the two monkes kneeling on theire knees before the altar and incensing it all the time that the rest of the whole quire was in singinge the foresaid anthem of Christus resurgens, the which anthem beinge ended the 2 monkes tooke up the cushines and the picture from the altar supporting it between them, proceeding in procession from the high altar to the south quire doore where there was 4 ancient gentlemen belonginge to the prior appointed to attend their comminge holding upp about with redd silke, and gold fringe, and at everye corner did stand one of the ancient gentlemen to beare it over the said Image, with the holy sacrament carried by two monkes around about the

24. Sheingorn, *The Easter Sepulcher in England*, p. 30.
25. Sheingorn, *The Easter Sepulcher in England*, p. 33.

church the whole quire waitinge uppon it with goodly torches and great store of other lights, all singinge rejoyceinge and praising god most devoutly till they came to the high altar againe, whereon they did place the said Image, there to remaine untill the assencion day.[26]

This liturgical action is the one to which Wolfram's Grail procession might be compared in some particulars rather than just to an ordinary singing of the Mass, especially since the Mass, which necessarily involves a celebration of the Resurrection, may not, by long tradition, properly be celebrated on Good Friday itself. The ritual of Good Friday commemorates the Passion, the Crucifixion, the death with the accompanying spear thrust into the side of Christ, and the burial of Christ by Joseph of Arimathea in the tomb cut out of stone. Early on Easter Sunday morning, the ritual can be completed in a dramatic fashion as described at Durham, in which the Host, the sacramental body of Christ, is raised from its tomb amid all the "goodly torches and great store of other lights" as at the Holy Sepulcher in Jerusalem in the celebration of the holy fire, re-presenting the holy light that passes through stone.

Wolfram's procession with the moving altar stone, the Grail, the lights and the aloewood incense, the spear and the weeping suggest an allusion not just to an ordinary Mass but to a Holy Week liturgy with lights passing before all. The garnet table stone is translucent to sunlight, Wolfram tells his audience. The radiance of the Grail's bearer is so bright that everyone thought that the dawn of day was breaking. That light passes through stone as the procession moves with the decorum of solemn liturgy, causing no damage or disturbance, passing through space and time.

26. Sheingorn, *The Easter Sepulcher in England*, p. 130.

4

The Frame Story

Feirefiz, Parzival, and Their Father

Wolfram clearly used the text of Chrétien's doubly named *Perceval,
or The Story of the Grail,* and he, too, wove together what Jean Markale feels are two perhaps quite different tales, the folktale of the naive young man who goes forth to seek his fortune, and the more
mysterious tale of the enigmatic Grail castle and its inhabitants.[1]
The magical Question that must be asked of the company at the castle—and the young man's failure to ask it—holds the two different
plots together. Chrétien added to the interest and complexity of his
story by having two heroes sally forth, Perceval and Gawain. Wolfram follows this double narrative outline as well, and goes beyond
the unfinished Chrétien romance by bringing both the Grail tale
with its Question and the Perceval-Gawain tale to a common conclusion, but not before he has added a third hero who brings a critical
third strand to the plot: Feirefiz, the heroic pagan brother of Parzival. For a reader who began with the German version of the story,
it comes as a surprise to see that in the French version, the hero
Perceval, almost to his very last line in the story, is searching for his
mother and not for a, or the, Grail, and most surely not for an unknown brother. It is also a surprise that the problem of baptism and
paganism and the crusader wars of Christian versus Muslim are
simply not present in Chrétien's version. Since Wolfram did follow

1. Jean Markale, *The Grail: The Celtic Origins of the Sacred Icon* (Rochester, Vt.: Inner Traditions International, 1999), pp. 1–22. Originally published as *Le Graal* (Paris: Éditions Retz, 1982).

Chrétien's story line, however, it is helpful to attempt to contrast the two versions in order to determine with some surety what the authorial intent of Wolfram was, especially if Wolfram's version is seen in the light of inventions of plot and gemstone symbolism found in the framing chapters 1 and 2 and 15 and 16. We will examine Wolfram's vision of the Grail, contrasting it with that of Chrétien whenever appropriate and possible, and first and most of all, by examining it in the light of the Christian-pagan frame story invented by Wolfram.

Chrétien's *Perceval* adventures might be divided into ten segments:

1. The young Perceval and his mother
2. The damsel in the tent
3. Killing the Red Knight
4. Gornemant's instruction on chivalry
5. The rescue of Blancheflor and her castle
6. Pentecost—the Grail procession; failure to ask the Question
7. The damsel with the decapitated knight
8. The haughty knight of the heath (Orilus)
9. The hideous maiden on the mule
10. Good Friday, the Hermit, Repentance; Easter Communion

These we will go on to consider in chapter 6 after examining the frame story. It will be necessary here to omit the parallel and more amorous adventures of Gawain, who in Chrétien, as in Wolfram, fits more the image of what has come down to us as the knight errant searching to be of service to damsels in distress. For both Perceval and Parzival it is different.

Much more important for having a key to the Parzival thread of the narrative, as I have said, are three extensive additions that Wolfram made to the foregoing narrative structure: the new beginning, books 1 and 2, a completion of the Perceval and Gawain strands in a confrontation of the two in book 14, and a new ending to stand parallel to the new beginning: books 15 and 16. By extending Chrétien's work in this way, Wolfram gave crusader Europe, and every period thereafter, a new model and insight into the nature of what he would have assured us was the true nature of the real Holy Grail. It is necessary and fair to Wolfram's work to consider the nature of the Grail in the context into which he put it. He wants the reader, too, to be able to humbly submit to the question that was thrown at his hero: "Haven't you realized the nature of the Grail yet?"

Wolfram von Eschenbach is often thought of as the inventor of the *Bildungsroman,* or novel of development, in German literature. Actually, because of his addition of a new beginning and a new ending to the basic story of the

Grail, he should also be given credit for being the first creator of the frame story in German literature. Wolfram's Feirefiz framework, books 1 and 2 at the beginning and books 15 and 16 at the end, encloses and gives new meaning to the Arthurian Grail material he received from Chrétien. By the creation of the action of the Feirefiz story and by confining it to the frame chapters, Wolfram both shows respect for the integrity of the traditional Grail material as he (critically) received it and literally places Parzival and the Grail quest in a new theological and poetic framework: the context of salvation for Christian and Muslim and, in that context, the propriety of their current relationship to one another. The frame chapters constitute a new and compelling context that forces the voice of legend and heroism to speak of the contemporaneous world of Muslim-Christian warfare. The reader is confronted with the complex discourse of an epic that is both legendary and contemporary and whose very structure forces him or her to assess the military world of chivalry and knightly warfare in the light of the world of kinship and religious loyalties. More to the point, it forces the reader living after the failed Third Crusade and between the fratricidal Fourth and the possibly then current preaching of the Fifth Crusade to examine the moral purpose and religious validity of these enterprises in the light of the Grail and of kinship loyalty. The reader is prompted by the frame story to ask, or to be aware of not asking, a religious question of Christendom—in the style of Parzival: what ails us? Why are we who are baptized engaging in religious warfare for the sake of the Holy Sepulcher in Jerusalem if, in fact, in the light of the real nature of the Grail, we already possess the Holy Sepulcher in all its power? Why indeed, if war for possession of Jerusalem and the Holy Sepulcher is fratricidal, and if the Person for whom the crusade is waged permits Himself to be transported in every movement of the Grail?

Despite the clever distraction of learned discourse on laws of inheritance as given in the legal traditions of the Germanic and Romance worlds with which the frame story purports to begin, underneath the learned explanation one hears the first echoes of a story and genre far older than the romances of Chrétien: the biblical parable. "Once upon a time there was a father who had two sons . . ."

> Once there was a man who had two sons. The younger of them said
> to his father, "Father, give me the share of the property that will be-
> long to me." So he divided his property between them. A few days
> later the younger son gathered all he had and traveled to a distant
> country, and there he squandered his property in dissolute living.
> When he had spent everything, a severe famine took place through-
> out that country, and he began to be in need. . . . When he came to

himself he said, "How many of my father's hired hands have bread enough and to spare, but here I am dying of hunger! I will get up and go to my father, and I will say to him, "Father, I have sinned against heaven and you, I am no longer worthy to be called your son; treat me like one of your hired hands." So he set off and went to his father. But while he was still far off, his father saw him and was filled with compassion; he ran and put his arms around him and kissed him. . . . And they began to celebrate. Now his elder son was in the field; and when he came and approached the house, he heard music and dancing. . . . He became angry and refused to go in. His father came out and began to plead with him. He answered his father, "Listen, all these years I have been working like a slave for you, and I have never disobeyed a command; yet you have never given me even a young goat so that I might celebrate with my friends." . . . Then the father said to him, "Son you are always with me, and all that is mine is yours. But we had to celebrate and rejoice because this brother of yours was dead and has come to life; he was lost and has been found." (Lk 15: 11–32, RSV)

The disguised parable of the frame story is the perfect vehicle for Wolfram because of a parable's intrinsic moral imperative to the hearer: "Go and do likewise." Both the story of the prodigal son (with the roles of the father and the older brother) and the parable of the good Samaritan (where, of the three travelers who passed the stricken man lying by the side of the road, it was only the Samaritan who did anything, because—and this is the crucial point for Parzival—he felt sympathy for the man's sufferings) have contributed quietly to Wolfram's structuring of the story. The parable of the prodigal son gives the kinship obligations and feelings because of the single (though compassionate) father and his two sons, and the parable of the good Samaritan shows compassion's ability to create human relations that defy social convention.

Wanting to justify his [previous question], the lawyer asked Jesus, "But who is my neighbor?" "Once a man was going down from Jerusalem to Jericho, and fell into the hands of robbers who stripped him, beat him, and went away, leaving him half dead. Now by chance a priest was going down that road; and when he saw him, he passed by on the other side. So likewise a Levite, when he came to the place and saw him, passed by on the other side. But a Samaritan [considered, like Feirefiz, to be both ethnically or racially mixed and to be religiously in error] while traveling came near him; and when he saw him, he was moved with pity. He went to him and bandaged his wounds, having poured oil and wine on them. Then he put him on his own animal, brought him to an inn, and took care of him [Feirefiz's chivalry: Feirefiz threw away his own sword even before, as Parzival tells everyone, Feirefiz knew that the two of us were relatives]. . . . Which of these three, do you think, was a neighbor to the man who fell into the hands of the robbers?" "The lawyer said, "The one who showed him mercy." Jesus said to him, "Go and do likewise." (Lk 10: 29–37, RSV)

Wolfram's only change is to reconceive "neighbor" as "family relative."

Turning now to Wolfram's frame story, the beginning of the frame and the end are set in parallel and can be characterized as revolving around three main themes in which the dilemma is set up in part 1 and resolved in part 2.

Books 1 and 2:

1. A father has two sons, one pagan and one Christian, who do not know each other.
2. Baptism's water is misused, against love, by the father: misused against wives' tears and against matrimony, and to enable further knightly warfare in the East.
3. The gravestone of the baptized is of ruby and emerald. They grant sight of the dead person's salvation from death. There are tears of compassion by the pagans over Gahmuret (whom the diamond helmet was unable to protect).

Books 15 and 16:

1. The Christian and the pagan brothers fight, then stop and realize that they have the same father.
2. Baptism's water is used in harmony with love, by the sons: it saves the pagan brother and fosters matrimony. It enables blissful happiness, not fighting, to overflow to the East.
3. The baptismal font is of two gemstones, ruby and (green) jasper. The water of baptism coming from the Grail grants sight of the Holy Grail and salvation. There are tears of compassion as the question is asked that heals Anfortas on Mount Salvation (whom the gemstones were unable to heal).

Water, the omnipresent element, in its gem form, tear form, and baptismal form, is the underlying, unifying element that unites the sacramental strands of human, jewel, and divine manifestations in Wolfram's framework. How does the hero get from book 1 to book 16? In the inner story, books 3 to 14, how does Parzival go from his cold-blooded blinding and killing of the Red Knight, and from his convention-conditioned failure to be moved when he first sees the Grail, to his emotional recognition that he almost killed his own flesh and blood in fighting Gawain? In Wolfram's reading, it is due to his development of compassion, the ability of his human heart to express its essence in the form of tears. This journey is not just one to full emotional maturity but to having any compassionate feelings at all, and in this development he is helped mainly by the women of the story. Three of these women, with their Wolfram-given names (one in German, two in French), outline the sequence: Herzeloyde, Condwiramurs, and Repanse de Schoye—Suffering Heart; Love Leads the Way; Overflowing Happiness.[2] If we then insert Sigune and Cundrie, Cousin and Knowledge, into this sequence, we have the road of penetrating light that brings Parzival the gem to the radiant point where his heart overflows with the waters of compassion, which prompts him to ask the Question. This is the road to taking possession of the Grail and also the only way to bring healing to all those who live on Mount Salvation. This is an important recognition, since the Grail is not so difficult to find, according to Wolfram, but without overflowing sympathy in its presence, one will remain bound to conventional expressions of propriety and not come to realize that one is in its mysterious and holy presence.

If Wolfram's Grail really is the consecrated stone of the portable altar, as I believe, then it is revealing to think how often Mass is said in *Parzival*. Before every major tournament, sometimes simply at daybreak, it is sung by the chaplain "for God and his master." Not one of these Masses could be said without an altar stone, the Grail, being there to consecrate the altar table, and to support the Body and Blood of Christ made mystically present in the liturgical action. The Grail is always there, in every chapter, but no one realizes it, and this is expressed with deft simplicity by having the Mass in the epic generally given only a half line or so. By this means, Wolfram has put the very problem that his hero has in the tissue of the story, and into the laps of his readers. Insofar as they, too, are not aware of the lack of recognition, neither on their part nor on the part of the characters in the story, Wolfram can smile again at his readers, Christian warriors all, crusaders and Knights Templar, living in the Land of Salvation, unaware of the need to ask the Question, one that might cause them to realize how sick they may have become and how beautiful they could be.

Let us examine the three interwoven themes as they are found in the frame

---

2. See appendix 1 for methodological considerations in explicating the meaning of Wolfram's names for the sequence of women.

story. First, the father who had two sons. Gahmuret is, as the story owns, a man in whom there is much black and white. As a chivalrous knight fighting for ladies' favor, he is without peer, and yet as a father and husband he displays much more of his human weakness. Several scholars have attempted to see an image of Richard the Lion-Hearted in Gahmuret, especially because of Gahmuret's friendship with the Baruch. Henry Kratz has replied to this identification in a convincing and balanced way.

> While these parallels are striking [Kratz cites nine from Panzer], it should be pointed out that there are many ways in which the two men do *not* coincide. For example, the three best-known facts about Richard are his kingship of England, his participation in the Third Crusade and his being held for ransom in Austria. There is no parallel to any of these facts in the career of Gahmuret. Even though Richard was known to have been on friendly terms with Saladin, it is a far cry from this friendship between two enemies to the outright service that Gahmuret renders the Baruc. Also, while Gahmuret marries a pagan woman, Richard did not. . . .
>
> If one excepts the name of Anjou, there is very little, actually, that Gahmuret had in common with Richard that he did not equally well have in common with many other crusaders . . . while Bumke's contention that the similarities between Richard and Gahmuret are confined to a few superficialities dismisses the evidence too easily.[3]

The evidence should be seen, I suggest, as evoking the time period of the Third Crusade by suggesting the time of friendship with the Baruch by a Christian king of Anjou, Richard the Lion-Hearted. The description that Wolfram gives of the character of Gahmuret as being willing to serve only the greatest of lords, and that lord being the pagan caliph of the Orient, is already to have slipped a provocative statement about power past the reader. The statement obliges Wolfram to give his famous equalizing description of the religious nature of the powerful paganism of the Orient at the time of the Third and Fourth Crusades. Gahmuret wished only to be of the household of the

> one who had supreme power on earth over all lands. Such was his heart's will. He was told that in Baghdad there was a man so power-

3. Henry Kratz, "The Crusades and Wolfram's *Parzival*," in *Arthurian Literature and Christianity: Notes from the Twentieth Century*, ed. Peter Meister (New York: Garland, 1999), p. 129–34. In this essay, Kratz takes his careful stance on the question between the positive evaluations of Friedrich Panzer and Willem Snelleman on the question of the identification of Richard with Gahmuret and the negative evaluation of Joachim Bumke but does not attempt to describe Wolfram's purpose in introducing such an allusion.

> ful that two-thirds of the earth, or more, was subject to him. To hea-
> thens his name was so great that he was called "The Baruch" ["the
> blessed one"; from Hebrew], and such was his power that many
> kings were vassals to him and subject were their crowns. The office
> of Baruch exists today, and just as Christian law looks to Rome, as
> our faith enjoins, there the heathen order is seen and from Baghdad
> they take their papal rule—deeming it entirely proper—and the Ba-
> ruch gives them absolution for their sins. (13, 12–25; 14, 1–2; Mus-
> tard, 9)

Wolfram's explanatory addition, "the office of Baruch exists today," and so on,
serves to remove the office of Baruch from the world of the story alone and
suggests the possibility of equating the two religions from the point of view of
how they are organized and, theologically, how both receive sacramental forgiveness of sins. They look to Baghdad as we look to Rome; they have equiv-
alently a pope whom they call the Baruch, who also promises them the remis-
sion of sins. This gracious, but surely provocative, text is aimed at creating
Muslim-Christian understanding and sympathy for one another's religion. The
text is important since it introduces the polar dilemma of the epic and the
frame—how then does the chivalrous Christian knight balance ecumenical
understanding of Islam with loyalty to Christ through baptism?

Bumke lists the many religious issues that are found in the text by
scholars, but they are restricted to the inner story of the hero Parzival's personal spiritual development, and thus Bumke's list misses the central problem of the text, revolving around the conflict of spiritual *triuwe*, religious loyalty—between ecumenism and fidelity, between religious respect for the
water of pagan tears on the one side and loyalty to the waters of sacramental
baptism on the other. Bumke writes: "The Christian theme of sin and grace
is what most obviously differentiates *Parzival* from the other Arthurian stories" ("Die christliche Sünden- und Gnadenthematik unterscheidet den Parzival am auffälligsten von den anderen Arthusromanen"),[4] and no one could
doubt the accuracy of his observation in the many examples he gives: Parzival's riding away from his mother, his killing of the Red Knight, Parzival's
silence at seeing the Grail and the suffering Anfortas, Parzival's renunciation
of God. All of which are true and can be contrasted with Chrétien's version.
Bumke's thoroughgoing analysis of scholarship on religion in the text, however, shows the degree to which the implicit religious problematic of the
frame story, ecumenism-fidelity, has not been made the focus of analysis,

---

4. Bumke, *Wolfram von Eschenbach*, p. 74.

and thus, I believe, the heart of the religious nature of the text and the Grail's nature itself has remained elusive.

In books 1 and 2, Wolfram creates two impressive processions for Gahmuret, depictions that many feel may not have been atypical for the traveling tourney knight of the day. Noise, music, a certain real or feigned nonchalance point to a rather self-assured person, but perhaps a bit more self-glorifying than unselfish. Wolfram enjoys, it seems, giving the description with a taste of irony of this knight who believed in moderation, was not given to haughtiness or boasting, but who, on the other hand, would only be in the military service of the most powerful ruler on earth, a man whose escutcheon bore the anchor but who never found a place where he wanted to stay:

> Ten pack horses he ordered loaded, and through the streets they
> went, twenty squires riding behind them. His household staff were
> seen up ahead, for pages, cooks, and the latter's helper lads had
> gone up front. Stately was his retinue: twelve highborn youths rode
> next after the squires, all well bred and with sweet manners, several
> of them Saracens. Next came eight horses, caparisoned in sendal-
> silk one and all. The ninth bore his saddle while a shield . . . was
> carried by a squire of cheerful mien walking alongside. After these
> rode trumpeters, who are still required today, and a drummer kept
> hitting his drum and swinging it high in the air. The master would
> not have thought much of the lot if flute players had not been riding
> along with the rest, and three good fiddlers. None of these was in
> any great hurry. He himself rode last, and with him his ship cap-
> tain, a man famed and wise. (18, 19–30; 19, 1–16; Mustard, 12)

There is more than a small hint in the presence of a ship's captain at Gahmuret's side that Gahmuret's anchor is one that will not hold. Wolfram contrasts this loud and showy procession, centered on the knight himself and on those who serve and glorify him, with the two reverent processions of the Holy Grail in which the loudest noise is that of light passing through the room. In book 2, once again Gahmuret processes into town with much the same fanfare, except that Wolfram adds:

> Now we must not neglect how their master approached. Fiddlers
> rode alongside him, and the warrior worthy had one leg stretched
> out in front of him on top of his horse; he displayed two boots
> pulled up on his bare legs. His mouth shone in its redness like a
> ruby or as if it were on fire, and a full mouth it was, not thin at all.
> His whole body was noble; fair and curling was his hair as far as it

> could be seen outside his hat and that was a rich headgear. Of green
> samite was his cloak, with sable trim showing black on the front of
> it, and set off against a shirt that was white. (63, 10–25; Mustard, 36)

Courageous indeed, but perhaps also a little style-conscious, and designed for
"love's reward." Gahmuret's colors are the two Wolfram prefers, red and green,
warmth and life, and these are worn against a trim and background of black
and white. Wolfram may be tweaking the stylishness that goes with chivalry,
but again, the presence of a ship's captain gives warning that, though the lips
are red and full, "of love's color," knights and crusaders move on and leave
families, women and children, behind.

The two processions introduce the two love affairs that will give birth to
the two sons of one father. Since the first procession is to come to the rescue
of Belacane, the black and pagan queen of the besieged town of Patelamunt,
the first son will be of mixed race, black and white, and since the father leaves,
the son will not know his father nor be baptized. Not until the end of the frame
story in book 15 do we learn that Gahmuret's son Feirefiz has been spending
his life looking for the famous warrior Gahmuret, not knowing that this man
whom he was seeking to find was his own father.[5] The critical question, and
for Wolfram one of the greatest import, is the poetic exploration of the status
of baptism and, as we have seen in Gyburc's prayer in his *Willehalm*, faithful
advocacy of the positive status of the nonbaptized before God. Thus the issue
of the baptized and the nonbaptized arises immediately in the first book.[6]

Belacane not only is black and beautiful, as in the *Song of Songs*, but is
radiant in her own way: her crown is a light-transmitting ruby (*ir krône ein
liehter rubîn;* 24, 12) so transparent that through it her head can be seen, and
she has a genuine and heartfelt regret that her beauty has caused the death of
her suitor.[7] She is like her crown; she is a living gemstone radiant with warmth

---

5. This is a curious parallel to Chrétien's Perceval, who is spending his time in Chrétien's version of the
tale looking for his mother.

6. Some (Jean Fourquet; A. T. Hatto) have suggested that the first book was not written first, but after
book 6. This seems highly improbable to me, due to the importance of the baptism question to the ending of
the epic and due to what I see as a clear frame structure integrated closely through books 2 and 3 with the
internal story. In any case, the theory of later composition has not met with acceptance. Bumke says with a
certain surety of voice: "Es wird deswegen dabei bleiben, daß Wolfram seine Dichtung mit der Erzählung von
Gahmuret begonnen hat, d.h. daß er von Anfang an mit einer eigenen Stoffauffassung an das Werk gegangen
ist." I am, of course, of the same opinion. See Bumke, *Wolfram von Eschenbach*, p. 86.

7. Belacane's name, which Wolfram seems to have picked or composed with care, sounds to the ear like
"bella" and "cane" or "Beautiful Song." In the *Song of Songs*, the love song of the Old Testament, the two lines
made most famous from liturgical usage are: *nigra sum sed formosa*, "I am black but beautiful," and the allusion
to spring lovemaking, *vox turturis audita est in terra nostra*, "the voice of the turtledove is heard in our land."
From the very beginning of his story, Wolfram hints by allusion to the *Song of Songs* that love despite difference

and light. In thinking about her, Gahmuret "reflected how she was a heathen, and yet never did more womanly loyalty glide into a woman's heart. Her innocence was *a pure baptism* [*ein reiner touf*, emphasis mine], as was also the rain that wet her: that flood which flowed from her eyes down upon the furs about her bosom" (28, 10-7; Mustard, 17). The similarity, if not equivalence, of pagan and Christian is suggested again in the presence in a pagan of what one would have supposed to be Christian virtues: loyalty, *triwe*, a chaste innocence in love, *kiusche*, and the rain of tears of regret over the warfare that is being fought over her.[8] This is such sympathy and even repentance that Wolfram has no trouble suggesting that the tears of such feelings bear a real similarity to the flowing waters of baptism, and may produce the same effect in the good pagan person: salvation. Alas, her Christian lover, Gahmuret, who is so aware of the holiness of her tears, cannot match her, either in loyalty or in the tears of honorable regret. When Gahmuret defeats a black prince, Razalic, the prince is described as a brave and black-complexioned pagan, to which Wolfram adds his theological hope editorially: "Far and wide went his fame, and if he later died *unbaptized*, may He who has all miracles within His power have mercy on that warrior brave" (43, 6–8; Mustard, 25).

When Gahmuret begins to grieve because he had no knightly activity, he became unhappy and deserted his black wife, even though she was dear to him. He then had his gold put on board ship, cast up his heraldic and real anchor, and deserted his wife for the sake of going off to the fighting. "And now I must tell you of departure. By night the worthy man went away, and it was done secretly. And when he deserted his wife she had within her body a child twelve weeks alive" (55, 10–5; Mustard, 31). He left a note: "I cannot conceal from you, Lady, the fact that were your faith of the same law as mine, I would yearn for you eternally, for I do suffer for your sake always. . . . Lady, if you will receive baptism, you may yet win me back" (55, 24–7; 56, 25–6; Mustard, 32). A curious note indeed, since before deserting his wife and child, Gahmuret had himself noted how close to baptism her innocence and her tears were. And, of course, Wolfram adds, she would be perfectly willing to be baptized: "To do honor to his God, the Lady said, I would gladly agree to be baptized and live as he desired." It is for this reason, no doubt, that Gahmuret left secretly by night and in haste before she could reply. The baby that is born six months later is the black-and-white child of them both,

---

will exist in the land, the voice of the lovebird, the turtledove, will be heard. The reader is being prepared for the paradox that this symbol, the turtledove, is the emblem of the fighting Knights Templar.

8. Both spellings are used in the MSS, *triuwe* and *triwe*.

Feirefiz.[9] As a parting shot, Wolfram writes that she kissed the child over and over again on his white spots, the part of his skin coming from her husband—she is still loyally in love with her husband, despite his inability to put *triuwe*, loyalty in love, above a career of knightly fighting.

As a last souvenir of this affair, and as a memento of his defeat of the forces of Isenhart, Gahmuret is given the dead Isenhart's helmet made of diamond, a gem supposedly impervious to the hardest weapons but, as we have read in Albert the Great, easily softened to mush by the blood of the lusty goat. The diamond helmet, the reward for fighting, will serve Gahmuret just as well as the sword of Ither, the Red Knight, will serve his son Parzival against his brother Feirefiz: both will fail at the crucial moment.

Gahmuret is a man like his son. He shares in black and white, though in a moral sense; however, as the preface assures us, he can still attain happiness. After deserting his wife and child and fleeing to Spain, Gahmuret is unhappy, but when he learns of the death of his brother in Anjou, the floodgates open, and this despite clear and authoritative instruction that he should mourn "with due restraint." "Unfortunately his grief was too great, and a flood of tears poured from his eyes" (93, 2–6; Mustard, 52). In Wolfram's poetry, this is the sure sign of a true human being. A good person is a gem of pure water and as such will inevitably send up an almost baptismal flood of tears from heart to eyes whenever sympathy or suffering come home to it, whether or not convention and instruction find such behavior appropriate. This sure sign of humanity, on the other hand, reaches its nadir when Gahmuret's son Parzival in his tutored simplicity fails to be moved even to question, let alone cry, at the suffering of Anfortas.

Just as Gahmuret finds himself flooded with grief, and just as Mass is being sung for Gahmuret, in comes the lady Herzeloyde, Sorrowing Heart, and she, appropriately, stakes her claim on Gahmuret. Since he is already married to Belacane, whom he abandoned, using baptism as the cover or excuse, once more baptism is invoked in order for the procession-loving knight to get his way. This time it is Herzeloyde who tells him, "You should renounce the Moorish woman for my love's sake. The sacrament of baptism has superior power [*des toufes segen hât bezzer kraft*; 94, 13], now give up your heathenry and love me by our religion's law" (Mustard, 53). Mustard's comment on this subject is that Wolfram's audience would "readily accede to the notion that marriage

---

9. The name could mean "Doer of Deeds" or "Performer of Feats," and possibly as well, "Brother and Son." The latter (*frère et fils*) would make sense in view of the ending and the double relationship to Parzival as brother and godson.

between a Christian and a heathen had no validity." This needs more than a little nuancing.

According to the biblical principle of the "Pauline privilege" a Christian may leave a marriage in which the partner—St. Paul was thinking of a Jewish partner—refuses to convert to Christianity. This principle could be extended to a nonwilling pagan partner. It seems, however, that Wolfram has presented an abuse of that privilege (one that itself seems to violate the prior principle of Christian charity). In this case, the non-Christian queen, Belacane, was deserted (while pregnant) by the Christian for the sake of fighting, and second, she was quite willing to become a Christian and be baptized. Wolfram has made it hard for his readers to accept such dismissive treatment of a family relationship to a pagan as Herzeloyde is suggesting, whether canonically legal or not. He is taking care to show through Gahmuret's behavior that one can make use of the sacraments shamefully and dishonorably—unchivalrously (a category not invoked by St. Paul). Gahmuret has no right to abuse the "superior power of baptism" in this way to bring further injury to the already injured party. Thus I think Wolfram has set up the text in the story in such a way that what is true is the opposite of what Mustard believes. The reader has been prepared by the situation to see any use of baptism to justify desertion of one's pagan wife and child as a violation of *triuwe*, personal loyalty, in other words, a completely underhanded misuse of the sacrament of baptism. And this is what Gahmuret does.

After his rejection of Belacane (and of the French queen) and his embracing of Herzeloyde, Gahmuret once again warns that he will not be kept from the business of knightly fighting and tells his second wife it's an old story how he will react if she objects. When he then goes off and is killed in the service of the Baruch, Herzeloyde is left alone, nine months pregnant with the second son of the parable, Parzival. In her distress she is near to death, but a wise man forces her jaws open and pours water into her mouth, and with the water, Wolfram's favorite element, she comes back to consciousness. Praising her husband's fidelity, she prays to be relieved of her intense distress and mourning for fear she could kill Gahmuret's child and thus give him a second death. Instead she thinks of the milk in her breasts and describes it, echoing the tears of Belacane, as a kind of human baptism:

> The lady found satisfaction in seeing that nourishment lying above her heart, that milk in her breasts, and pressing some of it out, the queen said, "You come from faithful love. If I had never received baptism, I would want you to be my baptismal water. I shall anoint

myself with you, and with my tears, both in public and in private—
for I shall mourn for Gahmuret." (Mustard, 62)

> Diu frouwe ir willen dar an sach,
> daz diu spîse was ir herzen dach,
> diu milch in ir tüttelîn:
> die dructe drûz diu künegîn.
> si sprach "du bist von triwen komn.
> het ich des toufes niht genomn,
> du wærest wol mîns toufes zil.
> ich sol mich begiezen vil
> mit dir und mit den ougen,
> offenlîch und tougen:
> wande ich wil Gahmureten klagn." (III, 3–13)

Lest any theologian or cleric rush to say that milk may not in any sense be
called an appropriate form of the water used in baptism, Wolfram is quick to
add an example that no medieval theologian would take lightly. Looking at the
baby she is nursing, the lady Herzeloyde imagines that she has prayed Gahmuret back into her arms and muses in a religious way:

> Wisely the Lady Herzeloyde said, "The supreme queen gave her
> breasts to Jesus, Who afterwards for our sakes met a bitter death in
> human form upon the Cross and Who kept faith [triwe] with us." . . .
> The country's mistress [Herzeloyde, Sorrowful Heart] bathed in the
> dew of her heart's affliction, and upon the boy rained down the tears
> of her eyes. A woman's true fidelity [triuwe] was hers. (113, 18–30;
> Mustard, 63)

Wolfram in the first part of the frame story associates baptism with fidelity
by associating water with tears and with motherly milk flowing out of loyalty,
and associating her loyalty with Mary and with that of Jesus crucified. Thus
family love and kinship association are connected through baptism with divine
activity as mother and son, husband and wife, brother and brother are made
"two in one flesh," just as Wolfram composed in his initial invocation to his
Willehalm. This overflowing of loyal affection is something that he sees as
enabling the human person to express humanity, and thereby to transcend the
boundaries of societal convention and society's instructions on conventional
behavior. Without experiencing family feelings, a knight can become a literal
obey-er of standard instructions—of exhortations to crusading—and runs the
danger of becoming a heartless servant of societal instructions, not seeing them

as something that must often be transcended in the name of human family love. The tears are the water of the clay that is the material of common humanity. Thus Herzeloyde, Sorrowing Heart, who has a title and a function that associates her in this text with Mary the Sorrowful Mother, says that she will anoint herself with her tears and her milk "both in public and in private," whether that is conventionally acceptable behavior or not, for she is so filled with fidelity that she must mourn the one who loved her and whom she loved— as did Mary.

"And so the adventure's die is cast and its beginning is set" (*hiest der âventiure wurf gespilt, / und ir begin ist gezilt;* 112, 9–10; Mustard, p. 63), that is, we have the two sons of one blood who do not know each other, one baptized and one not, though both are baptized in tears, and their common father will remain unknown to them both. They will meet. But the story has to deal with Gahmuret's death. And so we start with the diamond helmet that failed through the treachery of goat's blood and the death and burial of the Christian knight who died in the service of the pagan ruler of Baghdad. The sarcophagus is the most important and striking symbol in the initial half of the frame story, and has its parallel in the final half and the end of the story, since it alone has to deal with the ultimate *zil* of the human condition, death itself.

Gahmuret dies in the state of grace. His chaplain comes to the mortally wounded Gahmuret, who makes his confession and repents the sins of his life, and he receives the sacramental forgiveness of his sins from Christ through the absolution given him by his chaplain. In his forgiven and purified condition, enclosed in gold and precious stones through the kindness of the Baruch, his lord, who covers all the expenses, Gahmuret can now be called, as expressed by the incorruptible state of his body and by the gems that surround him, the pure one (*der reine*).

> He was laid to rest in Baghdad. The Baruch gave no consideration to the costs. With gold [the coffin] was adorned, and great treasure of precious stones was expended on it. Within it lies the pure one. His youthful body was coated with aromatic balsam [*gebalsemt*; balsam as in the Grail procession] and many were those that mourned for him. Over his grave was set a precious ruby through which he clearly shines [*ein tiwer rubîn ist der stein / ob sîme grabe, dâ durch er schein*]. We were permitted to place a Cross for his comfort [*im ze trôste*] and for the defense of his soul, after the manner of the Passion by which Christ's death redeemed us, on his grave—its cost was borne by the Baruch—and the Cross consists of a single precious emerald [*ez was ein tiwer smârât*]. . . . His manly fidelity and

his contrite confession give him a bright radiance in heaven [*diu manlîche triwe sîn / gît im ze himel liehten schîn, / und ouch sîn riwic pîchte*]. (107, 25–7; Mustard, p. 60)

Wolfram's depiction of Gahmuret's death-place uses medieval gemstone language but follows St. Paul on burial with Christ and on baptism:

> Don't you know that all of us who were baptized in Christ Jesus were baptized into his death? We were therefore buried with him through baptism into death in order that, just as Christ was raised from the dead through the glory of the Father, we too may live a new life. If we have been united with him like this in his death, we will certainly be united with him in his resurrection. (Rom 6:3–5, NIV)

> We do not want you to be ignorant about those who fall asleep, or to grieve like the rest of men who have no hope. We believe that Jesus died and rose again and so we believe that God will bring with Jesus those who have fallen asleep. (1 Thes 4:13–14, NIV)

> Listen, I tell you a mystery: we will not all sleep—in a flash, in the twinkling of an eye, at the last trumpet. For the trumpet will sound, the dead will be raised incorruptible, and we will be changed. (1 Cor 15:51–52, NIV)

The grave of Gahmuret, its gold and its two precious Augustinian gem-stones, is entirely the creation of Wolfram, and one might ask why he makes it such an impressive focal point at the end of the initial half of his frame story. Wolfram's rich and gem-filled climactic description brings the grave into a mysterious parallel with the grail on Mount Salvation by having the gold and precious stones adorn the (coffin) in which Gahmuret is placed be elucidated in detail, while a word for the "coffin" is not even present. Instead, Wolfram says of it only "the place wherein the pure one lay" (*dâ inne lît der reine*; 107, 4), thus putting all the emphasis on the gold and the two precious stones, and letting the reader have an inkling of a similarity to the mysterious but analogous function of the Grail stone. Like a third gem, the person in the grave is pure: he remained true to Christ, and his feelings of regret overflowed in his final confession, and he was absolved by his chaplain. He is aware of Christ's Passion and salvation from death, *als uns Kristes tôt lôste* (107, 11), in the emerald Cross, the gem of Christ's living loyalty put above him for his consolation *im ze trôste* (107, 12), and thus Gahmuret, too, is radiant. Enclosed in gold, visible through the transparent ruby and encouraged by the emerald, though he is subject to death, he is preserved in life. Gahmuret is thus a majestic parallel to the mortally wounded Anfortas, who is kept in life by the Grail stone.

Gahmuret is seen through the gemstones of Eden as a corpse mysteriously intact; in his incorruption he is mystically connected to Paradise, and he shines with a bright radiance in Heaven (*ze himel liehten schîn*; 107, 26). Both of the two stones above him are from the primal river Phison of the Garden of Paradise. Through the transparent or translucent ruby, the buried Gahmuret can be seen in radiance, like Augustine's carbuncle or ruby, the *anthrax* or "live coal," undimmed by the black darkness of its outer layer and not ever to be extinguished by the blackness of the grave or death. In the green translucency of the enormous emerald that is the cross, Christ's death and resurrection glows as the source for Gahmuret's verdant hope for eternal and vigorous life. And the emerald is not there to be a future hope but rather his consolation in the present—his resting in a grave notwithstanding. Both gems here are fulfilling their paradisial functions from Eden as described by St. Augustine, and the person-gem in the grave is shining in his forgiveness and in his soul's virtue as elucidated by Bishop Marbode. It is no wonder that the pagans treat this miracle of Christian faith as giving Gahmuret in his sarcophagus a divine status. As we saw, this miracle was commented upon in the *Willehalm* by the great pagan king of land and sea, Terramer:

> The baptized men have the advantage [against heavy cavalry] that Jesus the sorcerer has bestrewn the field with many stone coffins. Their bodies and bones lie inside, yet they are whole. He Who on the cross wore the thorny wreath upon His head as a harsh helmet performs such miracles for them. (357, 22–30; Passage, pp. 200–1)

It seems that not only is the use of the sword entirely the improper way to attain the Grail, it is also the improper way to show the nonbaptized the benefits of the baptismal waters. The ruby and the emerald have the power of themselves to show what God is capable of, and Wolfram comments that the pagans deemed the dead baptized man, shining through the gems, a divinity. The Baruch in his ecumenical and feudal loyalty to his knight Gahmuret is mentioned twice as bearing the expenses and doing so gladly. Surely this is both a remembrance of Saladin's kind generosity to Richard the Lion-Hearted and an indictment of the nonecumenical behavior of baptized lords and knights, including the same Richard, toward the Muslims in the Holy Land.

The epitaph is written on the diamond helmet, and a parallel epitaph is discovered on the Grail in book 16 discouraging ethnic and racial bias, thus testifying to the epitaph's importance. It is attached to the cross on top of

Gahmuret's grave, giving clear witness to the superiority of admiration on the part of the pagans, rather than to violence against them on the part of the Christians, when it comes to winning them over to being saved from death by the kindness of Christ:

> He was born in Anjou and yet before Baghdad he gave his life for the Baruch . . . he was baptized and supported the Christian law, yet his death was a grief to Saracens [*er truoc den touf und kristen ê: / sîn tôt tet Sarrazînen wê;* 108, 21–2]. This is true and no lie . . . he triumphed over falsity. Now wish him bliss who lies here! (Mustard, p. 61)[10]

---

10. In a nice touch, Wolfram creates a harmony in rhyme between Christain law, *ê*, and Saracen grief, *wê*.

5

The Frame Story Ending

The Overflowing Grail

Helmets, when they work effectively, and because they work effectively, enable violent fighting to occur because they make personal recognition of kinship impossible. So begins the ending of the story of Parzival. In book 14, Wolfram brings the heroes of the two strands of the inner Grail story (from books 3 to 14) together, Gawan and Parzival. The two relatives and fellow knights of the Round Table meet each other in a fight like no fight in the story, with their helmets, of course, on. Parzival's experience in this penultimate fighting contest is one of realization; he becomes aware of the helmet's unexpected relationship to blindness. He began his fighting career by fighting the Red Knight, whom he killed by throwing a javelin with stunning accuracy through the helmet's eye slits, a helmet's one clear vulnerability, thus at the same time managing to both blind and kill his noble and chivalrous opponent. Parzival was the blind one, however; he did not recognize that he was acting shamefully in three ways: in taking advantage of the eye slits, in using a throwing weapon, and, above all, in killing a kinsman. Then he went on to strip the corpse of its armor without even a tinge of regret, much less a feeling of compassion. There was no thought of burial in a sarcophagus with or without gems. Parzival rode on.

At the Grail castle in book 5, although technically he did not have a helmet on, Parzival did not see whose green cloak was on him, nor did he recognize a suffering relative in Anfortas, and so he did not feel called to take the social risk of asking the saving question. Finally at the end of the inner story in book 14, Parzival is blindly engaged in a ferocious encounter with a nonrecognized Gawain: a joust between loyal baptized man and loyal baptized man. In this penultimate sword fight, Parzival comes to a very important recognition of the negative effect of the helmet, and when he does, significantly, he tosses his sword away.

> Now hear how the joust proceeded. Both galloped hard to the charge yet neither had cause to rejoice, for here with the force of courage renowned kin [*sippe*] and noble friendship closed in sharp struggle. Whoever wins the prize must forfeit his joy to sorrow. Each dealt such a powerful thrust with his hand that the two kinsmen [*mage*] and comrades brought each other down, horses and all. Then with their swords they slashed and hacked until all around the green grass and splinters of shields were a blended froth. . . . The battle had very nearly reached the point where Gawain's foe was the victor when Gawain's squires, recognizing him and moved by their devotion to him, cried out aloud at his peril, calling his name in their grief, then the other one who till then had pressed on hard in the struggle lost his zest for battle and *cast his sword far from him* [*verre ûz der hant er warf daz swert*; 688, 21]. . . . "Accursed and dishonored am I," cried the stranger and wept. . . . "I admit myself guilty [of sacrilege]. . . . Alas that I fought with the noble Gawain! It is myself that I have vanquished." . . . Gawain said, ". . . Your hand gained victory over us both, now may you grieve for the sake of us both. It is yourself you have vanquished—if your heart knows true faith" [*Du hâst dir selben an gesigt, / ob dîn herze triwen phligt*]. (690, 1–2; Mustard, 357, 360–1)

Due to the devotion of his squires who were able to see despite the helmet, Gawain is saved from the helmet's blinding anonymity. Parzival is saved from what Wolfram tries to make into the most outrageous of sins to his contemporaries, slaying a kinsman. Parzival weeps at the close call—he now cares very much—and tosses his sword away, a gesture made famous because of the Christian defeat at Hattin in Galilee in 1187, signifying a desire to contend no further, and to yield oneself to the enemy. Parzival puts the feelings of kinship over the conventions of knightly combat. He weeps, following the example of his female relatives, thinking of the close call, and throws away the sword.

Wolfram of course goes further. Of killing a baptized person the Council of Sens had declared officially: "Who sheds the blood of a Christian, sheds the blood of Christ." Wolfram's other tack, however, is to suggest an older and more fundamental principle: "Who sheds the blood of a relative, commits an unnatural sacrilege and follows the path of Cain's fratricide." This sin has just been averted from the count of misdeeds of the slayer of the Red Knight by the devotion of Gawain's youngsters (at one point the text calls them *kint*; 688, 18).

One cannot help but think that this happy ending is a poet's reply to the Christian tragedy of 1204, then inadequately unrecognized as dire and unnatural, when Western Christianity fought Eastern Christianity to military submission. The defensive armor of the ancient walls of nine-hundred-year-old Constantinople fell to a Christian army, and the capital of the Christian East was ravaged and plundered of its arms and treasure, as was the Red Knight, Parzival's kinsman, of his arms and armor. How much better would this ending have been, suggests Wolfram, I believe, if, instead of continuing the lethal fight at the Golden Horn, upon hearing the familiar cries of *Kyrie, eleison* from the "youngsters," the soldiers on the walls, the Western Parzivals, had "felt the zest for battle disappear from them," had taken off their helmets and thrown their swords far away from them, and wept at what they had almost done. "It is yourself you have vanquished." Fratricide is suicide.

Why does Wolfram use blood relationship as his argument against knightly killing rather than the Council's argument about killing a fellow Christian? The answer is, of course, in the final framework of the epic, books 15 and 16, in which the brothers of the frame story's initial parable meet and are not fellow Christians. The question then becomes: may brothers who have the same father but who do not both have baptism, engage in lethal combat without incurring grave shame? Wolfram's account of the brothers' hostile meeting and recognition is full of authorial insertions begging God, and anyone who will listen, not to let them kill one another because they are really one, while at the same time not hesitating to entice the reader on by promising to reveal the secret of the martial virtue of both brothers.

In book 15, Feirefiz is introduced as "a master over all warfare" and "this courteous man was a heathen who had never known baptism." He is, baptism or no, as a human being, a gem of the purest sort, as is demonstrated not only by his conduct but also by the fact that he is covered with gemstones.

> All that lay within the power of Arthur's hand in Britain and in England would not match the worth of the jewels of noble water and pure that studded this hero's surcoat. Rubies and chalcedony would

> not have paid for it. This surcoat gave forth a blaze of light . . . genu-
> ine precious gems lay dark and bright upon it. I cannot name their
> virtues. (Mustard, p. 384)[1]

Not only these signs of power and of the pursuit of love are on him but also, pagan though he may be, he wears on his helmet as his insignia the ecidemon, the mongoose—the destroyer of the serpent. As these two brothers meet and fight with real intensity, Wolfram is forced to comment: "These pure men without a flaw each bore the heart of the other, and in their strangeness to one another they were still intimate enough. Well, I can't part this heathen from the baptized man if they are determined to show hatred" (Mustard, 385). And again: "I cannot refrain from speaking up: I must mourn their fighting from loyalty of heart because one flesh and blood are doing one another such harm. Both of them were, after all, sons of one man, the foundation stone of pure loyalty" (Mustard, 386). In a cry that is surely a protest against the Christian-Muslim warfare of his crusading day, the author interjects: "God shield Gah-muret's son! That is my wish for both of them, the baptized man and the heathen" (Mustard, 387). Alluding to the statement of Genesis 2:24 concerning the relationship of Adam and Eve that the two become one flesh, Wolfram interjects his comment on the fighters, "One may say 'they' were fighting if one wants to speak of them as two, but they are indeed only one, for 'my brother and I,' that is one flesh, just as good man and good wife" (Mustard, 386).

As the fighting continues, the source of the strength of both of the brothers is revealed: Parzival's strength comes from the Grail and from Condwiramurs. When Parzival is losing, the author's prayer is "Avert it Grail of power! Avert it, Condwiramurs the beautiful!" This is an appeal to the Christ of the altar-stone sepulcher, and an appeal to Parzival to remember his wife—loyalty to both will motivate Parzival. The Rock will provide strength, and the remem-brance of Condwiramurs will provide the motivation to fight harder. In a line I consider one of Wolfram's finest, Parzival begins to recover the advantage in the fight as he remembers Condwiramurs and begins shouting her name as a battle cry: "And just in time Condwiramurs came across four kingdoms with the sustaining power of her love" (*Condwîr âmûrs bezîte / durch vier künecrîche aldar / sîn nam mit minnen kreften war;* 744, 4–6; Mustard, 388).

The strength of Feirefiz also comes from two parallel sources: "one was the love that he bore steadfastly in his heart, the other was the gems which by their pure and noble kind taught him high spirits and increased his power"

---

1. From this point in the story, the Lachmann numbers will be given only where the original is cited. They are also to be found in the margins of Mustard.

(Mustard, 387). Love motivates both men, as chivalry, humanity, and religion demand, but standing parallel to Parzival's Grail are Feirefiz's gemstones. Granted that their power is accepted in his day, and that Augustine, Marbode, Hildegard, Albert, and Thomas Aquinas all grant gemstones an origin that is with God the Creator, God the Father, in Eden's rivers, in the glory of the angels, or in the quintessence of the stars, they possess, as Bishop Marbode wrote: *divinitas*, "divinity," or "God's power." This is Wolfram's way of acknowledging, I believe, that the pagans, too, in their way are in possession of divinity and divine powers: they, too, are cared for and strengthened by the primordial gifts and precious stones of God from the Garden of Eden and its rivers. The stones are a sign that heathen and baptized have one common place of origin, with its one benevolent Creator, their one Father.

Finally the fight ends as Parzival's sword shatters and he is helpless to continue. The two fighters sit down in the grass, and Feirefiz, the noble and courtly pagan, behaves in a manner similar to that of Saladin, and in a manner drawn directly in parallel to Parzival's throwing away his sword when he recognizes his kinsman Gawain as his opponent. Out of a chivalrous sense of fair fight, Feirefiz took his sword and "hurled it far away from him into the woods" (*ez warf der küene degen balt / verre von im in den walt;* 747, 15–6; Mustard, 389). And this is even before he has recognized that his opponent is his brother; Feirefiz does it sheerly out of noblesse oblige. Then both brothers remove their war helmets, and the blindness of war helmets is replaced with sight as the two recognize that they are the sons of one father. As he sees the black-and-white markings of the magpie on his brother's face, Parzival, like Belacane so long before, kisses his brother and is kissed in return.

The fighting is over now that their two-ness is seen as a one-ness. Yet their manful fighting ability came both from love of their families and, in both cases, from a second more mystical source, the precious stones. The fact that Parzival's Grail and Feirefiz's gems are both of stone serves to suggest that the Grail's helping power and the gemstones' helping power both ultimately come from a common transcendent source. If the Grail's power comes from Christ, from the Communion Host that arrives on Good Friday brought by the Dove, the gemstones' power comes from the Garden of Paradise, and thus from Creation's Father. Feirefiz's strength comes from the Father. If, moreover, God the Father and God the Son are One in the unity of the divine Spirit, then the strength of both brothers comes from one source: the Trinity. Baptism is seen to divide the two brothers, but only seemingly, because Christian baptism cannot be given in the name of the Son to the exclusion of the Father. It is not possible to perform a baptism saying "I baptize thee in the name of Christ." Though heathen and baptized are divided, their power comes from one source, and neither the one that is baptized nor the heathen should feel that his power is religiously unrelated to that of the other if God is Triune. Baptism is bestowed in the unifying Spirit of the Father and of the Son and not in the divisive name of the one or the other alone. God is One, but, as Wolfram keeps insisting, Three in One.

Wolfram's sedulous avoidance of the term "Christian" may find its explanation here. "Christians" should be called "the baptized" (as he always does!) because the baptized are baptized into the Trinity, into the relationship of the Father and the Son in the Holy Spirit. For Wolfram, "Trinitarians" might be a preferable designation for "Christians," but this is not a term in common use (except occasionally by pagan figures in both poems). Baptism into Trinity does not divide good Christian from good heathen, nor is baptismal water utterly foreign to pagan human tears, but rather Trinitarian baptism shows Christian and Saracen their divinely originated union in a Trinity that is indivisible. Baptism, then, most surely cannot be used and should not be misused as a reason for attacking the nonbaptized, who quite clearly enjoy the support of their Father within the Holy Trinity. As Trevrizent tells Parzival in book 14, "God has many secrets. Who hath ever sat in His council or who knoweth the end of His power. . . . God is man and also His Father's Word, God is Father and Son: this Spirit can lend great aid" (Mustard, 416, modified). St. John insisted that God is love (1 Jn 4:8), in Wolfram's version, as we have seen: God is kinship, loyalty existing in Trinity. Thus Wolfram addressed God in the second line of his *Willehalm*: "You who are Three and yet One" (*du drî unt doch einer*). For Wolfram, in Christ, human nature and the Second Person of the Godhead stand in the tightest of loyal relationships. God is Father and Son in eternal relationship; the Spirit, depicted as the Turtledove, is the loving spirit of that relationship; God himself is the original infinite pattern of family that establishes human relatedness. Kinship becomes in Wolfram's spiritual poetry the primal tripartite expression of the Godhead as it overflows into the Creator's human world.

Wolfram formulated a theology in which to interfere with kinship is sacrilege, and Cain's unfeeling murder of his brother Abel, shedding his blood on Mother Earth, becomes for him the first story giving an account of this original sin against the kinship-creating Trinity. It is the Trinity that is called on in baptism, not Christ alone, the Trinity source of all the waters of Creation and of redemption and of the tears of joy and sorrow. The doctrine of the Triune nature of God is Wolfram's brilliant resolution of the dilemma between loyalty to Christ in baptism's brotherhood on the one hand and on the other equal loyalty to one's pagan brotherhood in God the Father.

It is for this reason that at the climactic moment of the entire epic, when

Parzival is about to ask the long-awaited question of Anfortas, Parzival is accompanied by his heathen brother Feirefiz. With tears pouring down his own face in a human, heathen, baptism that had been missing the first time he saw the Grail, Parzival asks first where the Grail is kept, then turns in that direction and genuflects, not once but three times, in honor of the Trinity (*drîstunt zêrn der Trinitât*; 795, 25; Mustard, 414). Only then, rising to his feet, does he ask the question.

Perhaps the one embarrassing thing about this recognition that both sides are being loyal to God in his inner Triune nature is that it is the pagan heroes in the story, both the Baruch and Feirefiz, who first recognize the seriousness of the loyal religious commitment of the other party and are the first to act on this recognition. Feirefiz implicitly recognizes the Trinitarian pattern of relatedness as he rejoices that the brothers recognized each other, and Wolfram has him do it in words that are almost Pauline:

> "If I am to grasp the truth, my father and you and I, we were all one, but this one appeared in three parts. . . . You have fought here against yourself; against myself I rode into combat here and would gladly have killed my very self; you could not help but defend your own self in fighting me. Jupiter, write this miracle down! Your strength helped us so that it prevented our deaths!"—He laughed and wept, though he tried to conceal it, and his heathen eyes shed tears as in honor of baptism. Baptism must teach fidelity [*triuwe*] since our new covenant was named for Christ and in Christ you can see what fidelity is. (752, 7–30; Mustard, 392)

It is Wolfram's own insistence that it is fidelity to family that is taught by baptism—rather than alienation from members of it. He cleverly uses Christ himself (who could be proposed as the reason for hostility between Christian and Saracen) as the very reason and exemplar of loyalty to the human family *usque ad mortem*. Once again in the story, both baptized and unbaptized men have been able to recognize that the law of kinship is of divine origin. The pagan hero thanks his god Jupiter, the Christian author thanks Christ, and baptism is described not as an occasion for having an excuse to separate oneself from and to abandon (as did Gahmuret) fellow human beings, much less crusade against them with the sword, but as an occasion instead to realize how loyal the Holy Trinity was to Its human race in the Incarnation and Passion of Christ, loyal even to the divinely unthinkable, death. And as before, it is the pagan who sheds the tears of joy over recognized kinship, tears that are, as Wolfram insists once again, most surely the waters of a kind of baptism.

For someone whose tears are so good-hearted, is further baptism, Christian baptism, necessary for salvation? We know from Gyburc's plea in the *Willehalm* that Wolfram, using her voice, begins with the Magi and Job, and gives many scriptural examples of God's children who were far from church or the people of Israel and with whom God was well pleased. St. Thomas Aquinas, Wolfram's thirteenth-century near contemporary, cited St. Augustine to say what Wolfram had felt before him: "some have received and benefited from invisible sanctification without visible sacraments,"[2] and some can attain salvation because of their desire for baptism (*propter desiderium baptismi*), which originates from faith operating out of affection (*quod procedit ex fide per dilectionem operante*; Gal 5:6), a loving feeling by which God performs an inner sanctification of the person (*per quam Deus hominem interius sanctificat*).[3] God's power is not restricted to the visible sacraments. (*Cujus potentia sacramentis visibilibus non alligatur* [*alligatur: ad* + *ligare*, lit. "to tie to," here, "is not tied to"].)[4] This is an important line of thirteenth-century argumentation, and it is anticipated by Wolfram. It is exemplified in the case of Feirefiz, who already has a fine sense of nobility and family, and who has so fallen in love with the Christian woman who carries the Grail that he is gladly willing to be baptized. The incident almost literally anticipates Thomas's dictum earlier about a desire for baptism to be able to constitute a real and genuine baptism *ex fide per dilectionem operante*, through faith that comes from the workings of love.

The question of baptism in Christ's name, rather than in the name of the Trinity, came up in the thirteenth century, perhaps motivated by the more narrow and aggressive Christian spirit of the Crusades, and especially by the zealots who preached them. Thomas Aquinas briefly discussed the possibility. He rejected it on the ground that it was not traditional and not grounded in Scripture, which quite clearly says, "Going therefore baptize all nations in the name of the Father and of the Son and of the Holy Spirit" (Mt 28:19). It seems Wolfram had a more poetic and ecumenical reason.

If pagan tears of human feelings are a kind of baptism, and if the good pagan recognizes, albeit implicitly, human kinship, the Trinitarian pattern, as divine, and can be thereby saved, is there any further need or advantage to be obtained from a proper Christian baptism? The baptism of Feirefiz begins with the question of the now cured and beautiful Anfortas to Feirefiz: "Sir, do you see the Grail lying there before you?" Feirefiz answers that he sees nothing but a green cloth—an *achmardi*—and the lady who carries it. Anfortas then tells Parzival, "Sir, I do believe that your brother has not yet seen the Grail." The

2. *Summa Theologiae*, 3a pars, quest. 68, 2, sed contra.
3. *Summa Theologiae*, 3a pars, quest. 68, 2, responsio.
4. *Summa Theologiae*, 3a pars, quest. 68, 2, responsio.

wise old man Titurel hears of this and sends back the message, "If he is a heathen man, then, without the power of baptism he has no use wanting his eyes to join the company of those who do see the Grail." Sight is Wolfram's reason for the baptism of the nonbaptized: this sacrament of water has the power to grant sight of the Grail; the power to see with the eyes of faith what "that magician" does for Gahmuret in death and will do for Anfortas in life.[5]

It is little noticed that there is a second question in Wolfram's version of the Grail legend. Wolfram has Feirefiz put a question to Parzival and the Grail community: "If I come to baptism for your sakes, will baptism help me in love?" (*Ob ich durch iuch ze toufe kum, / ist mir der touf ze minnen frum?* book 16; 814, 1–2; Mustard, 424.) He is, of course, referring to Repanse de Schoye, but this question to the baptized must have rung loud and clear on more than one level in the crusader era. Does baptism help the baptized to love? Is not the question an innocent convert's sincere inquiry and simultaneously an inadvertent, sly rebuke? It is as if the Saracen were asking Christianity if its sacraments are of any help in doing what Christianity is essentially all about. Do the followers of the Turtledove just receive help in fighting? The question gently proposes Wolfram's dream for the way Christianity should be spread— let the heathen members of the family fall in love with the happiness the baptized have been given. Neither the Grail, nor sight of the Grail, can be won by fighting. Let the pagans fall in love with the Grail, with what it promises, and with the only person by whom the Grail will, in any case, permit itself to be transported from place to place, from one culture to another—Repanse de Schoye, Overflowing Happiness, The Spread of Joy.

In accordance with the renunciations required in the liturgy of baptism, Feirefiz is told that he will have to give up all his gods, especially the Jupiter to whom he so often turns, if he wishes to receive baptism. He agrees, and in view of the role that Jupiter and Mars play in Anfortas's suffering, there is an irony here to which we will return. The heathen is called into the temple. As we might have expected from Gahmuret's grave, "the baptismal font was a single ruby, and it stood on a circular step of jasper" (*Der toufnapf was ein rubbîn, von jaspes ein grêde sinwel, / dar ûf er stuont;* 816, 20–2). Since "templum" is ecclesiastical Latin for "church," it is now quite clear where he is standing

5. Albrecht Classen wrote that Parzival and Feirefiz are "connected through blood though separated through their beliefs." There is a further critical separation at stake, one that is remedied here: they are separated by "sight," the ability to see the Grail. Thus I think it is mistaken to suppose that Feirefiz has not truly "converted to Christianity," or that his baptism is an "external badge without true religious meaning," just because it was occasioned by love. On the contrary, Feirefiz's baptism has given him full sight of the Grail and enabled him to be joined to Overflowing Happiness. See Classen, "Jewish-Christian Relations in the German Middle Ages," in *Amsterdamer Beiträge zur Älteren Germanistik* 58 (Amsterdam: Rodopi, 2003), p. 138.

among all the knights and squires. The Augustinian stones from Genesis are there, ready to grant their meaning to the ceremony: the ruby to speak of inextinguishable light, of unfailing fidelity; the green jasper to signify life that can never wither and to speak of granting sight to the eye.[6] The baptismal font is at first empty; then it is tilted slightly in the direction of the Grail, and the Grail invisibly overflows, performing its ancient paradisial function. The Grail is the source of overflowing baptismal water that flows outward from it, invisibly, as the water did from the original single source of the four rivers of the Garden of Eden. Suddenly the baptismal font is full of water. Having described the filling of the ruby font in this miraculous way, a font whose waters would now appear blood-red to anyone looking at the ruby font, Wolfram distracts the reader from this miracle in his usual style by making the very casually distracting comment that the water was neither too hot nor too cold. Well, if the people who look at a baptismal font generally do not realize the miraculous nature of the waters they are looking at, the remark is slyly apropos of the type of comment one might actually hear at a baptismal ceremony, despite that fact that this water grants eternal life and the light of sight to Gahmuret's mixed-blood son.

The priest is also provided by the Grail, which in its invisible outflow does not just create sacraments and kings but also designates priests. Though sometimes mistakenly understood as ironic, Wolfram's comments on priests, granted that he associates them with the love-radiating and conducting function of Condwiramurs, have to be understood positively. Priests may not have killed or kill. By the ancient tradition and the canonical prohibition to which Wolfram alludes, a man with blood on his hands may not be ordained a priest. The priest's hands have to be free of blood and sword fighting, since he stands close to the Trinitarian and sacramental function of the Grail:

Women and priests, as is well known, bear no weapons in their hands. Yet God's blessing watches over priests. Serve them with unswerving devotion, and if your life is to have a good end [recall here Gahmuret's final confession to his priest, guaranteeing his heavenly radiance], you must show good will to priests. Nothing your eye sees on earth is like unto a priest. His mouth proclaims that martyrdom which cancels out our damnation. And his consecrated hand takes

6. Modern jasper can be of more than one hue; however, in antiquity and up to the Middle Ages, especially due to the references to jasper as the transparent foundation stone in the heavenly Jerusalem, *jasper* referred to transparent green stones. See Walter Schuman, *Gemstones of the World*, rev. and exp. ed. (New York: Sterling, 1977), p. 146. The stone being referred to is most probably, I believe, the peridot from Egypt. It was brought back by the crusaders to Europe, where it became very popular for ecclesiastical and liturgical use.

and holds the highest pledge [the eucharistic Body of Christ] that
ever was given for guilt. (Mustard, 268)

In other words, the function of his hands in holding "the highest pledge"
makes his role analogous to that of the sepulcher-chamber in the Grail stone
itself. The Grail stone in the frame story is the source and provider of all the
sacraments of the church, as well as their ministers. The Grail provides the
Eucharistic banquet for those on Mount Salvation; the sacrament of penance
and last rites for Gahmuret, as indicated by the chaplain, the ruby, and the
emerald; baptism and holy orders as seen in the miraculous overflow of water
and the ancient priest; and finally, the Grail gives its own bearer to Feirefiz in
the sacrament of matrimony.

The derivation of baptism and the sacraments from the Grail is another
way to connect its true identity with Christ and with his Passion. In the *Summa
Theologiae*, St. Thomas gives his view of the origin of the sacraments in the
Passion by first citing the *Glossa Ordinaria*: "The sacraments by which the
church is saved flowed from the side of the sleeping Christ" (*Ex latere Christi
dormientis fluxerunt sacramenta per quae salvata est ecclesia*).[7] He adjoins his
agreement:

> It is obvious that the sacraments of the church have their power in a
> special way from the Passion of Christ. . . . As a sign of this, there
> flowed from the side of Christ as he hung on the cross water and
> blood. One of these refers to baptism and the other to the Eucharist,
> and these are the most powerful sacraments.
>
> Manifestum est quod sacramenta Ecclesiae specialiter habent virtu-
> tem ex passione Christi. . . . In signum cujus de latere Christi pen-
> dentis in cruce fluxerunt aqua et sanguis, quorum unum pertinet ad
> baptisma aliud ad Eucharistiam quae sunt potissima sacramenta.[8]

What Wolfram has described in his frame story in vivid thirteenth-century
imagery is what the theologians of his era were saying in more abstract fashion.
The Grail has to be a container for the "side of Christ asleep" in his Passion,
but pouring out his mystical life and light, blood and water. The lance is not
mentioned either by Thomas or the *Glossa*, but it did not have to be, since
everyone knew the legend of Longinus, especially after the controversial but
effective finding of the lancehead in the First Crusade. The bleeding lance is

---

7. *Summa Theologiae*, 3a pars, quest. 62, 5, sed contra.
8. *Summa Theologiae*, 3a pars, quest. 62, 5, sed contra and responsio.

present in the Grail procession in book 5 and becomes an immediate cause of lamentation in the hall because of the recollection of John 19: 31–34, and the role of one of their own, a soldier:

> Because the Jews did not want the bodies left on the crosses during the Sabbath, they asked Pilate to have the legs broken and the bod- ies taken down. The soldiers therefore came and broke the legs of the first man who had been crucified with Jesus, and then those of the other. But when they came to Jesus and found that he was al- ready dead, they did not break his legs. Instead one of the soldiers pierced Jesus' side with a spear, bringing a sudden flow of blood and water. (NIV)

At his baptism in this flow of water, Feirefiz is told by the priest of the faith that he shall accept: belief in the Triune God, the Highest God, whose help is everywhere of equal benefit and therefore of loyal help to baptized and nonbaptized alike. One should not expect of baptism any special feudal benefits in fighting or winning wars (another comment to the crusaders of the day). Following the actual baptismal ritual and its prayers fairly closely, Wolfram describes the virtues of water in words parallel to the ritual prayer for the blessing of the baptismal font. St. Thomas gave his own remarkably similar justification for the liturgical prayers over the water and adds his own insight showing the appreciation of the most vital of the four elements:

> By divine institution water is the proper matter for baptism—and this is fitting. First of all, from the very nature of baptism which in- volves a rebirth to spiritual life. This rebirth is in close concordance with the properties of water. Indeed seeds from which all living things both plants and animals are generated, are themselves moist and related to water . . . water by its diaphanous nature is receptive to light: therefore it is appropriate for baptism in that baptism is the sacrament of faith [aqua sua diaphanitate est luminis susceptiva: unde competit baptismo inquantum est fidei sacramentum].[9]

The moist nature of water makes it appropriate for giving life; the diaph- anous nature of water makes it appropriate for receiving and transmitting light; it is translucent to the light of divine faith, and it passes light through itself to the candidate. The power of all Three is within the water of the font like the divine power in the water of gems. The Son of God himself stepped into water

---

9. *Summa Theologiae*, 3a pars, quest. 66, 3, responsio.

The baptismal font (c. 1225) of the cathedral of Hildesheim. The bronze font has four kneeling figures pouring water from amphorae, representing the four rivers of Paradise. This makes the baptismal font itself into the single source of water, the *fons vitae*, at the center of the Garden of Paradise from which all four rivers spring, and suggests that the water of baptism returns the baptismal candidate to the Garden of Paradise, seeing Christ Himself as the original fountain of water in the Garden. On the lid, Mary Magdeline adds her tears to the baptismal water, as did Herzeloyde. This iconography of water is remarkably similar to that of the Bamberg Paradise Altar, in which the four rivers are similarly depicted as men with amphorae, who pour forth their water while looking back to their source, the stone sepulcher of Crucifixion and Resurrection. *The Bridgeman Art Library, New York.*

This detail of the Hildesheim font shows one of the four rivers of Paradise which support the baptismal font, thereby suggesting that the baptismal water in the font springs from the primal fountain in the Garden of Eden, making baptism a return to the Garden of Paradise. The ancient priest who baptizes Feirefiz similarly expounds on the universal life-giving and sight-giving function of water. The four rivers of the Eden pour out their waters toward the four directions of the whole world, kneeling with their amphorae in the anthropomorphic style of classical antiquity. *Könemann Verlagsgesellschaft, Cologne.*

for his baptism in the Jordan. The priest continues. "From water trees derive their sap," he says; "water fructifies all created things . . . from water man has his sight. Water gives many souls such radiance that angels cannot be more bright" (Mustard, 425–6). The critical realization that sight comes from water may refer not only to the transparency of the element itself but also, I believe, to the very aqueous humor that fills the eyeball and makes the human eye itself diaphanous enough to be receptive to light and thus capable of physical sight. Were the human eyeball filled with blood or any other less "diaphanous," substance our sight would be dark indeed. Many a soldier struck in the eye by arrow or bolt, dagger or sword thrust must have lost an eye on the field of battle. Medieval illustrators are generous in showing parts of bodies strewn on the field of fighting. Many may have witnessed the horror of the end of sight in an eye with the oozing out of the aqueous humor from a wound suffered in the eyeball. Wolfram must have known of this. Most seriously for his hero Parzival, this very act is what he is responsible for: killing Ither, the Red Knight, by striking him in the eye slit of his visor with a javelin, penetrating as no light beam would, causing instant blindness and death, and the oozing out of the sight-giving watery substance. At the beginning of the epic tale of *Parzival,* sight was taken away, and at the end of the tale, sight is restored.

Feirefiz can now see the Grail. Under the influence of love, the light of faith has entered his eye. Feirefiz is illuminated, water by light, light passing through diaphanous water, penetrating through the translucency of person, revealing him to be a gemstone possessed of, in Marbode's word, divinity. And, as Terramer would have said, the light passed through the pagan gem without any noise or commotion, causing no damage. Now one of the baptized, he does not become a son of God—he has been that since his creation; but now he can see the stone that made him a translucent gemstone, and has given him a transparency to radiance that is a rival to that of the angels. He can see with Parzival and all the Grail community how the Passion of the Savior is present sacramentally in the broken Bread of the altar stone.

This scene reveals that Wolfram was thinking of the Grail as the fountain, the source of the water of the sacrament of baptism. The source of all the sacraments is Christ, and as we have seen, Thomas Aquinas and the *Glossa*

Detail from a battle scene from the "Crusaders Bible." At the left is a gruesome act reminiscent of the death of the Red Knight. A helmeted knight stabs his opponent in the eye, as the victim vainly attempts to pull on his enemy's helmet. All the knights on the left side are wearing Wolfram-era helmets with the familiar, if vulnerable, eye slits. *Photograph: The Morgan Library, New York. MSM.638, f.40.*

Ordinaria testify that these two sacraments flowed from the side of Christ in his Crucifixion (as can be seen in the iconography of the Mauritius altar of St. Servatius in Siegburg). To see the Grail, then, is to be able to see Christ in the altar stone as the Grail, as the source and enabler of the effectiveness of the sacraments, most especially of baptism and the Eucharist as they once flowed from his Passion in Jerusalem on Good Friday and now flow from the Grail. The Grail stone is a description of the function of the altar stone with the Body of Christ within it, given not in the language of theology but in the language of stories of wonder and cast in the language of the knightly activity and quest. Baptism grants sight of Christ in all his humility in the Sepulcher and in the wonder stone of the altar that grants outflow of gem-like *divinitas* to those who are attracted to baptism not by threat of Christian sword and fire but by the promise of falling in love with and marrying Overflowing Happiness.

And now to the Question. What is wrong with Anfortas, the keeper of the Grail and the head of the Grail community on Mount Salvation? It is interesting that the healing of Anfortas and the return of the sick man to wholeness

A twelfth century portable altar with its central altar stone. This is the Mauritius altar, preserved in the treasury of St. Servatius in Siegburg. It about 14 inches long, and about 6 inches wide. The stone covering the sepulcher compartment is of red porphyry from Arabia, possibly removed from some object of Roman antiquity. The edge of the upper table has a repeated geometric motif. *Schatzkammer der St.-Servatius-Kirche, Siegburg.*

The Mauritius portable altar from above. To the left of the stone is the Crucifixion of
Good Friday, and to the right of the stone is the Resurrection of Easter Sunday. The
stone being between the two represents the transitional period, Holy Saturday,
between the two events, the time Christ was in the sepulcher-tomb. In the left panel
the Trinity (Trinitas) acts to save Adam. The Father is above, the Dove of the Holy
Spirit hovers between heaven and the cross on earth, Christ's blood pours down onto
Adam in his sepulcher, who rises up from the grave as the blood reaches him. In the
right panel, the Ascension is above, Mary Magdeline speaks with Christ below, and in
the middle the three Mary's come to the tomb with spices on Easter morning. The
sarcophagus of the Resurrected is red in analogy to the altar stone. *Schatzkammer der
St-Servatius-Kirche, Siegburg. LVR-Rheinishes Amt für Denkmalpflege. Photographer:
Michael Thuns.*

requires only that spontaneous interest and sympathy for the sufferer prompt
the questioner to ask the question. At his first visit in book 5, Parzival was too
concerned with proper behavior to condone such a spontaneous feeling push-
ing him to break protocol. The unasked original question was literally "How
stands your lordship's suffering?" (*hêrre, wie stêt iwer nôt?* 484, 27) The rather
distant and formal address (*hêrre* and *iwer*) is an inquiry that is polite but
betrays indifference toward the sufferer. It asks politely for the degree of distress caused by the disease but not what the sickness is. This formal question
is replaced in the final book 16 by a family form of address (*œheim* and *dier*)
that shows that real kinship feelings have grown up in Parzival's heart; and by

a switch from "how?" to "what?" "Uncle, what are you suffering from?" (*Oeh-eim, waz wirret dier?* 795, 29).[10] Both the subjective concern for the sufferer and a concern with the nature of the sickness that were missing in Parzival's first visit are now present. If it is Christendom's suffering caused by its non-sacramental activity that is being called into question, the questioning must be done in a family way; it must come from a concerned relative. In this way, conducted by love, the nature of the ugliness-causing affliction can be faced and thereby remedied.

Since the spontaneous asking of the question alone effects the cure, no one gives a direct answer to Parzival's question. Wolfram leaves it to the reader. The reader is thus pushed by the author to reflect on the symptoms and the condition of the Fisher King in the light of the care and the cure. What was Anfortas suffering from? And just who is Anfortas? The answer that is concealed in the text, I would like to propose, is based on the dominating presence of Saturn, Jupiter, and Mars. The most significant change, moreover, in Anfortas's condition is one from a stench-emitting ugliness to one of incredible beauty, exceeding that of Parzival, and from near-suicidal depression to happiness. These are not biological sicknesses but psychological and spiritual ones based on insecurity and vacillation, *zwîvel*, based on the men's identity as swordsmen who yet wear the turtledove.

Who is this Fisherman who is in charge of the baptized Grail community? In view of the Third and Fourth Crusades, it might be possible to suggest Innocent III, successor to St. Peter the fisherman, but I prefer to see Wolfram as not restricting his story to simple one-to-one correspondences. As in the case of Gahmuret of Anjou being associated with Richard the Lion-Hearted of Anjou, I see the text rather as eliciting a time, suggesting an era, whose behavior should be subjected to asking the Question, rather than being a text susceptible to easy one-to-one personal equations. Wolfram's text is valid for many eras of Christendom, as well as the one in whose context he wrote it. When I think of Anfortas, whose name, as classical as the three gods causing his suffering, can be said to contain a Greek alpha privative joined to the Latin root for *strong*, then *An + fort* signifies human weakness. It is parallel to the Latin word for a sick person, *in-firm(-us)*. He is thus the embodiment of Christianity in its full human weakness, and his name steers the reader away from simply assigning him a role as one specific historical person. Perhaps, more specifically, Western Christendom is being pointed to, in its painful need of healing through the second coming of its spirit of simplicity, Parzival, and in

10. See Leslie P. Johnson, "Parzival's Beauty," in *Approaches to Wolfram von Eschenbach: Five Essays*, ed. Dennis Howard Green and Leslie Peter Johnson. (Bern: Peter Lang, 1978), p. 288.

deep need of simplicity's questioning of what its crusader knights are attempting to do in the Land of Salvation.

All attempts to ease the sufferings of Anfortas, whether based on the medicinal value of stones or of herbs, fail to work in his case. Trevrizent reports that it is a wound in the testicles from a poisoned spear that struck Anfortas in a joust as he was pursuing a love not allowed to him by the Grail. If this love was Orgeluse, and she is the one who is happy at the coming of Anfortas's cure, then Anfortas found himself in love with Prideful Arrogance. The pagan Feirefiz fell in love with Overflowing Happiness, while the Christian Anfortas became enamored of the maiden Arrogance. Once again we have in the text a reflection of the condition of the crusaders and of crusading Christendom at the time of Wolfram's writing—Western Christians who will not be made whole again until they first, by themselves and spontaneously, become aware of the fact that they are sick.

The hopelessness of conceiving of this illness in standard terms, curable by standard medicine, is shown by the ineffectiveness of all the medical knowledge of stones and herbs used by the Grail community to help Anfortas.[11] Why cannot the wound be cured? After all, Munsalvaesche community uses all the herbs that can have drifted down the four rivers from the Garden of Paradise. In book 9, Trevrizent tells of all the books of medicine that they tried to no avail, all the herbs that are useful against snake venom, to no avail.

> God himself denied us their aid. We sought help from the Geon,
> and the Fison, the Euphrates and the Tigris, the four streams flow-
> ing out of Paradise, and to Paradise we came so near, where its
> sweet fragrance has still not faded away, to see if perhaps there
> might come drifting some herb that would take our sorrow from us.
> It was labor lost. Our grieving began afresh. (Mustard, 257)[12]

Every precious gemstone known to Augustine, Marbode, Arnold, are listed as being present and only of palliative use.[13] Wolfram lists one whole thirty-line manuscript page of them, beginning with "carbuncle and moonstone,

---

11. For a delightful and learned account of all the Arabic, classical, and medieval methods being used to cure Anfortas, see Arthur Groos, *Romancing the Grail: Genre, Science, and Quest in Wolfram's Parzival* (Ithaca: Cornell University Press, 1995), pp. 144–69 ("The Enchanted Body") and 197–219 ("From Medicine to Miracle: Healing the Fisher King").

12. Medieval cartographers showed Eden at the eastern edge of the world, sometimes just off the eastern border of the map. One could have gotten the impression that a journey to the edge of the Garden of Eden was possible, where one could stand near the headwaters of the four great streams.

13. Arthur Groos makes the comment on the list: "This description concludes one of the longest unsuccessful cures in medieval literature, emphasizing again the antithesis between divine wisdom and worldly knowledge." *Romancing the Grail*, p. 208.

balas and gagathromeus, and ending with beryl and topaz" (Mustard, 412–3), but they are unable to help remove the affliction; God is preventing their paradisial effectiveness from helping Human Weakness—Anfortas—escape his pain. The stones are effective, however, as far as they go. The green stones continue to exert the power to disperse poison in the air; the sapphires maintain the power to inspire courage and serenity. Above all, the stones remain as part of a life-support and pain-alleviation system; like the Grail stone, they help keep Anfortas from death and help make his condition bearable. The nature of his illness must be unusual indeed, for the stones and herbs obtained by the Grail community do all that medicine can do, that is, keep Anfortas alive, but they have no power to restore "human weakness" to beauty.

The sickness comes not from the type of entity that the medicinal herbs and stones of Paradise can cope with but from the very gods of the heathenry whom baptism is intended to fend off. When the priest baptized Feirefiz, after Feirefiz had renounced Jupiter and all his gods, he prayed: "May this water fend heathenry from you with the full power of all Three" (Mustard, 426). In Arthur Groos's work, cited earlier, he feels that Wolfram is hinting at the malevolent effect of a conjunction of Jupiter and Mars that occurred in 1208, during the time of Wolfram's writing of *Parzival*, as being the cause of Human Weakness's—Anfortas's—illness.[14] I find this a very interesting and creative suggestion.[15] It is not a celestial conjunction of these two planets in the astrological sense, however, that is causing the problem but, symbolically, the conjunctive dominance of these two pagan, planetary deities over Christian Human Weakness, Anfortas.

At the time of Parzival's first visit, there was fear of Saturn, which is the fear of Chronos, the ancient god of the passage of time. This is the fear of the very ultimate coldness that this planet brings to human life and to the wound. The wound is in the testicles, since that is the place of reproduction and the human attempt to defeat the ultimate power of Chronos. Anfortas is afflicted with the fear of mortality, the ultimate human weakness, one that is relieved only by the Trinity, not by a forbidden dalliance with Orgeluse. Anfortas's ultimate death can be held at bay by the One whose power of Resurrection resides

14. Gross, *Romancing the Grail*, pp. 202–3. The conjunction could indeed have been understood as an analogy revealing the nature of the contemporary situation on earth.

15. Using revised computer models, Raymond Pfeiffer, professor of astronomy and physics at the College of New Jersey, assures me that Mars and Jupiter were in a very close conjunction in October 1208. The two were no longer in Cancer, however, as Gross had it, but were at 143 and 144 degrees along the ecliptic. This places them in Leo. In Stahlman and Gingerich's tables, Leo extends from 120 to 150 degrees. This event, Wolfram, a.k.a. Flegetânîs, could have read as a very serious analogue illuminating the current situation, as I indicated in the prologue. See William D. Stahlman and Owen Gingerich, *Solar and Planetary Longitudes for the Years −2000 to +2000 by Ten-Day Intervals* (Madison: University of Wisconsin Press, 1963), pp. xiii and 454.

in the Grail. So it is that the Grail and the stones can keep him alive, against Saturn.

But what of the ugliness of Anfortas and his stench? In the conclusion of the frame story, Anfortas has also come under the domination of Jupiter and Mars, two pagan entities his baptism should have fended off from him—but did not. Jupiter is the god of domination and rule, and Mars is the god of war; put those two together in the heavens, and as they reach their zenith, they exert the desire for domination and war, domination through war. Feirefiz has already learned that the Grail cannot be attained by war. Wolfram and the events of his day made it embarrassingly clear that Western Christendom had not renounced what Feirefiz renounced. Western knighthood's holiest community is suffering from their spiritual and cultural enthralldom to Jupiter and Mars. Though the knights of Christ fight for the Holy Sepulcher, whose dome is crowned with the cross and the Dove, and though all wear the livery of the turtledove, the bird of loyal love, still, as sinful human beings, they are in thrall to the power of time, the desire for dominance, and the method of war. The implication is that this state of profound ambivalence, of *zwîfel*, must be seen as something that is ailing the West, a condition that must be subject to Question. The baptized must reject their service to the god of domination and the god of war and see, through the gift of sight that comes with baptism and possession of the Grail, that they are sick, wounded by their own actions, and will not get better until they ask the question: what is wrong with us? Could the crusades to liberate the Sepulcher be an action controlled by the very gods we renounced in baptism? In the Grail stone, portable everywhere, the baptized already possess all that the Holy Land could give—the Sepulcher of Resurrection, the happiness of Paradise.

Anfortas's wound, symbolic in several senses, expresses the same ailment of the baptized: first, the wound is one inflicted by the poisonous spearhead of paganism, namely, the service of alien gods, especially preference for Jupiter, and having relationships to other peoples based on preponderance of power, in clear dissatisfaction with the family-kinship ways of relating to people, the ways that originate in the Trinity. The spearhead's heathen name is on it, and the poison of its heathenism remains in its victim until its presence is made subject to question as inappropriate for Christians. Second, the wound was made and is ameliorated by a spearhead and would suggest that the affliction is that of winning and losing in warfare, the service of Mars. Third, the wound is in the testicles, meaning that the sinful condition of being subject to Mars and Jupiter in seeking military dominance for possession of the Holy Sepulcher will go on from generation to generation—as a form of original sin— Cain killing Abel and spilling blood on the virginity of the earth.

When Parzival and Feirefiz enter to ask the question, they find Anfortas seated not on a throne but in a bed. Cardamom, cloves, and nutmeg were sprinkled everywhere to "kill the stench of the wound" (Mustard, 392). Anfortas's fire was of wood aloes, a precious aromatic wood normally sold in small chips, as I have found out, because it is so enormously expensive. Anfortas's room, shockingly, has whole logs of aloe wood burning to cover the smell. Massive amounts of incense used to cover the smell of the Christian affliction. His bed is covered with every precious stone known in the lapidaries in order to disperse the poison, as I mentioned earlier, and the bedposts—and this is a very pointed confirmation of the reading that has gone before—are covered with snakeskin! It is not only Jupiter and Mars who have power over him; Anfortas needs to be free also of the poison of the snake, whose ancient temptation to arrogant pride, "You will be like God," now has tempted him successfully to follow the wrong gods. Anfortas's mysterious and unyielding sickness is sin, falling in love with prideful arrogance, with Orgeluse, the ancient sin of auto-idolatry. When Parzival and his brother approach the snakeskin bed, they will be wearing a most appropriate helmet: the ecidemon—the mongoose.

No matter how ugly and odiferous the human weakness of the community of the baptized on Mount Salvation has become, through acceptance of the Question, when it comes from a sympathetic heart, they can be cured. Wolfram's dream comes to its fulfilment as he has the crying Parzival, weeping over himself and the condition of Anfortas and the Grail community, bend the knee three times to the Holy Trinity and the Grail, and then ask the Question in friendly concern: "Uncle, what are you suffering from?" At the sight of familial compassion, God relents. Anfortas's wound is cured, his paganism disappears as he concerns himself for Feirefiz, and he is restored to incredible beauty, beauty exceeding that of Parzival himself. Parzival, who in fighting Gawain realized that he was fighting himself, and who in fighting Feirefiz came to see that he was fighting himself, when he comes to weep over Anfortas's human weakness, is weeping over himself and over the deeds he, too, performed in honor of Mars and Jupiter. In curing Anfortas through genuflecting to the Trinity, and in asking with compassion about his uncle's condition, Parzival finally recognizes his own kin-relationship to the Triune God and to Anfortas, Human Weakness. In so doing, he cures himself and his kinsman.

> The lustre which the French call 'fleur' entered his complexion—
> Parzival's beauty was as nothing beside it [Absalom, Vergulaht, and
> Gahmuret are mentioned]. . . . The beauty of none of these was
> equal to that which Anfortas carried out from his illness. God's
> power to apply his artistry is undiminished today. (Mustard, 359)

And so it is clear by his return to the healthful condition of beauty that Anfortas's sickness was ugliness, and a singularly repulsive form of ugliness. God's Grail and the community's concern had kept him alive. But not beautiful.

In imagining the Grail community as the community of the Western Church, one can hear an objector saying to Wolfram that he has ignored what Christ promised to the first fisherman, Peter: "You are Peter, and upon this rock I will build my church, and the gates of hell will not prevail against it." I think Wolfram has answered well. The church will always be there, nothing will destroy it, Christ guaranteed its existence; but Christ mentioned nothing about protecting it from ugliness, from becoming ugly by its actions and enthrallments, nor did he promise protection from inflicting or receiving wounds that can render the inflictor as well as the receiver sad and ugly.

It doesn't matter, Wolfram seems to say; God was able to raise St. Silvester's bull, and the dead Lazarus as well, even after he had begun to smell. Ugliness is curable by the Artist of family feeling. Thus as Wolfram ends this section, he reassures his readers, contemporary and modern, in his usual upbeat way, that the miracle induced by the acceptance of questioning and presence of tearful compassion can still happen: "God's power to apply his artistry is undiminished today."

6

The Grail in the Inner Story

It is so clear that you almost miss it. The Grail is there, often unnoticed, but the cross of the crusaders is almost completely absent. The cross comes to be mentioned nine times in the poem, and it is therefore present, but in the case of Wolfram's temple knights and their proud livery, it is simply not there. In Wolfram's time, all the military orders of knights wore the cross as their emblem. By papal concession, the Knights Templar wore a red cross, the Knights of the Hospital a white cross, and the Teutonic Knights a black cross. All crusader knights wore the cross, in proud recognition of the fact that they had "taken the cross." This was especially associated with the military orders who were the protectors of the relic of the true cross, the Holy Sepulcher, and Mount Zion. In devout honor of Jesus, their cloaks had the cross sewn off center, on the shoulder, since that is where he had carried his cross. Wolfram, however, has his Templars wear the turtledove as their emblem—not the Dove, symbol of the Holy Spirit, but going one step further, the Turtledove, the more erotic symbol of human and divine love. This is perhaps totally ahistorical, but it is profoundly true in the theological context of his epic poem and a telling symbolic expression of their spiritual predicament of wielding the sword out of loyalty to the Triune God—who is love.[1]

1. This use of the turtledove is perhaps not totally ahistorical. The crusaders had placed a cross surmounted by a Dove, both apparently of gold-plated silver, on top of the small dome above the

Then, to make it worse, they find themselves sitting in defeat after failing to defend their Lord's desmain by military force. In the course of the story, Parzival will have to travel away from his father's attitude, in which anything worthwhile can be gained by knightly fighting, an attitude in which one's ideal is to be of service to the strongest possible earthly ruler (whether it be the Baruch or King Arthur), and toward the compassionate feelings of his mother Herzeloyde, toward the mutual love of Condwiramurs, through the sad self-knowledge imparted to him by Sigune and Cundrie, to the overflowing feelings of happiness of Repanse de Schoye.[2] After this journey, he will not only find the Grail but find and recognize the Grail, and it will recognize him.

Brian Murdoch has written of the irony of this journey that the hero is "permitted to see" but "cannot yet gain access to his own intended paradise." "He does at least see" the Grail with its very clear "link to paradise. Feirefiz, later on, will not even be able to see it until he is baptized. . . . The grail, borne by Repanse de Schoye, *is* paradise, it is the ultimate goal."[3] This irony is important because it underlines that "seeing" consists of more than observing. Without the accompanying feelings, the tears of regret of which the eye is also capable, there is no seeing of the Fall, nor of Paradise regained. In this sense, Murdoch adduces the "seeing" of the priest and the "highest pledge." As he mentions, book 9 says: "nothing your eye sees on earth can be compared to a priest" (*swaz dîn ouge ûf erden siht / daz glîchet sich dem priester niht*; 502, 13–4), and the reason for that is the visible/invisible nature of the spiritual entities the priest brings from the Grail: he pronounces the Passion, which "invisibly" forgives sins, he holds the "unseeable" pledge (the Eucharist) in his hand.[4] The journey to Paradise is one that leads to a simultaneous seeing and feeling of compassion, to conversion and regret—as in the case of Gahmuret, to the double function of the water in the eye: sight and tears.

This is also the type of journey on which Anfortas and his Templars find themselves. Badly defeated and depressed in the context of war for military domination of Mount Zion, they must travel on to the acceptance of another way of dealing with the heathen and of finding happiness, the happiness of the holy Grail stone. Wolfram uses the Trinity and the bedroom, women and

---

burial chamber, the edicule of the Holy Sepulcher, under the dome of the Church of the Holy Sepulcher. It remained there until the crusaders lost Jerusalem to Saladin in 1187. A drawing of the fourteenth century shows Christ sending the Dove down into the church through the oculus in the dome. See Martin Biddle, *The Tomb of Christ* (Phoenix Mill, England: Sutton, 2000), p. 36; and p. 84: "Theoderic recording (by 1174) that the cupola was then topped by a gilded cross on which was a gilded dove."

2. See also appendix 1.

3. Brian Murdoch, "*Parzival* and the Theology of Fallen Man," in *A Companion to Wolfram's Parzival*, ed. Will Hasty (Columbia, S.C.: Camden House, 1999), p. 156.

4. Murdoch, "*Parzival* and the Theology of Fallen Man," p. 156.

priests/hermits/ex-knights, all the sacraments and their Origin—he uses laughter and tears, blind killing and merciful forgiveness, foolishness and wisdom all to elicit feelings of kinship and family love.[5] It is on this journey of the heart that Wolfram hopes to bring his readers and listeners, a journey of the transformation of feelings from indifference to sorrowful feelings of loss to the overflowing happiness of repossession, a journey that will replace his contemporary world of prolonged Muslim-Christian warfare with a world led by the model of faithful women, by Christ's loyalty kinship to the human race to the point of death, by the Turtledove. If Christ's cross had become a symbol used to urge Christians against this vision, to urge them to engage in familial killing, Wolfram would replace it with the Dove of the overflowing love of the holy Trinity.[6]

Wolfram modifies Chrétien's story, as he goes along, in accordance with his interpretation of this journey and of the nature of its goal, the Holy Grail. It is impossible to detail every change he makes, nor would it be desirable to attempt to do so in the case of an author who constantly attempts to connect everything to everything;[7] but it is useful to see if the poet's conception of the holy Grail stone is present by its effects, as it should be, as Wolfram transforms the tale. As in the case of most quests, what is sought is already there. It is just that the seeker, a *homo viator,* slowly wise, takes a while, a journey of time, to realize it.[8]

The Young Parzival and His Mother

Wolfram gives a name, and thereby gives a function in the realm of human feelings, to many of the anonymous figures of Chrétien. Perzival's mother,

---

5. The question has been raised as to the appropriateness of hermits instead of priests in Wolfram's pastoral and sacramental situations with Parzival. I think the reason is that canon law forbade (and forbids) anyone with blood on his hands from becoming a priest. If Wolfram wanted to have ex-knights as spiritual advisors, a most appropriate thing for his purpose, then he would have to settle for hermits or monks. Since many monks backed the crusades, that left hermits. Wolfram's hermit figures, absent the canonical prohibition, would have been, I believe, priests.

6. For a delineation of the importance of the Dove see: Anne Huntley-Speare, "The Symbolic Use of a Turtledove for the Holy Spirit in Wolfram's *Parzival,*" in *Arthurian Literature and Christianity: Notes from the Twentieth Century,* ed. Peter Meister (New York: Garland, 1999), pp. 107–25.

7. I am not the first to express this thought and the consequent difficulty of writing about Wolfram's work. Professor Hatto, reflecting on a previous paragraph of his own commentary and its apparently jumbled state, combined a gentle complaint and a compliment, "But it is typical of Wolfram's art, as of few others', that so much is linked with so much else." Wolfram von Eschenbach, *Parzival,* trans. A. T. Hatto (London: Penguin, 1980), pp. 433–4.

8. The term *homo viator* is used of Parzival by Gary Shockey. Cited by Albrecht Classen, "Self and Other in the Arthurian World: Heinrich von dem Türlin's 'Wunderketten,' " *Monatshefte* 96, 1 (spring 2004): 23.

known from the frame story, is one of the first. Herzeloyde, "Sorrowful Heart," has been concealing her son from knighthood by keeping him in the forest.[9] Wolfram has given a justification for her attitude by showing in the frame story how her husband, Parzival's father, had deserted her to go off a-knighting and got killed, and how she treated the young baby Parzival almost as her husband returned to her again. She is an image of loyal love and the consequences of such love.

She is also an image of the lack of success that attends all attempts to protect a child from the surrounding world. In both Chrétien's version and Wolfram's, the boy is almost completely overcome by awe when he sees his first knights. Chrétien's Perceval thinks he is seeing five angels, one of whom he thinks is God. Wolfram's Parzival thinks in seeing the three knights who approach him that he is seeing God. Wolfram changed the number of shining knights from five to a more Trinitarian three. Both boys make fools of themselves over the knights, and in this, both poets are holding up the mirror to their contemporary world. Chrétien has Perceval say to the knights, "You are more beautiful than God." Wolfram has his young charge address the divinities in more traditional Germanic-Christian feudal manner: "Help, God, You surely have help to give."[10] Wolfram has a fourth knight come forward, so that there are now three, and one. The hilarity, and naive idolatry, that anyone would mistake a knight in armor for God Almighty, whether there were three of them or five, must have made audiences in France and Germany laugh. Some knights may even have felt flattered by the irony, but both poets are not out to flatter, but rather to show the tragedy that strikes a family when the desire for knighthood or crusading befalls a family member. The price is paid immediately because of a woman's loyal love of her son, when the boy goes off to engage in the world of fighting.

Chrétien's Percival asks his mother, before he leaves, "What is a chapel or church?" in response to her parting advice that he frequently pray to the Lord in the beauty of a chapel or church. This is a wonderful lead-in to Perceval's first comic adventure, where he blunders into the beautiful tent of the sleeping lady (Jeschute in Wolfram) thinking that it must be a church. Wolfram could

---

9. The etymology of Herzeloyde, "Sorrowful Heart," is based on identifying Wolfram's technique of what Fourquet calls "reprise," i.e., giving a parallel definition in the following or preceding lines, also suggested in appendix 1. Wolfram uses the technique, for example, in the case of Repanse de Schoye to suggest "overflow of happiness." See Jean Fourquet, *Wolfram d' Eschenbach et le Conte del Graal, Les divergences de la tradition du conte del Graal de Chrétien* (Paris: Presses Universitaires de France, [1938] 1966). See also Mustard, p. 78, n. 9.

10. The tradition was already old at the time of Wolfram. The ninth-century *Heliand*, for example, in treating God as a chieftain, translates the "daily bread" from the petition in the Lord's Prayer "Give us this day our daily bread" as "give us this day 'Your holy help,'" *thina helaga helpa*. See *The Heliand: The Saxon Gospel*, trans. G. Ronald Murphy, S.J. (New York: Oxford University Press, 1992), p. 54.

have used this comic device as well, especially since he must have liked the humor, but he transforms the boy's question to one bearing more on his theme: "Oh mother, what is God?" (*Ôwê muoter, waz ist got?* 119, 17). Her answer emphasizes divine characteristics that are most important to Wolfram: light, humanness, loyalty. "Son, I will tell you in all earnest. He is brighter than the daylight, yet he took upon himself the features of man. Son, mark this wisdom and pray to him when in trouble, for his fidelity [*triwe*] has ever offered help to the world" (Mustard, 68). Both mothers urge their sons to pray, but Wolfram implies that God, who is pure light, took on some nonlight, almost like Feirefiz, when he became a human being. Christ's loyal help, if understood foolishly as applying only to oneself and only to the baptized members of the family, is what will cause Parzival and Anfortas's Templars grief on Mount Salvation following the battle of Hattin. Wolfram's crusade against literalism has begun. If God is not understood as being human as well as divine, and if God is not understood as Triune in his very essence, then the problems of human warfare, Cain and Abel, will not be understood by his Christian audience as being against the very nature of God.

Biblically, human beings are made "in the image and likeness of God." It is, therefore, of crucial importance to the poet to ask the question "Then what is God like?" If God is understood as a non-Trinitarian Monad, never-Incarnated, a simple Self, then the hero could feel justified in feeling that the appropriate form of human imitation of God might be restricted to one centered on self. Heroic behavior need not, of its essence, include concern for others-as-family as being something derived from the very nature of the Godhead. Being created in the image of God would then not of itself so clearly constitute a prohibition against hostilities. Wolfram always seems to mention both the Incarnation (*Menschwerdung*, in German, significantly, "becoming human") and the Trinity when he writes of God. Because of his animus against the sin of Cain, against human fratricide as justified in the Crusades, Wolfram thinks it far more important to raise the question of the nature of God rather than that of a church.

Wolfram softens the initial moment when the young hero leaves his mother at the bridge. This is where there is a clear parting of the ways, not only in the narrative itself but also for the two authors. Chrétien's tragic hero commits the terrible mistake of putting task over people, and Chrétien depicts this in an extreme form. It becomes the root cause for all of his Perceval's failure in his quest for chivalry.

"Fair son," she [his mother] said, "God be with you. May He give you more joy than remains with me." When the boy was but a

> stone's throw away, he looked back and saw that his mother had
> fallen at the head of the bridge and was lying in a faint as if she had
> dropped dead. But he whipped his horse across the crupper with his
> switch and rode away. (Kibler, 388–9)[11]

It would seem that Wolfram could have used this scene as it stands, since it
describes the first act of Perceval's journey to be a chivalrous knight as a sinful
act of disregarding suffering, and the sinfulness consists of such task- or quest-
orientation that he feels no compassion for his mother who has fallen to the
ground out of her feelings for him. However, Wolfram changes the scene in a
most interesting way. First he sees to it that his Parzival does not observe his
mother's fall, and so, though Parzival is the cause for her collapse and death,
at least he does not see and turn away from it, like the priest and the Levite in
the parable of the Samaritan. Wolfram also pauses to make the reader or hearer
think of the divine-like loyal love (*triuwe*) that caused the mother such sorrow.
As the Grail is the container of the Passion, she too is an image of compassionate suffering, *Herze-loyde,* an image of kinship like that of God in Christ,
and Wolfram turns his attention from Parzival to her.

> Next morning when daylight came the lad made up his mind
> quickly that he would go straight to Arthur. Lady Herzeloyde kissed
> him and ran after him. Then the sorrow of the world ["reprise" of
> her name] befell. When she no longer saw her son—he rode away:
> who could be glad of that?—then the lady without falsity fell upon
> the ground, where grief stabbed her until she died.—Her death
> from sheer loyalty saved her from the pains of hell. Well for her that
> she became a mother. Thus she traveled the journey that brings re-
> ward, a root of goodness she, and a branch of humility [*ein wurzel
> der güete und ein stam der diemüete*]. (128, 27–8; Mustard, 72)

The last comparison of this lady without falsity is suggestive: "a root of
goodness and a branch of humility." The phrase is a distant echo of the Grail
itself, which is carried by a lady of pure loyalty, without any falsity, and the tree-
like image suggests one of the descriptions of the Grail as the bliss of Paradise,
"both its root and branch" (*bêde wurzeln unde rîs;* 235, 22). There is no wonder
then that Wolfram has her go straight to Paradise. In her faithful love and
falling to the ground stabbed by wounds inflicted through fidelity she reincar-
nates the Passion and Death of Christ and is an image and likeness of the

---

11. For translations of Chrétien, I am using Chrétien de Troyes, *Arthurian Romances,* trans. William W.
Kibler (New York: Penguin, 1991).

Grail.[12] Like Condwiramurs, in the intensity of her faithful attachment to her own, she obtains salvation and thereby shows the way to the Grail. Her eyes both saw and wept. Parzival sees but does not weep; Feirefiz weeps but does not see. Both will journey until they have the human eyes that do both.

The Damsel in the Tent

Chrétien's version of this little episode is especially successful, since he is able to have his poor hero think that the tent of noble lady is a church. It fits his mother's description of a church as being beautiful and containing treasures. His treasure, however, is not amused to wake up with this strange, uncouth, and hungry young man in her arms. Both authors make the hero a buffoon at this point, especially when young Parzival wants to take the lady's ring, "because his mother told him to."

Wolfram does not essentially change the plot, except for one small detail: he removes the gemstone from the lady's ring. Chrétien: "Yet her resistance was in vain, for the boy kissed her repeatedly, twenty times as the story says, regardless of whether she liked it or not, until he saw a ring set with a shining emerald on her finger" (Kibler, 389–90). Wolfram: "Loudly the lady protested, but he paid no heed to what she said and he forced her mouth to his. Then it was not long before he hugged the duchess to himself and took her ring besides" (Mustard, 73–4). Gemstones mean so much to Wolfram, and especially the emerald, with its condensed power of vibrant life and sight, that this green stone is not one that for him would fit into such a burlesque scene—especially since he had used the emerald so solemnly in the cross of the burial of Gahmuret in the preceding book.

There is now a curious insertion on Wolfram's part, one of the unexpected and mysterious appearances of Sigune (Wolfram's anagram for "Cousin") cradling the body of her dead lover, the knight Schionatulander, as she grieves for him faithfully and without cease. She appears three times, almost surrealistically, in the plot—her sudden appearances are never caused by events in the storyline—and she tells Parzival his own name. She is thus the person who is

---

12. Salvation through fidelity is not as unorthodox as it may sound. "Faith" was often translated into German as early as the ninth-century *Heliand* by the word *triuwe*, meaning "to be true" or "to keep faith with" (in English, in the older marriage ritual, "to plight one's troth"), meaning marital or warrior fidelity. This Germanic tradition, that "faith" is person-to-person fidelity, and therefore loyalty to Jesus as a person (rather than the more intellectual acceptance of his doctrines), is a continuous strand in German literature extending from the *Heliand* to *Parzival* and to Martin Luther's concept that the faith by which one is saved is *fides qua*, personal fidelity, *triuwe*, to Jesus Christ.

the first to say what his identity is, and tells him as part of his identity that her knight, who is covered with the oil of balm, died defending Parzival's land. This alone would give pause as to the identity of the dead knight, since Parzival's destined land is the Terre de Salvaesche, "Land of Salvation"; and then there is the curious description of the knight who died for her and for Parzival as being in a constant state of being fully covered with oil of balm.[13] It has been observed by scholars that there is a curious resemblance to the Pietà, in the disposition of the two figures and in the description of the completely faithful and yet virginal love of Sigune for her knight.[14] I think that it is significant for an approach to the images of the Grail stone in the story text that the dead knight is anointed with balm, covered with ointment. Wolfram would have known that "anointed" in Greek is "Christos," "Christ" meaning "the Anointed One," and that the traditional Christian rites of Baptism and Extreme Unction contain a "chrismation," an anointing with chrism or specially blessed oil, which is used to express sacramentally the mystical union of Christ and Christian, about which Wolfram wrote so movingly in his invocational prayer at the beginning of his *Willehalm*.

This image of Christ depicts him as a relative being held by a relative, as if the faithful were not only the relatives of God the Father but also, because of Christ, cousins of the Virgin Mary, and perhaps inheritors of her role, as here shown. Parzival wears the cloak of the Queen in the Grail scene. Thus this recurring and almost surreal apparation of fidelity, of *triuwe*, on the part both of the dead knight and of his lady who is holding him faithfully even in death, suggests the scene of the Deposition from the cross, so often depicted in medieval church art. The mourning of the virgin cousin reminds the reader/hearer of the feelings of the Virgin Mary as she held Christ's body before his burial in the rock and suggests the appropriate disposition of those who hold the Grail as their faith-possession. This image, not present here in Chrétien's text and repulsive when it comes, but so carefully presented by Wolfram, is another suggestion, one that will be repeated, of the nature of the stone Grail as reverently holding or containing the Body of Christ. It is this very Sigune who will later put the question to Parzival: "Haven't you found out the nature

13. This is sometimes rendered as "embalmed." This is a too-literal and quite misleading translation, since embalming in our day is no longer associated with covering the body with balm as in the story, but rather with procedures that introduce preservatives like formaldehyde into the corpse. In thinking of such "embalming" procedures rather than one of "anointing," the reader is effectively led away from the suggestion being made in the text.

14. Schwietering is an example. "Sigune embodies Wolfram's thoughts on faithfulness, *triwe*, being intensified and transfigured by suffering, in so pure a form . . . that she awakens in one the image of the Mother of God with her dead son on her lap." Julius Schwietering, *Philologische Schriften*, ed. Friedrich Ohly and Max Wehrli (Munich: Wilhelm Fink Verlag, 1969), p. 320.

of the Grail yet?" (*Habt ir geprüevet noch sîn art?* 441, 1). This she asks, even as she, almost as an icon, depicts its nature for him.[15]

The Killing of the Red Knight

Both authors agree that the Red Knight behaves in a chivalrous manner toward the country bumpkin who comes toward him on his nag ordering the knight to take off all his armor and weapons and simply give them to him. How simple indeed to think that wearing the armor and carrying the sword brings one to chivalry. Chrétien excuses his Perceval's bad behavior more than Wolfram, in that he allows King Arthur's court to go ahead and give the young man permission to challenge the Red Knight and to take his armor. During their brief joust, Chrétien has the Red Knight use the side of his lance and not the point against Perceval: "he raised his lance with both hands and struck the boy such a mighty blow across the shoulders with the shaft of his lance that it drove him down over the neck of the horse" (Kibler, 395). Painful, perhaps, and embarrassing, but not lethal.

Wolfram makes the Red Knight even nobler. The Red Knight turns his lance completely around so that it is the butt end and not the blade end that hits the boy. "The knight reversed his spear shaft and struck the lad with such force that both he and his pony were tumbled onto the flowers" (Mustard, 86). Parzival does not perceive the courtesy, hurt as he is and ignorant of chivalrous behavior, and seizes a hunter's throwing weapon, something no knight would do, and with his sure eye, throws his hunting javelin right through the eye slits of the Red Knight's helmet. As blood and aqueous gel ooze out the back of the man's head, the gallant Red Knight falls dead. In both authors, the ungallant Perceval/Parzival next strips the corpse of its armor with the help of a young squire. Wolfram's Parzival has made his first kill, and is now robbing a corpse to achieve knighthood. To make it worse, Wolfram both names the Red Knight, Ither, and reveals to the reader that Ither is a relative of Parzival. Chrétien neither names the dead knight nor makes him a relative of Perceval, and so has his hero ride off to meet the teacher who will give him the instructions in chivalry that he sorely needs. Wolfram, on the other hand, lingers over the scene of the dead kinsman, as he did with Gahmuret.

Through the squire Iwanet (Yonet in Chrétien, who at this time is giving

---

15. For a treatment of *faithfulness* or *triuwe* in Wolfram's thought, see Anne Huntley-Speare, "Wolfram's Willehalm and Triuwe: A Model for Society," Ph.D. diss., Pennsylvania State University, 2001 (available from UMI Dissertation Services, Ann Arbor, Mich.).

a detailed report of the fight to King Arthur), Wolfram introduces two Grail elements, the spear and the portable Blessed Sacrament. Since most readers are led to concentrate on the awful scene of Parzival's ungainly efforts to get the armor off the dead hero and the details of corpse robbery being carried out by the desperately struggling youngster, the modestly inserted event with the squire usually goes unattended. This I believe is intentional on Wolfram's part. He must have felt that the way of distraction was the poetically appropriate presentation of the event—it is true to the way the Grail is (not) seen.

> Ither of Gaheviez he [Parzival] left lying pitiably on the meadow,
> who was so fair in death and who had, in life, known the fullness of
> joy. If knightly action had been the cause of his death in a joust,
> with a spear through his shield, who then would mourn the great
> calamity? But he died from a javelin. Then Iwanet brought him
> bright flowers for a covering. The shaft of the javelin he set in the
> ground at his side and in the manner of Christ's Passion this lad
> pure and proud pressed a piece of wood through the javelin blade to
> make a cross . . . at the news many a woman was dismayed and
> many a knight wept as they gave vent to their faithful grief. . . . The
> Queen rode forth from the city and bade them lift up the holy Sacra-
> ment [daz heilictuom] over the King of Kukumerlant whom Par-
> zival's hand had slain. (Mustard, 88, modified)

The passage bears a great deal of thought. The mere presence of a bloody spear, a cross, and weeping women, together with weeping knights, suggests a memory of Calvary but also gives the reader a proleptic glance at the Grail procession, where lamentation by the women and knights occurs as the bloody spear is carried into the room. The death of the Red Knight is associated with the death of Gahmuret, whose grave was associated with that of Christ, Gahmuret whose demise in a fight caused the same outbreak of weeping. Gahmuret's grave was made of sacred paradisial red and green stones, thereby associated with divine fidelity, eternal life, and sight, and was thereby associated with the grave of Christ. The death of Ither is also made to resemble that of Christ, not by the stone of the sarcophagus but by the presence next to his corpse of the lance that killed him—and if the reader does not see the association, young Iwanet makes it clearer by pressing a piece of wood onto the blade of the lethal javelin to make a cross of it. It is now associated with the lance related to the death of Christ and with the outpouring of blood and water and the removal of blindness from the legendary Longinus.

At that moment, into the death scene, at the orders of the Queen, enters the portable altar shrine with the Body of Christ within it, and it is lifted up in benediction over the corpse of the knight killed "by the hand of Parzival." It is as though Wolfram wishes the words of the Council to echo across the flowery meadow: "He who sheds the blood of a Christian, sheds the blood of Christ." This the good knight Parzival has done. And then the portable shrine disappears once more from the narrative.

The word used here for the portable shrine, *daz heilictuom* (159, 28), deserves a moment's further consideration. The word has several meanings. Obviously it can indicate a holy thing or sanctuary, a shrine or reliquary, relics, or, in this case, with *daz*, "the," *the* holy thing: the Eucharist. In one of the earliest uses of the word, Notker employed the word to translate the Latin for sacrament, and to signify the body and blood of Christ (*diu heiligtuom mînes lîchamin und bluotes*).[16] In medieval times, *heilictuom* could also mean a shrine or reliquary containing relics. Mustard and A. T. Hatto combine both of these notions and translate the terms as "the Monstrance," an ingenious possibility that, however, liturgically implies too much and, in a Grail story, suggests too little. A monstrance requires a solemn procession and, above all, visible exposition of the Sacrament; Wolfram's story does not want such visibility; it revolves around the hero's nonrealization of the enormity of what he has just done. Wolfram also does not use the word for monstrance. A recent German translation (by Peter Knecht) simply renders the word *heilictuom* as the Blessed Sacrament, *das Allerheiligste*, without specifying the nature of the vessel that acts as the container.[17] The Sacrament here is in a container that is portable (the Queen orders it brought), it is lifted up in blessing over the dead, and it is without the ceremonies attendant on the use of a monstrance. The *heilictuom* is therefore most likely a portable altar shrine, containing, under its stone, the Eucharistic wafer, the Body of Christ. It is, in other words, the Grail.[18]

Gornemant's Instruction on Chivalry

Chrétien has his hero next come to Gornemant for instruction. Perceval both begins and ends his session by telling his vavasour that he must be off on his quest to find his mother. The instruction is short and consists of four principles Perceval must learn before his spurs are attached and he becomes a knight. The first is mercy. If you get the upper hand against an opponent and he is no

---

16. Notker Labeo was a monk of St. Gall, famed as a teacher and as a translator. He died in 1022 AD.

17. Wolfram von Eschenbach, *Parzival: Studienausgabe, Mittelhochdeutscher Text nach der sechsten Ausgabe von Karl Lachmann*, trans. Peter Knecht, intro. Bernd Schirok (Berlin: de Gruyter, 1998).

18. For further examples of *heilictuom*, see the Grimms' *Deutsches Wörterbuch* (Leipzig: Hirzel, 1877), 10: 844–5.

longer capable of self-defense, show him mercy and do not kill him. The second is not to talk too much; people who talk too much soon discover they've said something they regret. The third is to console any woman who is disconsolate in any way, and the fourth is to go to church and pray to be a good Christian all your life. Having received the instruction and the spurs from his vavasour, Perceval is off, for he "was very impatient to reach his mother and find her alive and well" (Kibler, 402). His quest is still, and will remain, to find his mother whom he saw fall to the ground before he rode off.

Wolfram may be said not to have heeded Gornemant's instruction on re-straint in words, for he has his Gurnemanz go on to extend them. More im-portant, he changes the locale of the first point and transforms Chrétien's general instruction to go to church or chapel whenever you can. Wolfram has Parzival actually attend Mass as they speak, the place and time of the Grail's actual presence, and there learn how to participate in the Sacrament. "Then our simple-witted hero went where Mass was being sung for God and for his host. During Mass the host taught him the things that increased blessedness: how to make his offering, how to make the sign of the Cross, and how to foil the devil thereby" (Mustard, 93). Parzival's instructions on chivalry are, therefore, begun in the presence of an altar stone, and his first instruction is on and during actual participation in the Sacrament of the altar.

The four instructions of Chrétien's Gornemant are paralleled by four fur-ther teachings of Wolfram's Gurnemanz. First: let mercy go along with daring, let the defeated man live; and do not forget to wipe the armor rust off your face. Mercy and rust together? That is Wolfram's humane style. Second parallel principle: do not ask too many questions. Third parallel: let women be precious to you; be loyal to them; and a welcome note: be cheerful. Fourth, here there is no parallel mention by Wolfram of churchgoing in general—Wolfram seems to prefer realizing what occurs in church: Parzival has just been instructed while at Mass. The instruction continues: never lose your sense of shame, because if you have no sense of honor, hell awaits. Furthermore: have com-passion on the needy and protect them; treat rich and poor equally; stay out of quarrels among the boorish. And finally, about matrimony: "Husband and wife are one, as are the sun that shone today and the thing called day itself, neither can be separated from the other, they blossom from a single seed" (Mustard, 93–5).

And so, after having been at Mass, and therefore in the presence, though without realizing it, of an altar stone, the Grail, Wolfram's Parzival first learns that to be a chivalrous knight he must practice compassion, and that husband and wife are two but one, like daylight and sunlight, an image of the undivided quality of the Trinity.

The Rescue of Blancheflor and Her Castle

Wolfram tells his version of the siege of Biaurepaire, which he transcribes as Pelrapeire, with the battle incidents such as the unexpected arrival of the grain ships and the ruse of sending well-fed prisoners back to their own lines, and the defeat of the two leaders of the besieging army. There is one sad repetition of Parzival's own behavior, however, that Wolfram introduces: "The knights he struck down came to a bitter end, for this is what was done: at the gussets of their armor the citizenry took their revenge and stabbed them through the slits. This Parzival forbade them to do" (Mustard, 112–3). He is learning—a good man slowly wise.

He also takes Gurnemanz's advice seriously about man and woman. In Chrétien's version, after Perceval (and the grain ships) have lifted the siege, the grateful and enamored queen, Blancheflor ("White Flower"), offers herself and her lands to Perceval in marriage. He declines, despite their nights in bed together, because he wants to leave. "He remembered his mother whom he had seen fall in a faint and he wanted to go see her more than anything else" (Kibler, 417).

In Wolfram's version, Parzival accepts marriage.

> To him there often came the thought of embracing her, as his
> mother had counseled him—and Gunemanz too had explained to
> him that man and wife are one. And so they entwined arms and
> legs. . . . The custom, old and ever new, dwelt with the two of them
> there, and they were glad. (Mustard, 110)

Wolfram also changes her name, significantly for his version of the story, to Condwiramurs, "Love Leads the Way." Parzival too, however, soon wanted to go and asked his wife's permission to leave, "to see how things are faring with my mother, for I know nothing at all as to whether she is well or ill. So for a brief time I will travel to her, and also for the sake of adventure" (Mustard, 121). He does not yet know that she died of grief at his parting, but Parzival is honest enough to give his wife a Gahmuret-type of admission, namely, that he wouldn't mind having a knightly adventure or two on the way—purely so that she could reward him when he returns. Parzival is still the son of his father.

Condwir + *amurs* ("Love Conducts" or "Love Leads the Way") is well named by Wolfram. Retaining the French "White Flower" would not have helped. Condwiramurs's husband still needs to be "conducted" for some distance along the way toward becoming a spontaneously humane human being. Without love, he will not be moved to defy convention and ask the Question. He will not weep. He will not realize what he ought to feel in the presence of the Grail and its wounded. Condwiramurs will exemplify the compassion that must spontaneously well up in him in order to find his way to realizing the nature of the Grail.

In the Presence of the Grail at the Grail Castle

It seems that both authors are quite similar in describing how their heroes find their way to the place where the Grail is, but this is not entirely true. Chrétien's hero stumbles upon a stream that he cannot cross while riding along all absorbed in prayer that he might be able to find his way to his mother. Wolfram's Parzival also finds the waters that cannot be crossed while in a daze. He has let the reins of his horse go, the reins dragging along the ground, so that no human hand has guided him there. Wolfram also says it is hard to say if it was a far ride or a near one. Both authors imply that the Grail mountain is not found with a roadmap or by conventional planning and calculation. You have to let go of the reins. Neither hero can cross the waters when they are reached, but both head up into the rock after they have been told by the Fisherman where to go for the night.

While Chrétien has two fishermen speak to him, Wolfram makes it more explicit that one Fisherman is preeminent, and thus hints that the reader might have entered St. Peter the Fisherman's realm. In order to be properly clothed, Chrétien's Perceval is given a cloak of scarlet to wear, while Parzival is given the cloak of Repanse de Schoye (together with a Wolframian distractive reason, there hadn't been enough time to make him proper clothing). By entering the Grail hall wearing her mantel, Parzival is associated immediately with Repanse de Schoye's function of bearing the Grail, and also with her name, Overflow of Happiness. This is indeed Parzival's future, but not his present state, and the castle itself is described as a place of deep sadness, despite the striking contradiction of having within its walls Overflow of Happiness, the person who carries the Grail. Wolfram compares the scarcity of activity there with the lack of banners at Abenberc. Abenberc is usually understood as indicating the fortress of Amberg, which is quite close to Wolfram's Eschenbach.[19] In any case, there is here suggested on the part of the Templars a joyless lack of ac-

---

19. Because of several ties that I believe exist to artifacts at Bamberg, both the papal sarcophagus and statue of Clement II, as well as the altar stone (see chapter 7), I wonder if perchance this Abenberc could be Bamberg. One of the major manuscript groups does indeed have "Babenberc," instead of Abenberc, and that would mean some scribes thought it was Bamberg, and thus this could be another possible link to the portable altar stone at Bamberg.

tivity that is not alluded to in Chrétien's description of the approach to the great hall.

Wolfram has been accused by one critic of being too compromising with knightly activity and not opposing it as completely as does Chrétien.[20] The next episode shows that this charge is off the mark. Just before entering the great hall, Perceval is armed with a sword with a pommel of gold, whereas Parzival is completely disarmed. In order to make it visibly clear that he is not following Chrétien on this issue, Wolfram creates a little scene in which his hero gets angry at an imagined slight from a courtier and reaches for his sword, and clenches his fists when he finds none at his side. I think, therefore, that one must make a distinction here—Wolfram's main thrust is against the crusades as fratricidal war against the nonbaptized; concerning chivalry and knightly activity, he sees the bad side of them but is more able to make compromises. In the presence of the Eucharist, moreover, by liturgical tradition, swords were not to be drawn or even worn, or, significantly, presented. Wolfram hints again, by taking away Parzival's sword for the Grail procession, that the Grail's nature is more sacramentally related than his French counterpart realizes. It is not until the end of the meal, when the carts are being removed, that Parzival is presented with the sword. Wolfram seems anxious to downplay and be rid of this sword in the story as soon as possible so that he can end with Parzival's corpse-robbed sword breaking on his heathen brother's helmet.

In Chrétien's version, the guest is now seated on the bed with the Rich Fisherman. The action begins as a squire

> came forth from a chamber carrying a white lance by the middle of
> its shaft, he passed between the fire and the middle of the bed. Every-
> one in the hall saw the white lance with its white point [la lance
> blanche et le fer blanc] from whose tip there issued a drop of blood
> [une gote de sanc], and this red drop flowed down to the squire's
> hand. (Kibler, 420)[21]

There is no reaction to the sudden appearance and the miraculous single drop of blood. Not only does the amazed Perceval keep his questions to himself, as

---

20. "Besonders schwer verständlich erscheint aus Chrétiens Perspektive Trevrizents Einstellung: *wand in der wirt von sünden schiet / und im doch ritterlîchen riet.* Indem Wolfram den Hang zur Gewalttätigkeit der menschlich Natur einschreibt, hat er Chrétiens radikale Kritik an der Kriegerkaste entschärft." ("From the perspective of Chrétien, Trevrizent's attitude is especially difficult to comprehend—*his host absolved him from his sins / but encouraged him to knightly deeds.* When Wolfram ascribes to human nature the tendency to violence, he blunts Chrétien's radical criticism of the warrior caste.") Elisabeth Schmid, "Wolfram von Eschenbach: Parzival," in *Interpretationen: Mittelhochdeutsche Romane und Epen,* ed. Horst Brunner (Stuttgart: Reclam, 1993), p. 193.

21. *Le Conte du Graal (Perceval),* in *Les Romans de Chrétien de Troyes, Édités d'apres la Copie de Guiot (Bibl. Nat. Fr. 794),* ed. Félix Lecoy (Paris: Librairie Honoré Champion, 1973), p. 100.

he has been taught, but also there is no reaction whatsoever on the part of anyone in the room.

Wolfram obviously thought this was not in accord with the function of the lance as a preparatory gesture signifying the nature and immediate entrance of the Grail. Knowing the allusion, he assumes that all would remember the blood on the lance and react. "This custom was effective for provoking lamentation," Wolfram notes, and then he veers away from the somewhat delicate and semimagical description of the spear as having but a single drop of blood and substitutes a flow of blood.

> Blood gushed from the point [*an der snîden huop sich pluot;* 231, 20] and ran down the shaft to the hand that bore it and on to the sleeve. And now there was weeping and wailing throughout the whole wide hall. The people of thirty lands could not have wept so many tears. (Mustard, 127)

The blood "gushing" rather than a single pearling drop, and the parallel human reaction of the people gushing tears in such quantity that it could be compared to the tears of thirty lands, shows how far Wolfram is reinterpreting the lance scene, toward the gushing of blood and water from the side of the Crucified and toward the reaction of the weeping and lamentation of the whole Christian world, "thirty nations," to the death of Christ. The tremendous reaction is appropriate to the Good Friday event itself and to the legend of Longinus's spear connected with it, to say nothing of the finding of the lance during the First Crusade. The lamentation fits subsequent liturgical commemorations of the event every Good Friday. Even so, Parzival is not moved to be human enough to cry and to defy literal instructions on proper behavior. This is more serious than the situation of Perceval in Chrétien's more sober version, where Perceval does not have the massive emotional reaction of so many nearby to guide his feelings, there being no reaction whatsoever on the part of the assembled guests to the entrance and passage through the hall of the lance with the single drop of blood. Perceval's lesser fault, therefore, is that of not letting his curiosity overcome his literal obedience to instructions.

The condition of Anfortas (unnamed in Chrétien) is treated differently by Wolfram. His historical model may possibly have been the brave young Leper King of Jerusalem, Baldwin IV, who led the Templars and soldiers of the kingdom despite his terrible sickness, once famously leading them into battle despite weakness, almost echoing Anfortas, by being carried in his bed. In the year 1183, his leprosy began its fatal and final spread over his whole body. Wolfram must have ascertained that in that year of 1183 the planet Saturn was in Leo, exerting its cold and leaden influence on the mortality of the suffering king of Jerusalem. Three fireplaces are burning to keep the coldness from Anfortas. In the fireplaces are whole logs of *lignum aloe*, the precious and extremely expensive imported wood, burned as incense. The hall must have smelled like a Western cathedral or an Eastern Orthodox basilica! The fact that there are three incense fires blazing at once (there is one in Chrétien) is again a pointer to opposition to Saturn-Chronos, unfeeling Coldness itself, in its/his capacity as the unemotional opponent of the Trinity and of mankind. So, too, is the fact that Wolfram's Fisherman, in the midst of all his furs, is wearing a red gemstone on his head: on his sable cap there shines a translucent ruby, *ein durchliuhtic rubîn*, Augustine's stone of Paradise, containing the power to remain a live ember, an *anthrax*, with the capacity to glow of its own power inextinguishably in the cold darkness. The condition of Anfortas is made into the human condition by these elements. Wolfram adds a comment, as if it were needed: "his life was but a dying" (Mustard, 126), almost a citation of the old Latin proverb, *media vita in morte sumus* (in the midst of life we are dying).

The additional ominous element, that the very framework of the bed on which Anfortas lies is covered with snakeskin, is something Wolfram leaves for the second coming of Parzival. At this point in the narrative the enemy is death, the death caused by the lance: the mortality of the Crucified, that of human nature, that of the father of Parzival, and that of the Red Knight— brought to pass by the hand of Parzival. And therefore "all thirty nations weep." The god Chronos, Saturn, whose star is at its zenith, is the sovereign threat, and its coldness afflicts the very core of "human weakness" itself, which, in heavy furs "because of his ailment," is put on display in the Man on the bed. Wolfram's fires and furs serve the same purpose here as the many powers of the gemstones in book 16: they hold off, they alleviate, though they cannot overcome or cure. In the same place in his narrative Chrétien merely mentions the Fisherman as sitting in furs before a single large fire of unnamed dry logs with a brass chimney supported by four columns, with room for four hundred men around it. All the elaboration just described is Wolfram's invention, pointing to the nature and function of the Grail before it appears.

The entrance of the Grail. In Chrétien's version, two squires enter the hall first, each carrying a candelabrum with at least ten candles. The boys are very handsome; they are accompanied by a maiden.

> A maiden accompanying the two young men was carrying a grail
> [*un graal antre ses II mains / une demeisele tenoit*; 3208–9]; she was
> beautiful, noble, richly attired. After she had entered the hall carry-
> ing the grail, the room was so brightly illumined that the candles
> lost their brilliance like stars and the moon when the sun rises. . . .

The grail which was introduced first was of fine pure gold [*de fin or esmeré estoit*; 3221].[22] Set in the grail were precious stones of many kinds, the best and costliest to be found in earth or sea: the grail's stones were finer than any others in the world, without any doubt. The Grail, like the lance, *passed* [*trespasserent*; 3229] in front of the bed and went [*alerent*; 3230] into another chamber. The young knight watched them *pass by* [*passer*; 3221] but did not dare ask who was served from the grail [the lord of the castle then orders the table prepared; they wash their hands]. . . . Two squires carried in a broad ivory table: as the story relates, it was entirely made of one piece. They held it a moment before their lord and the youth, until two squires came bearing two trestles . . . of ebony. The table was placed on these supports with the tablecloth over it. The first course was a haunch of venison cooked in its fat with hot pepper . . . a squire carved the haunch of peppered venison . . . and he placed pieces of it before them on whole loaves of flat bread. Meanwhile the grail *passed again* [*retrespassa*; 3279] in front of them and again the youth did not ask who was being served from the grail. . . . But he kept more silent than he should have, because with each course that was served he saw the grail *pass by completely uncovered* [*trespasser . . . tot descovert*; 3289] before him. But he did not learn who was served from the grail. (Kibler, 420–1, modified; Lecoy, 3208–90; emphasis mine)

The astonishing thing is of course the continual movement of the Grail as it passes by to bring food to someone in a mysterious other chamber. It passes by with each course and is not once set down in front of the lord or placed at the lord's table. The other surprise is the prominent focus of the text on the first course: haunch of venison in hot pepper sauce (*hanche de cerf an gresse au poivre chaut* [3268–9]—given almost like a menu item!) served on flat bread. The grail itself is very clearly a serving dish of gold encrusted with the finest jewels, and when it is brought into the room by the unnamed maiden, the whole room is bathed in light, presumably from the brilliance of the gem-

22. The word *esmeré*, very unusual according to Fourquet, and not understood by French copyists or by the Norwegian translator, might have meant "decorated with" but was understood by Wolfram as pertaining to color and thus is related to his use of green for the *achmardi*. (Understandably so, I believe, since "esmeraude," already evidenced in 1120 AD, according to *le Robert*, was used for emerald.") See Jean Fourquet, *Wolfram d'Eschenbach et le Conte del Graal, Les divergences de la tradition du Conte del Graal de Chrétien* (Paris: Presses Universitaires, [1938] 1966).

stones and the gold. The hero is intimidated by his instructions from indulging his curiosity about who the person might be in the other room who is being served from the beautiful dish that keeps passing in front of his eyes, at one time completely uncovered.

Wolfram, for his part, also keeps the intimidation of the young hero intact, and for the same reason: Parzival fails to ask a question because he does not want to exceed his literally understood instructions on chivalrous behavior. The rest Wolfram transforms radically in order to bring the banquet and the Grail from the realm of the magico-religious into the realm of the religious and mystical—and the contemporary.

As the entrance of the Grail begins, a great steel door opens to admit the procession, as though the separation of two realms was being changed by an opening. This opening of the steel door together with the solemn rite of the lance has reminded scholars of the Byzantine Rite of the Mass with its use of a small lance during the *proskomidia*, or preparation of the bread and wine.[23] In this preparatory ritual for the Divine Liturgy (Mass), the bread is symbolically pierced in the side, after which water and wine are poured into the chalice, in memory of the lance thrust of the Crucifixion. There follows later a solemn Great Entrance, in which the veiled chalice and *diskos* (paten) with the bread and wine are brought in procession with incense and candles from the place of preparation, carried through the Royal Doors, brought into the sanctuary, and then placed on the altar. It must be admitted there seems to be something to this, and Wolfram could easily have been influenced by descriptions of the Eastern divine liturgy given by overawed crusaders returning from the East and, ironically, from the conquest of Constantinople. There are other items that have an Eastern cast, such as receiving the bread in white napkins. This can be seen in Eastern Church mosaics of Christ administering Communion to the apostles who wait with cloth-covered hands to receive the food of the heavenly banquet.

Other elements, such as the stone Grail itself placed on the table, the almost excessively orderly groupings of the procession, the propriety of the bowing, and the presence of the unusual table, however, suggest the Roman liturgy, so that Wolfram is combining elements of Eastern and Western sacramental liturgy, together with the familiar paraliturgical services of Good Fri-

---

23. Konrad Burdach thought that even Chrétien's Grail procession was based on the Byzantine liturgy of St. John Chrysostom. See his *Der Gral: Forschungen über seinen Ursprung und seinen Zusammenhang mit der Longinuslegende* (Stuttgart: Kohlhammer, 1938; reprint, Darmstadt: Wissenschaftliche Buchgesellschaft, 1974), p. 130.

day and Easter, as at Durham, described earlier, to create a generalized, overall medieval depiction of the sacramental meal itself, the Mass, as lordly largesse emanating mysteriously from the Passion and the Grail stone.

Wolfram's depiction of the Mass of the Grail is his own poetic recreation of the essence of the sacrament: an anamnesis, a living memory, of the events of Good Friday and Easter, the Passion and Resurrection embodied in the lance and the altar stone. These sacred events reenter Wolfram's contemporary world by crossing time in a Great Entrance from the realm beyond the "steel door," with its gray mist of time past, accompanied by brilliant light and incense. Their arrival makes the room diaphanous. The Holy Grail is accompanied not by the movement of the familiar twenty-four elders of the heavenly liturgy (Rev. 4:10) but by twenty-four women, analogous source on earth of heavenly over-flow of light and feeling. All are present in a mysterious theophany contemplated first in lamentation and then in bliss, and culminating in an opulent feeding of the multitude with miraculously served bread and wine in a banquet of delights on earth that is almost the banquet of heaven. How graciously ecumenical a protest is this combined Rite of the Eastern-Western Grail Mass against the fratricide of the Fourth Crusade, against the destruction and death of those who participate in the self-same banquet in the church of Constantinople. In 1204, as Wolfram was writing, a repetition of Cain's attack on Abel reentered time, in service to the wrong gods. The combined Grail rite, on the contrary, is a depiction of what the true nature of the celebration of the non-territorial lordship of Christ actually is.

Women, instead of men, are the part of the procession that gives radiant light to the room. This too is a part of Wolfram's feeling for what occurs during the Mass/Divine Liturgy. The divine light, that is, women, enter the room with the candles—not the squires of Chrétien. Women, since they represent feelings of loyalty to the point of death, Herzeloyde, and Sigune, are fidelity itself; thus they point the way, and lead men by love (condwir-amurs), to realizing the nature of the presence of the Grail—Christ's loyalty. Wolfram again puts men and women together as sunshine and daylight, or here, as gem and light. If men are gems and women are light: radiant light passes through precious gemstone, and the result of the combination is the famous brilliance. This is not a literal description of any liturgy in Christianity but a spiritual and theological representation of what happens in the sacraments given in Wolfram's emotional terms. Wolfram's ideal vision of the Mass is one that combines not only Western and Eastern liturgy, Good Friday and Easter, the heavenly banquet and medieval banquet but also the virtues, as he sees it, of men and women.

The women all bow and stand with perfect liturgical decorum as they enter in groups, each carrying one candle, unlike the squires carrying candelabra with ten or more candles apiece. Finally four bring in the table, which is not ivory but "a precious stone so clear that in the day the sun shone through. It was a garnet hyacinth long and wide, and he who measured it for a table top had cut it thin that it might be light to carry" (Mustard, 128). Women represent the fidelity, the overflow of faithfulness, without which there is no attaining the Grail, no understanding of what Christ did in death (Mustard, 128). Now the ivory appears, but not in the form of a table but as the trestles that support the stone so that light can shine through.

Wolfram pulls us back again to the language of the stones. A garnet hyacinth is a blood-red stone, and so the light that shines through it will be reddened. Like the baptismal font of Feirefiz and the grave of Gahmuret, the color of the stone, with its powerful ability to transmit light, guarantees the continuance of loyalty and life, not overcome by darkness or cold. It is related to the hopeful ruby that Anfortas is wearing as the tabletop is brought to him. The garnet, moreover, has the special property, as we saw in Albert the Great, of being able to "gladden the heart and dispel sorrow." The daylight pouring through passes through stone and adds a sustaining gladness, despite the condition of Anfortas—a note of hope to the community of the Grail. The ritual celebrated upon this stone has happiness and the celebration of the transmission of light through stone as its goal. Thin tabletops of this type were indeed cut during the time of the Crusades to enable Mass to be said in some solemnity while on the road, but they were not as large as this one. Wolfram is magnifying the glory of his Grail. When all is ready, in comes the queen. Unlike Chrétien's Grail bearer, who is simply a maiden who is carrying it in her two hands, this Grail bearer has a name and rank, and, in direct correspondence with the sadness-dispelling garnet hyacinth that is the tabletop, she is radiantly happy.

> After them came the queen. So radiant was her countenance that everyone thought the dawn was breaking. She was clothed in a dress of Arabian silk. Upon a deep green achmardi [green silk cloth with golden thread] she bore the bliss of Paradise, both root and branch. That was a thing called the Grail, the overflow of all earthly bliss. Repanse de Schoye [Overflow of Happiness] was the name of her whom the Grail permitted to be its bearer. . . . Before the Grail came lights of no small worth, six vessels of clear glass, tall and beautifully formed, in which balsam was burning sweetly. When they had advanced a proper distance from the door, the queen and

all the maidens bearing the balsam bowed courteously. Then the queen free of falsity placed the Grail before the host. (Mustard, 129, modified)

In contrast to Chrétien's version, where the tabletop is of ivory, and where the moving Grail is never set down, in Wolfram's version the tabletop is of translucent stone, and the Grail is placed before the host—and that means upon the garnet tabletop through which sunlight shines. The Grail does not pass again and again in front of the lord and his guest. The tabletop upon which the Grail is placed is itself a precious stone, and therefore, with Augustine, Marbode, and Albert, it is a precious stone that has come from and with the overflow of the rivers from the Garden of Eden. That is, as Augustine said, it is part of the outpouring of divine pleasure in the overflowing rivers from Paradise, from the time of purity before the Fall. The precious stone from Eden's river points to the psalmist's banquet: "You will give them drink from your river of delights" (*torrente voluptatis tuae potabis eos*).[24] The stone comes from the mysterious time world behind the steel door. The steel door is a striking addition not found in Chrétien, and will be a help in locating the specific altar stone used by Wolfram as his model. As a precious stone, the garnet also points to the heavenly Paradise, the walls of the heavenly Jerusalem of Revelation 21. And with Hildegard we can say that it is there not only for paradisial beauty but also "for healing."

The Grail permits, lets, itself be carried, to the table and thus has a personhood not found in Chrétien's notion of the Grail, a fact that implies a great deal with regard to the nature of the Grail, a stone with personal characteristics, and commanding ones at that. In its being placed on the thin tabletop, Wolfram has given a visual clue as to the nature of the Grail: in the manner here described, the portable altar stone, in its small shrine or reliquary form, was placed upon a larger tabletop to consecrate it for the Mass or other service. The Grail here is the portable altar stone containing the overflowing and radiant Body and the presence of Christ, who is then responsible for the commanding personal characteristics of the Grail.

Chrétien's Grail is immediately responsible for a haunch of well-prepared venison; Wolfram depicts the Grail as responsible for far more: it is the perfect happiness, the bliss, of Paradise, the *wunsch von Pardîs* (235, 12).[25] It is the origin, the roots, of the happiness of Paradise, and that has to lie in the beat-

---

24. Ps 36:8. The verse continues: *quoniam apud te fons vitae* (for in your house is the fountain of life).

25. *Wunsch* signifies an ideal, perfection, "the most that one could wish for." It also refers to a high level of happiness (MHG *Wonne*), and so is perhaps best understood as "bliss," "beatitude," or "perfect happiness" when used in a religious context such as this one of Paradise.

itude of the Creator of Paradise, and it is the branching of that bliss, the spreading, the overflow, of that perfect happiness to those creatures who wish to have a part of it. In other words, the Grail is not a holy container of static divine happiness, but by being the root and branches of the bliss of Paradise, it is a thing of growth and of expansiveness. The Grail contains (and is contained by) the Person whose function is to spread bliss, to help the overflow of happiness go from its origin in Paradise through its loss in the Garden, to branching out everywhere. There is certainly no description like this in Chrétien. In Wolfram, the Grail is the fullness to overflow of perfect happiness, the bliss of Paradise, and for that reason it is appropriate that it be carried from place to place and time to time in the hands of Overflowing Happiness, and not be spread abroad by overflowing hostility.

The great steel door, perhaps indeed suggested by the Royal Doors of the Eastern liturgy, must be, as it is there, the Gate of Paradise, the Gate of Heaven, since it is from there that the Grail comes to provide the bread and wine for the guests, and it is to the world behind the door that it returns. The Grail, in other words, as the altar stone, wrapped in the green of life, is not one of the sacraments, but it is the origin, the root, and the vitality of them all and enables their branching. It is the stone that by containing the Body of Christ has the capacity to consecrate a garnet tabletop into being an altar from which bread and wine are miraculously distributed. Christ, crucified and buried in the Sepulcher and risen from it, has given the earth in the portable sepulcher a miraculous rock that cures our, and Anfortas's, greatest weakness. It is the Rock from which the water flowed in the desert, it is the primal fountain in the midst of the Garden of Paradise from which all four rivers overflow, especially the gem-bearing rivers, and thus on the green *achmardi* one sees the source, placed appropriately on a table of translucent red garnet.

This Holy Grail of human salvation can only be carried from place to place by one person, and she, accompanied by incense-burning vessels, is the only one who can lift it and bring it to the nonconsecrated table: Repanse de Schoye, Overflowing Happiness. And she is a she. Her face is radiant and lightens the whole room. In Chrétien, it is the Grail with its jewels and gold that spreads radiant light; in Wolfram it is the woman who glows with feeling and with an overflow of radiance. It is the women with their own radiance, the love and beauty peculiar to them, who are the ones who not only lead to the Grail but accompany it with their light, each one carrying her own single candle. This is, as I have said, a theologically poetic statement by Wolfram, and so some critics with nervousness about women acting in such an obviously liturgical setting being uncanonical should look again. Neither women nor priests take up the sword to reach their goal, says Wolfram, and yet they get there, and women easily overcome many a strong knight, and good priests instead of the sword take into their hands the greatest pledge ever given to remove guilt. Parzival notices that he is wearing a woman's cloak, the cloak of Overflowing Happiness. "She" is the way to deal with the Saracen brother whom Parzival will meet at the end of the story, and she is the way to spread the happiness, now ailing, called Christianity, to the Baruch's Middle East. After all, almost everyone is wearing some silk or brocade from Araby, and in the midst of the Grail procession West meets East even in the very cloth that the members of the Grail community wear, and in the very cloth that envelops the Grail, a green *achmardi*.

Wolfram anticipates that his audience will say of the Grail, "There never was anything like that." And he replies with perfect assuredness, "they will be wrong in their angry protest, for the Grail was the fruition of blessedness, such abundance of the sweetness of the world that its delights were very like what we are told of the kingdom of heaven" (Mustard, 130). The Grail is the fruition of blessedness, the final result of what the beatitude of salvation can bring, and must mean both communion in bliss with the Trinity and communion in happiness with the delights of the world. During benediction of the Blessed Sacrament, two verses are chanted by priest and people to which Wolfram may be alluding here: "You gave them bread from heaven / which had in it every delight." (*Panem de coelo praestitisti eis. / Omne delectamentum in se habentem!*) The allusion in the verse is to the manna in the desert, understood as a type of the delight of Holy Communion. Thus not only do the guests receive the bread from the Grail but also whatever wine the guest might think of desiring, "he found it in his glass, all by the power of the Grail" (Mustard, 130).

Despite the presence, indeed possession, of such an overflow of bliss, the host is suffering, and the guest does not ask the question why. The question is different in Wolfram. Chrétien's hero fails to ask the question why the lance bleeds, and to whom in the unseen chamber the Grail is being carried. Wolfram changed the question from one to satisfy curiosity about two intriguing events to one that would express feelings of sympathy for the suffering of his host, prompted perhaps as well by feelings of confusion over such sadness in the presence of such happiness. Both Chrétien and Wolfram depict their heroes as too restricted by conventional rules of behavior to have emotions capable of sufficient "overflow" to transcend these rules and ask their questions, and thus both heroes are "kicked out" of the Grail castle the next morning without quite realizing why.

The Damsel with the Decapitated Knight

As happened before the Grail castle scene in Wolfram, now again after its ending a mysterious apparition of the cousin with the corpse of the dead knight occurs. This is its first appearance, however, in Chrétien. Chrétien's damsel is holding her dead lover in her arms, but there is surely no suggestion of a Pietà: he is decapitated. The scene is therefore incredibly gruesome, and it is hard to forget that the woman is holding a headless corpse, which through loyalty she refuses to leave. She is a cousin of Perceval, as in Wolfram, and she tells Perceval how accursed he is for not having asked the two questions and thus having relieved the Grail castle of its curse. In Wolfram's version, the cousin is given the name Sigune, an anagram of *cusine*, and she serves a similar purpose. She informs Parzival that he is accursed, but for a different reason from deficient curiosity. "You should have felt pity for your host, on whom God has wrought such terrible wonders, and have asked the cause of his suffering. You live and are dead to happiness" (Mustard, 139). She accuses him of insufficient loyalty to a suffering fellow human being to have overcome his shyness.

She is sitting in (or possibly under) a linden tree, the tree to which the turtledove flies, according to Wolfram's folklore, when its lover dies. She is the very image of the all-overcoming sympathy and loyalty that Parzival does not yet have. In being seated with the corpse of the lover on her lap (no decapitation), she is again the very image of the emotions that should accompany loyalty to the fallen, and since there is a wooden tree behind her like a cross, she presents the reader and Parzival with a living icon of the nature of the Grail as a holder of the Body of Christ.

The Haughty Knight of the Heath

In Chrétien's version, the husband of the damsel in the tent finds Perceval, challenges him, and loses the fight. When the Haughty Knight asks for mercy, Perceval grants it and sends him off to Arthur with the message that his wife was innocent, and then Perceval adds the words "This I swear to you." This oath in a simple phrase is accepted by the Haughty Knight with no further ado, and the husband and wife ride off happily. There is nothing more than the words "I swear to you" to attest to the veracity of Perceval's statement, and the incident is over quite speedily.

Wolfram's version adds a very important element, another appearance of the reliquary shrine. Immediately after seeing his cousin, Sigune, Parzival

A knight and his wife as Wolfram might have seen them, carved from one piece of stone. The crusader with staff and scrip, cross sewn to his garment, his hand around his wife, appears to be either about to leave and his wife seems unready to let him go. Or, if he is returning from the Crusades, a look of weariness on his face and his pilgrim's staff in his hand, her hand says that she will not easily let go of him again. The tragedy of the separation of husband and wife caused by the fighting of the Crusades has been touchingly portrayed by the artist by having both crusader and wife be carved from one piece of stone. From the cloister of the priory of Belval in Lorraine. *The Conway Library, Courtauld Institute of Art, London.*

comes across the woman in the tent, Jeschute, and her still very angry husband, Orilus (the Haughty Knight of the Heath). Following Chrétien, in Wolfram's version Parzival fights with the husband to assure him that the lady in the tent has done no wrong. He likewise vanquishes the husband, Orilus, who still, however, refuses believe that his wife is and was innocent. Parzival forces him to kiss his wife, which Orilus does stolidly, and then Wolfram adds: "The three tarried there no longer, but rode to a hermit's cave in the wall of the cliff. There Parzival found a casket with holy relics [*eine kefsen Parzivâl dâ vant*, 268, 28] and, leaning beside it, a spear painted [*ein bemâlet sper*, 268, 29] in bright colors" (Mustard, 145). This can be none other than, again, an appearance of the Grail. It can be no accident that the spear, so recently seen at the Grail castle, is leaning against it. And the word *kefse* is the common designation for the box-type reliquary used with an altar stone to contain the sacramental Body of Christ. When Parzival is about to swear an oath to Jeschute's innocence, the

Siegburg: KK St. Servatius, Gregorius-Tragealtar, Motive auf der Deckplatte
© LVR-Rheinisches Amt für Denkmalpflege - Alle Rechte vorbehalten
Foto: Michael Thuns - Digi.- Bearbeitung Detlef Perscheid

The Gregorius portable altar from Siegburg, viewed from above. It is about 15 inches long and about 9 inches wide. The apostles are in the top row, including Paul. In a parallel row at the bottom are bishops. On the left edge are the saintly women and on the right edge saintly men. To the left of the altar stone are scenes of the childhood of Christ, on the right are the Passion and Resurrection, and the Baptism in the Jordan. The green altar stone covers the sepulcher containing the sacramental body of Christ. *Schatzkammer der St.-Servatius-Kirche, Siegburg.*

reliquary altar stone is also given the more Eucharistic designation *heiltuom* (269, 2), the word that was used in the case of the blessing of the corpse of the Red Knight. Parzival shows his awareness that he is standing before more than the sacred remains of saints: "[If I am lying,] may I stand disgraced forever before the world and all my honor lost, and as pledge for these words let my happiness, with my deeds, be offered here before the Hand Supreme—that I believe is the hand of God" (Mustard, 146, modified).[26] The reliquary with its altar stone is the place of the hand of Divine exertion of power (and not just that of saints). Later in the scene, Trevrizent tells Parzival that the reliquary stone is related to his father Gahmuret:

> He [Gahmuret] gave me his jewel treasure,
> and what I gave him in return pleased him very much.
> That reliquary casket [*kefse*] which you saw once before
> —it is even greener than grass[27]—
> I had it made from the stone which
> the pure, noble man gave me. (Mustard, 266, modified)

> er gap sîn kleinœte mir.
> swaz ich im gap daz was sîn gir.
> mîne *kefsen*, die du sæhe ê,
> —diu ist noch grüener denne der klê—
> hiez ich wurken ûz eim steine
> den mir gap der reine. (498, 7–12)

Wolfram is gradually letting his readers/listeners in on the mystery of the whereabouts of the Grail. In its mysterious way, it is easily and frequently within reach. Connected to the precious stone of Augustine, *lapis prasinus*, the paradise stone that is as "green as grass," it can be found over Gahmuret's grave; it has appeared many times in the story, over the Red Knight's corpse, in Sigune's iconic posture, in the *kefse* for Parzival's oath taking, placed on the altar table in the Grail ceremony, and now again it is placed on the bare altar of Good Friday in Trevrizent's cave.

---

26. Parzival is depicted here as referring to the hand of God in parallel to his own as he swears his oath. His one hand is on the *heiltuom*, with the body of the Crucified, and the other hand is raised to God's own almighty Hand.

27. Lit.: "clover."

The Hideous Damsel on the Mule

It would be quite a contest to see which of the two authors, Chrétien or Wolf-ram, describes this woman in more hideous terms. Chrétien gives her the eyes of a rat and the lips of an ass or an ox, teeth the color of egg yolk, and the beard of a goat. Wolfram gives her hair like the bristles of a pig, a nose like a dog's, two boar's teeth sticking out, and both eyebrows braided up into her hair. In Chrétien's version, she curses Perceval for not having asked the two questions: the reason for the drop of blood on the lance and what rich person was served from the Grail. "Cursed be the hour you kept silence, since if you had asked, the rich king who is suffering so would already be healed of his wound and would be ruling in peace over the land he shall now never again command" (Kibler, 438). After her quick appearance she leaves, and Perceval resolves, for the first time, to begin a quest to find out the answers to his two unasked questions.

Wolfram gives the hideous woman a name, Cundrie, and he adds a sur-name: *la sourcière* (*la surziere*). The names serve to indicate in German that she is knowledgeable, a person of learning, *kund*, and in French that she is a sorceress, a "wise woman," in a sense analogous to that of the Magi as the "wise men." There is a psychological underpinning here for her ugliness that is not present in Chrétien: she brings not just knowledge and advice on chivalrous behavior, as the teachers of Parzival have done but also something more frightening: self-knowledge. Nothing on earth can appear quite as repellent as the realization that one has been a personal failure—and this is the knowledge she brings. Like the Hideous Damsel, she too tells Parzival that he is cursed for not asking, but the whole context is different. He is cursed by Cundrie for being an unfeeling guest, for having violated the old custom of *Gastfreundschaft* toward his host, the "sorrowful fisherman." "He showed you his burden of grief. O faithless guest! You should have taken pity on his distress. . . . May your mouth become empty, I mean of the tongue within it, as your heart is empty of real feeling!" (Mustard, 170–1). She accuses Parzival, by reason of his not having felt compassion on seeing Anfortas in his suffering, of being an unnatural monster, of being far uglier than she is, her ugliness being merely external. This means that when he cures Anfortas of his ugliness, that is, Anfortas's own behavior, his failure, by feeling fraternal sympathy, Parzival will also be acknowledging his own ugly failure to have feelings, and will cure himself. He too is suffering from the same illness, the same ugliness, as Anfortas, and needs the cure of feeling pity to get better again. Wolfram has thus given a profound reason for the apparent ugliness of Cundrie in the story and used it to connect Parzival's problem to that of the Grail community. She, then, as a good scholar should, reminds Parzival of his past family history, speaking of both Gahmuret and Feirefiz as well as Herzeloyde—something, of course, that Chrétien could not have written, since he does not have Wolfram's frame story. She thereby connects Parzival's mission and his failure to a historical dimension of the Grail.

The failure goes back through Frimutel and Titurel to Mazadan, to Adam and his sin in the Garden of Paradise. The Grail is connected by her to both Feirefiz and to Gahmuret, and this Wolfram brings to a very satisfactory conclusion in books 15 and 16. Cundrie now practices what she preaches. As opposed to Chrétien's Hideous Damsel, who "ceased speaking and left without another word," Cundrie *la sourcière* "succumbed to grief. Weeping she wrung her hands, and many a tear overtook another as great sorrow pressed them into her eyes. It was loyal devotion taught the maiden to pour out her heart's distress" (Mustard, 171–2). Without the tears of sympathy, for Wolfram no human being, no matter how gem-like in appearance or knowledge, is truly a gem of the genuine element Water, the basis of all precious stones and of the Grail stone itself. Her tears show her to be a gem and a genuine part of the outflow of the Grail.

Perceval and Good Friday

This was the last scene that Chrétien wrote with his hero Perceval in it. Perceval comes to repent his sins, especially his fundamental one, one he is unaware of—that he rode off even though his mother had fallen at the bridge. He had not known that she died at the moment out of grief. His inability to ask the questions about the Grail is attributed to his root sin at the bridge. Five years have passed in which he has not gone near church or chapel, despite her advice. As he rides through a deserted region, he meets three knights and ten ladies walking barefoot and doing penance. They inform him that it is Good Friday, and tell him it is not good to bear arms on the day when Jesus died.

> On a day like today, in truth He was nailed upon the cross. . . . This
> was truly a holy death which saved the living and brought the dead
> back to life. The wicked Jews, whom we should kill like dogs,
> brought great harm to themselves and did us great good when in
> their malice they raised him on the cross: they damned themselves
> and saved us. (Kibler, 458)

(Wolfram obviously took his Good Friday scene from here, but just as obviously removed Chrétien's nonecumenical and noncompassionate remarks about the Jews.) The knights tell Perceval they are coming from confession to a hermit in the forest and urge him to go and confess to him as well.

Chrétien's Perceval follows the path they have marked, dismounts at the hermitage, and, weeping, goes into a small chapel where the hermit and a priest have just begun the service. Tears flow from his eyes down his cheeks as he is told of his role in his mother's death, and after he admits not having asked the Question of the Grail community. He is told by the hermit that the Rich Fisher is the son of the king served from the Grail, who is also the hermit's brother, and Perceval's mother is their sister. (Wolfram did not invent the idea of relatives at the Grail, but he extended kinsman status to everyone.) "A single host that is brought to him in that Grail sustains and brings comfort to that holy man—such is the holiness of the Grail" (Kibler, 460).

It is because of this passage in Chrétien that so many medieval French illustrators depicted the Grail as a ciborium. Perceval is given a penance to perform, which consists mainly of going to church, hearing Mass if possible, and doing penance in the church. He is advised to respect the priest by rising in his presence and to help the widow and the orphan. (Wolfram is much more elaborate on why one should rise in the presence of the priest: his mouth proclaims the Passion and his hands hold the Eucharist.) A secret prayer is whispered into Perceval's ear, consisting of the many and holy names for the Lord; one to be used only at the point of death. Perceval then on Easter Sunday "very worthily received communion. The tale no longer speaks of Perceval at this point." And thus the Perceval strand of the tale breaks off, never to be finished by Chrétien.

Wolfram too begins this segment of the tale, his book 9, with a hermit's cell, but "with a swift stream flowing through it" (Mustard, 234). The reader is not too far from Paradise. Wolfram's Parzival then finds a hermitess, rather than a hermit, and of course it is the faithful Sigune mysteriously appearing again. In her fidelity, she still watches over the coffin of the fallen knight, and on her finger she wears a ring. "The stone in it was a garnet which gleamed out through the darkness [ûz der vinster; 438, 7] like a little spark of fire" (Mustard, 236).[28] The stone bespeaks her unquenchable fidelity in the face of death in the familiar terms of the ability of the carbuncle stone to shine in the dark. It is at this point that she asks Parzival not if he has found the Grail but rather

28. Some translations give ûz der vinster as "in the window," but the noun here is feminine, and thus the phrase cannot mean "in the window," but rather "out of the darkness."

"Have you at last discovered its true nature?" When, at the end of the tale, he does at last genuflect and ask the Question, and the role of Sigune and her knight in the narrative as a didactic icon is no longer necessary, in book 16—that is when Parzival returns to Sigune for the last time, and burial is able to take place. Cundrie brings Sigune food from the Grail, and the wise woman always leaves her mule "where the spring flows out of the rock" (Mustard, 238). Wolfram uses biblical imagery to say that the Grail is near, and that its nature is rock and flowing water, rather than the more ecclesiastical, but less liturgical, language of Chrétien.

Wolfram's Parzival then meets the gray knight with two maidens; they make the same complaint to him that it is Good Friday.

> Today is Good Friday when the whole world can rejoice, yet at the same time sigh in grief. Where was a love more faithful [triuwe], ever shown than that which God showed to us, Who for our sakes hung on the cross? Sir, if you are baptized, you should lament that exchange. (Mustard, 241)

The women, of course, feel sorry for him and make significant mention of the fact that armor must be cold. Parzival rides on and repentance arises in his heart, and in feudal style asks God, his Lord, for help. If the crusader is upset at failure and disturbed that God did not give his help with the battles now lost, perhaps God will give his holy help to help his vassal to repent. Once more, he gives up control to God, lets the reins fall, and immediately his mount arrives at Fontane la Salvatsche, the Fountain of Salvation, where the hermit Trevrizent begs him to dismount, and (like St. Paul) to get down off his horse.

They stand in the snow and frost, parallel to the mortal cold that afflicts Anfortas—Saturn, Chronos, is in their skies as well—and then the hermit and Parzival go deep into a cave in the rock. Inside the rock, they enter another cave in which Parzival finds the holy books that the hermit reads, and then: "An altar stone stood there, bare, as is the [liturgical] custom on this day, and on it a casket with holy relics" ("nâch des tages site ein altarstein / dâ stuont al blôz. dar ûf erschein / ein kefse"; 459, 23-5; Mustard, 246). The Grail appears again, and in its proper liturgical form without an altar cloth, for the services of Good Friday. Going into the rock, something that does not occur in Chrétien, puts them in a parallel position to the Grail itself, in communion with the Holy Sepulcher, Christ, and Christian, in the stone together, on Good Friday, when Christ was placed in the rock, the cave tomb. The stream running by suggests baptism as the way into this rock. The hermit and Parzival are in the rock cave just as the Body of Christ is in the kefse, the altar-stone reliquary. Parzival recognizes the reliquary as what he has seen before, when he swore an oath upon it. Does he recognize the similarity to Sigune of the Pietà with her glowing garnet in her hermitage? It is up to the reader to recognize Wolfram's mystical suggestion that the two persons now in the cave, in the presence of the altar stone and spear, with the remembrance of Good Friday's entombment in Jerusalem, are all parts of the same profound mystery of faithfulness, *triuwe*, the mystery celebrated in the Grail ritual and held in the Grail stone.

Trevrizent's teaching goes far beyond anything in Chrétien and gives something of a catechesis based on salvation history—as Wolfram reads it. God is pure loyalty itself, God is the light that penetrates the darkness of our thoughts soundlessly and without being seen (as in his gem example in *Willehalm*). Then Wolfram explains the Grail. It cannot be found by searching, it is a vocation, one must be called. The knights who live with the Grail at Mount Salvation do so for their sins, whether they win or lose battles.

> They live from a stone of the purest kind. If you do not know it, it
> shall here be named to you. It is called *lapsit exillis* [468, 7].[29] By the
> power of that stone the Phoenix burns to ashes, but the ashes give
> him life again. Thus does the Phoenix molt and change its plumage,
> which afterward is bright and shining and as lovely as before. (Mustard, 251–2)

Now the description of the nature of the Grail is being given in even more ecumenical language. Before, at the Grail ceremony, the language was that of Western and Eastern liturgy; now it is that of "heathen" mythology. In this ancient language, Wolfram identifies the Grail as the place of transformation from life through death to life again. In Christian language, the stone is the Holy Sepulcher, and the Phoenix is Christ. The Grail is the place of "molting" from ugliness to beauty, as will happen spectacularly to Anfortas, "Human Weakness."

In the myth of the Phoenix, the stone, the place where this transformation occurs, is identified as an altar. The Phoenix must fly to the sacred altar stone at Heliopolis in Egypt, and it is only on that altar stone, *in Solis urbem et in ara ibi*, that the transformation of the firebird takes place and he rises from his ashes.[30] Good Friday, Easter, the Resurrection from the altar stone of the sar-

---

29. There are several variants of *lapsit exillis* in the manuscripts. I prefer *lapis exilis*, which would mean "thin stone." The copyists seem not to have been sure of Wolfram's original, whose poetic Latin, like his French, is often more suggestive than precise. Other variants of *lapsit* (an ungrammatical form of the deponent verb *labor, labi, lapsus est*; or of *lapsare*, "to fall,"or "to slip") are *iaspis* (jasper) and *lapis* (stone). Variants on *ex illis* (from them) are *exilis* (thin) and *exillix* (?) and *exilix* (?).

30. The quotation is from C. Plinii Secundi, *Naturalis Historia*, bk. 10, ed. Roderich König (Munichh: Artemis, 1986), p. 18. In the *Physiologus*, the bird brings incense to burn in its death and rises from the ashes

cophagus. The Grail, then, is the gemstone of all gemstones; it is the stone that makes death, in pre-Christian "heathen" terms, into a molting of feathers. With the new feathers, the soul flies again.

The transcendent power of the Grail is also described by Wolfram in the following passage in terms of the Holy Spirit and two altars. The Dove descends every Good Friday onto the stone, suggesting a strong parallel between the flight of the Dove to the Grail stone and the flight of the Phoenix to Heliopolis's altar stone, renewing its great transformative power.

> This very day there comes to it [the stone] a message wherein lies its greatest power. Today is Good Friday and they await there a dove, winging down from Heaven. It brings a small white host, and leaves it on the stone. The dove is of a penetrating white radiance [*diu tûb ist durchliuchtec blanc;* 470, 7]. Then the dove soars up to Heaven again. Every single Good Friday [*immer alle karfrîtage;* 470, 9] it brings to the stone what I have just told you, and from that the stone derives whatever good fragrances of drink and food there are on earth, like to the perfect bliss of Paradise: I mean everything the earth can produce! And further the stone provides whatever game lives beneath the heavens, whether it flies, or runs or swims—this is the way in which the power of the Grail gives gracious support to the knightly brotherhood [*der rîterlîchen bruoderschaft* 470, 19]. (Mustard, 252)

The introduction of the Dove reminds the reader of the function of the Holy Spirit during the Mass of the Eastern and Western liturgies: to come and bring the transforming power of the Trinity upon the inert bread and wine and change their natures into the Body and Blood of Christ. Though it is commonly thought that in medieval times such power was attributed to the priest alone, Wolfram attributes to the priest the privilege of holding the Body of Christ, and of invoking the Word of God, but it is the Holy Spirit of the Trinity, called on in the epiclesis and resident in the stone through the sacramental Body of Christ, that gives to the liturgy itself the power of transformation. The Dove is described not as being as bright as, or brighter than, the daylight but as being *durchliuchtec blanc.* This means that the Dove emits a brilliant, penetrating white light that shines through things, like light (to use one of Wolfram's favorite images) passing through gems, and thus is able to penetrate the altar

---

"on the third day." The Phoenix's resurrection is explicitly called an image of the Resurrection of Jesus. *Physiologus latinus versio Y*, ed. Francis J. Cormody (Berkeley: University of California Publications in Classical Philology, 1941). Wolfram could have had the story from either source or common knowledge.

stone with its more than solar divine radiance.[31] The Holy Spirit is also given as the cause for the great abundance enjoyed by all the temple knights on Mount Salvation, just as the Holy Spirit in Genesis 1 is described as hovering over all of the action of God's making the world. Above all, as Huntley-Speare has written, "the means by which divine aid and presence come to man is the Holy Spirit, making the power of Christ's death and resurrection (embodied in the wafer) accessible. . . . Wolfram marks the Grail society as under the command of the Holy Spirit."[32]

There is also a warning here, and a protest. The sacred stone upon which the host is laid is the bare altar of Good Friday (preconsecrated hosts for Communion are prepared at the Mass of Holy Thursday). There is only a simple piece of cloth on the altar on this day. It is called the corporal ("body cloth") in the West and the *iliton* in the East—both words indicate that it is the shroud. Though it is not Friday evening of 33 AD, the Body of Christ is laid on the shroud on a bare stone. This is not the stone of the Holy Sepulcher in Jerusalem, since it is the stone of every altar in Christendom and it is done every year. The Grail of Christ, the Phoenix, and the Holy Spirit cannot be isolated at the single altar of Jerusalem's Sepulcher if the Holy Spirit is invoked upon all—the altar is ubiquitous and, miraculously important, portable. The other innocent phrase, or not quite so innocent, that emphasizes this mystical fact is the strong *immer alle karfrîtage*—*always, every Good Friday*. The Holy Grail is not an item that can be located in one time zone, including the privileged dates of Good Friday and Holy Thursday of 33 AD. This is a direct reply to both Chrétien, and more strongly, I believe, to Robert de Boron. The Holy Grail is not a vessel—serving dish, chalice, or rock tomb—that was once used by Christ. It is indeed the container of the Body of Christ, and it is the stone that contained his body on the Friday evening of his death, and nothing from the Thursday of his Last Supper. It is not the rock tomb, however, so recently lost by the Knights Templar to the Saracens, which is an entity not transferable from Jerusalem. Wolfram's Grail is the stone tomb as portable over time and space into every country and era of the "Land of Salvation," reestablished in its full transforming power by the annual in-flying of the Divine Spirit. The Dove does not descend upon some serving dish in Cornwall or at Glastonbury Abbey, or appear in a cup at the time of Arthur. The Grail can be found easily, as Parzival does by letting the reins of questing fall to the ground, and can be

31. See Mario Huber's penetrating *Licht und Schönheit in Wolfram's "Parzival"* (Zürich: Juris Druck Verlag, 1981), p. 118. He accurately uses "durchleuchtend" as the translation of *durchliuchec*; in English this might be "[brilliantly] illuminating," "shining through," or "trans-radiant."

32. Huntley-Speare, "Wolfram's Willehalm and Triuwe," p. 116–7.

seen by the baptized—any Good Friday, the day when the altar stands uncovered. The Grail cannot be recognized so much in secular time, but rather in liturgical time, and especially "every single Good Friday," within the sepulcher of the altar stone.

This is not news that should be borne with sadness, Wolfram is saying to the knights who defended Jerusalem unsuccessfully, to his contemporary readers, and to us generations later. The Grail is full of the power of God, renewed every Holy Week, and this news should be borne by Overflowing Happiness herself. She alone, says Wolfram, Repanse de Schoye and no one else, whether made sad by the loss of Jerusalem, or sad over personal failure of sympathy with the suffering, should attempt to carry the Grail in sad determination. It is simply too heavy for the despondent. The reaction to the existence of the real Holy Grail should be full to overflowing happiness and nothing less. Saturn is defeated, and remains defeated, for Gahmuret and for Parzival, and for Anfortas, the temple knights, and Feirefiz. Not having defeated the Saracens

A side view of the portable altar at the Walters Art Museum in Baltimore. The side panel in the illustration appropriately depicts the holy women at the tomb early on Easter morning being spoken to by the angel. The altar with its rectangular stone on the top surface is shown by the iconography of the side panel to be the Holy Sepulcher, the place where the Resurrection of Christ is mystically made present during the Mass. *The Walters Art Museum, Baltimore.*

in 1187 in the Holy Land is simply nothing in comparison to this. Feirefiz will also come to the Grail, and he will be led to it and to its flowing waters by the Overflowing Happiness of the people of the Land of Salvation. This is the ultimate happiness of the Grail and its people, who wear the sign of the affection of the Trinity, the turtledove.

The inner story now makes a transition to Gawain's romantic adventures, which we will not follow. There is, however, a magic parallel to Parzival's stone Grail that should be mentioned. It is related to Gawain, and Wolfram presents it at the Castle of Wonders. Where Chrétien in his narrative simply has a high tower with a balcony from which one has a marvelous view of the surrounding countryside, "then he [Gawain] wished to see the view from the tower. He climbed a spiral staircase . . . until they reached the top of the tower and could see the surrounding countryside which was more beautiful than words can describe" (Kibler, 478–9). This becomes in Wolfram:

> At one end of the hall rose a narrow tower high above the castle
> roof, a winding staircase leading to it. Up there stood a shining pil-
> lar [it is, of course, surrounded by precious stones, from diamonds
> to emeralds]. It seemed to him [Gawain] that he could see in the
> great pillar all the lands round about; it seemed the lands were cir-
> cling the pillar, and the mighty mountains collided with a crash. In
> the pillar he saw people riding and walking, others running or
> standing still. (Mustard, 312–3)

Why is this here? I believe the stone pillar is a contrast, deliberately set in place to distinguish its magical and scientific nature (it seems almost to anticipate the quartz lenses of a telescope or periscope) from the nonmagical and sacramental mystery of the Grail, just as the gemstones and their powers in Anfortas's sickroom are set there to distinguish their limited powers from the power of the Grail and the power of sympathy.

Wolfram brings his inner story to an end in book 14, in which the two adventurers meet and fight. Parzival has now personally so matured that he rejoices when he realizes that Gawain is a relative and that he did not hurt a kinsman. "Alas that I fought with the noble Gawain! It is myself that I have vanquished," he says, and tosses his sword far from himself (Mustard, 360–1). How far he has come since coldly throwing the javelin through the eye slit of the helmet of the Red Knight. Book 14 is thus both a culmination and a seamlessly beautiful transition from the world of Parzival's personal, emotional growth as a Christian knight, full of peaceful loyalty to his kin, to the social world of books 15 and 16, in which he comes to recognition of kinship outside Christianity and to the recognition of Christianity's sore need through sympathy to be cured of its malignant devotion to Jupiter and Mars. While the inner story's narrative circles around the mystery of the Grail and its relation to the sacrament of the Eucharist, when the story reaches book 15 it makes a transition and returns to the world of Book 1, to the mystery of the Grail's relationship to baptism, and to the kinship of those baptized and those not.

At the end, Sigune the faithful is found dead with her knight by Parzival, the new keeper of the Grail, and is buried. It is as though even the most solemn forms of *triuwe* must sometimes be brought to closure and allowed to pass. The literal fidelity of the Templars to the Holy Sepulcher of Jesus in Jerusalem, the devout cause of the first crusaders, can perhaps now be brought to a final end, to be replaced by a less literal but just as devout fidelity to the portable altar stone and its sepulcher in which the Body of Christ is present and on which the Spirit descends to refresh its sacred outflow in the Mass and baptism. Christianity's Overflowing Happiness, with the help of the Dove and the Phoenix, can then lead the story back home to the East, to the Garden from which it all began.

7

The Paradise Altar
of Bamberg

As I followed the director up the beautiful staircase to the exhibition rooms at the Diocesan Museum, I thought *What a long journey this has been, and now I hope I have found what I am looking for.* I was following in the steps of the painstaking research of Josef Braun, S.J., who in the 1920s had catalogued just about every type of altar in existence in Europe, and had been minutely detailed in his description of every portable altar he could find, giving their location, their style, whether flat stones or plain box- or altar-type (*kefsen*), the blessings used in their consecration, and the symbolism and motifs used in the decoration of their upper surfaces and sides.[1] Because "overflow" is so important to Wolfram, as well as the theme of the rivers of Paradise, I was hoping there would be a handful of portable altars decorated with this motif.

According to Braun, despite the great number of medieval portable altars still in existence, there were only two with the theme of the four rivers of Paradise, one in Brussels and one in Bamberg, and the first of these was in the flat stone form.[2] Would it be pos-

---

1. Joseph Braun, *Der christliche Altar in seiner geschichtlichen Entwicklung* (Munich: Guenther Koch, 1924), 1:500ff.
2. Braun, *Der christliche Altar in seiner geschichtlichen Entwicklung*, 1:503. I later learned that the flat portable altar in Brussels had a brownish-beige stone. That would clearly seem to rule it out of consideration in the context of Wolfram's poetry.

sible to find the very altar stone that was Wolfram's Grail and to look at the very stone that inspired this great Christian ecumenical masterpiece?

Because Bamberg is in Franconia, Wolfram's heartland, and because there is a possibility that Bamberg is mentioned at one point in the narrative, as an alternate reading for Abenberc, and because its portable altar was in the reliquary-box form, I believe that the altar at Bamberg is the one that inspired Wolfram.[3] Nonetheless, I had gone to the Musées Royaux in Brussels just to see if perchance there might be something to the one there. It was, as I mentioned before, not on exhibition, and inaccessible for the foreseeable future. In any case, it was a simple flat stone, and not the reliquary type mentioned so often by Wolfram, and so I decided that I had better let it go and drive back to Germany. I left that evening. A friendly museum guard—he pretended with kindness and a straight face that my French was perfectly intelligible; the cashier had not done so—informed me that the following day was a car-free Sunday for Brussels, and that I should be careful where I stayed because I would be ticketed if I attempted to drive in the city the next day. On my way from Brussels, I passed several road signs indicating the direction to Waterloo. It was my turn to wonder and smile at the omens on that rainy day. I did not follow them.

Two days later, when the director of the Diocesan Museum in Bamberg turned around on the museum staircase and told me that he had been mistaken when he said to me on the phone that their altar had the twelve apostles on it and nothing more, he made me a very happy researcher. Braun wrote in 1924: "The rivers of Paradise, depicted as men with urns from which water is streaming, occur only on one flat portable altar in the Brussels museum and on one of the [two] portable altars in Bamberg."[4] Reliance on Braun, despite World War II and eighty years of change, was justified. When the director explained that not only were the four rivers of Paradise there but also the four trees, and that they were also on the top face of the altar, I could not hide my feelings. I could tell by his trace of a smile that he could see the expression that must have been on my face. Perhaps the word "repanse" might have described it.

When we reached the top of the stairs, a huge crowd was milling about, thronging especially around the exhibit of the astoundingly beautiful "star cloak" of the emperor Heinrich the Second, dating from approximately the year 1020 AD. I went into the next room full of glittering monstrances and

3. In the text is *z'Abenberc* (227, 13), which Mustard (p. 125, n. 2) understands as "the fortress of Amberg, near Schwabach, east of Wolfram's hometown of Eschenbach." This is generally accepted. Nonetheless, mss., *Gg*, actually have *datze babenberch*. Babenberch, Bamberg, of course, has my preference because of the altar stone. See chapter 6, note 18.

4. "Die Paradiesesflüsse, Männer, die Wasser Urnen entströmen lassen, kommen nur an dem Tafelportatile im Brüsseler Museum und an einem der Bamberger Portatilien vor." Braun, *Der christliche Altar*, p. 503.

reliquaries, threaded my way through more of the crowd behind the director—
and then I saw it. There were two portable altars under glass protectors. The
director turned to me and smiled, pointed to the one on the left, and bowed.
The crowd was giving it only a passing bit of attention. Wolfram would have
thought that appropriate. I'm afraid I did not.

It was somewhat off to one side, but as I approached it, I asked myself
whether I was going to look at it with the feelings of Parzival on his first visit
or on his second. I went through a little of both. It was so ordinary, and so
extraordinary. It was against a side wall, and yet I thought if people knew what
this small object might be, it would be in the center of the room. I wanted to
rush and look at it up close, and yet I was walking toward it slowly. What color
was the stone? I made myself take a quick glance at the top of the object to
see the stone. It was green. Relief and happiness. I kept looking. I was in some
kind of state. The personified rivers were right there, pouring their storied
water from the stone. There were the four trees of Eden at the four corners of
the stone. I tried to take it in, all of it. I knew that despite looking at it as
carefully and intensely as I could, and taking more than copious notes, I would
miss something, and so, despite the clear German sign saying no photographs
allowed, I proceeded to ask and was given permission to take pictures. I
climbed all over the glass to get at the object, and people didn't seem to mind.
As long as I kept my notebook and pen in hand, I was accepted by the streaming throng of visitors as doing research and therefore exempt from common
rules.

Let me give it a name: the (Bamberg) Paradise Altar. It has the small size
and proportions of an average medieval portable altar: it is 24.7 centimeters
(9.8 inches) long, 15.5 centimeters (6.2 inches) wide, and about 14.9 centimeters (5.9 inches) high.[5] It is dated to the second half of the twelfth century,
and thus was in use at the time (c. 1202–1210) Wolfram was composing his
Parzival. It is very hard to give a definitive place of origin for the altar, but it
seems to have been associated for some time with Bamberg. One of the reasons
for its preservation is that it may have been one of the portable reliquary altars
enclosed in a side altar in the seventeenth century to consecrate that altar and
was not removed until the restoration of the cathedral in 1836 when it was
discovered there. Of the four enameled plates that once formed the top surface,
two have been preserved, and two are lost. The two that are present, however,

---

5. For details, see Renate Baumgarten-Fleischmann, *Ausgewählte Kunstwerke aus dem Diözesanmuseum
Bamberg* (Bamberg: Bayerische Verlagsanstalt Bamberg, 1992), p. 34. Based on observation and on the dimensions given in *Ars Sacra* and museum guidebooks, the average length for portable altars varies from about 7 to
14 inches.

enable one to reconstruct what must have been on the other two. One of the inscriptions on the Paradise Altar is related to one on the Gregorius portable altar in Siegburg, but there is no other connection in terms of its treatment of its riverine theme or its curious water-based style of decoration to any other reliquary-type portable altar known. In this respect it is unique.

Let me attempt to describe the Paradise Altar and some of the reasons for its uniqueness, and attempt to explain why I think it is the stone that Wolfram was thinking of, or inspired by, when he came to his realization about the true nature of the Grail. Viewed from above, the center of the upper table of the little altar is the altar stone. It is, of course, as one would expect after reading Wolfram, green. This would not have been surprising in Wolfram's day, since green serpentine, which is just translucent, on the edges, was a commonly preferred material for altar stones. We need only go back to Augustine's reading of the green-grass stone to see why. This semiprecious stone in its greenness signifies that life cannot desiccate and that life and light can radiate through its function as a grave cover. The stone covers a rectangular recess cut into the oaken body of the little altar. This recess, the sepulchrum, is now empty. I asked to examine the altar, but because of the crowds and special exhibition, the director did not want to remove the protective glass covering. The recess, in any case, is now empty. As this was a portable altar, the recess would have once held three pieces of the sacramental Body of Christ, three grains of incense (in honor of the spices brought by the women and Joseph of Arimathea), and the relics of saints, all wrapped in silk and sealed in place by the stone.

To the left of the green stone is Abel rushing forward toward the altar stone with a lamb in his cloth-covered hands, ready to make it his offering. To the right of the altar stone is King Melchisedech hastening toward it with his offering of a round loaf of bread and a chalice of wine in his hands, as he reaches out to place them on the altar. This means that on the missing plaque below the altar stone would have been Abraham with the knife ready to offer his son Isaac on the altar, with the ram caught in the thicket nearby. These three figures are all considered to be Old Testament types of the offering made by Christ of himself by sacrificial death on the cross and by his being laid in the Sepulcher.[6] It is not uncommon to find these three figures on portable altars, since all three prefigure Christ's Crucifixion in patristic thought, and all three are mentioned by the priest at Mass during the anaphora prayer following

---

6. See Wilhelm Messerer, *Der Bamberger Domschatz in seinem Bestande bis zum Ende der Hohenstaufen-Zeit* (Munich: Hirmer Verlag, 1952). Messerer also reconstructed the missing parts of the inscriptions on the basis of portable altars in Siegburg.

the words of consecration in the Roman canon: "Look with favor on these offerings and accept them as You once accepted the gifts of your servant Abel, the sacrifice of Abraham, our father in faith, and the bread and wine offered to You by your priest Melchisedech."[7] They therefore point directly to the Mass as celebrated on this stone, and to the consecratory Body of Christ beneath it.

The four evangelists whose medallions with their symbols are in the four corners of the tabletop point to the story of Christ recorded in the four Gospels. Wolfram gives as one of the priest's distinctive functions that he proclaims with his mouth the redemptive sufferings of Christ written by the four evangelists (and, as his other function, that he takes into his hands the highest pledge given for sin).

To my happiness and amazement, to the left of Abel on the edge of the altar was a man pouring water. It was the personification of one of the rivers of Paradise, drawn as a man with an oriental cap and, in the classical manner, pouring a stream of blue water out of a large jar onto the earth. In the same way, on the extreme right of the tabletop of the altar, to the right of Melchise-dech, a male figure also wearing a Persian cap in the style of classical antiquity pours water out of a large amphora that runs in a blue stream behind him, reaching to the edge of the altar. Both personifications of the rivers are looking back to the green altar stone that covers the sepulchrum at the center of the altar table, their source, making the Sepulcher of Christ's Passion and Resurrection an analogue to the primal river rising in the middle of the Garden of Paradise. As their heads tilt in reverence toward their stone source, the rivers' urns are filled to overflowing with water, just as the baptismal font filled miraculously with water at the moment when it was tilted toward the Grail for Feirefiz's baptism. From the middle of Paradise miraculously and invisibly comes the water that divides into the headwaters of the four rivers, the Pishon ("where there is gold and precious stones"), the Gihon, the Tigris, and the Euphrates, that irrigate the whole world. The personifications of the other two rivers we can assume were on the top and bottom missing panels, their heads also tilted in reverence as they face back toward the altar stone at the center of the "Garden of Paradise."[8] St. Augustine would have been happy to see the design so indebted to his reading of Genesis.

7. The prayer can be found in the Catholic Missal as the "First Eucharistic Prayer" (nowadays there are four in the Roman Rite), also designated the "Roman Canon."

8. Braun's interpetation of the four streams is: "Die Paradiesesflüsse versinnbildlichen die Gnadenströme, die sich von dem einen Christus, dem Felsen, dem das lebendige Wasser entspringt (1 Cor. 10:4), segen- und fruchtspendend über die ganze Welt ergossen." (The rivers of Paradise symbolize the streams of grace which, welling up from the one Christ, the rock, poured themselves out over the whole world bringing blessing and fruitfulness.) *Der christliche Altar in seiner geschichtlichen Entwicklung*, p. 503. What Braun says of the portable

At each of the four corners of the altar stone (the serpentine stone measures 3¾ inches by 2½ inches) stands one of the four trees of the Garden of Paradise: "And the Lord God made all kinds of trees grow out of the ground— [1] trees that were pleasing to the eye; and [2] good for food. In the middle of the garden were [3] the tree of life and [4] the tree of the knowledge of good and evil" (Gen 2:9, NIV). It is pretty clear that the religious poet who designed this altar felt that the Mass was the mystical restoration of mankind to the once lost Garden of Paradise. This is so very close to Wolfram's constant description of the Grail as being the root and branch of paradisial happiness that it supports seeing the Grail ceremony as related to the restoration of the original bliss. The gate barring the return of human beings to Eden had been reopened in Christ's Passion, and the stone slab covering the grave had been made into an open door.

An inscription around the outer edge of the altar, restored, reads: "[What you see here is] witness to the heavenly [banquet] hall, the wide-open gate of heaven, for He is setting up places in heaven [lit.: "in the air"] for His holy ones" *(aule celi testis, pervia porta celestis, sanctis enim eius componit in ethere sedes)*. The significant expression *pervia porta celestis,* "the wide-open door of heaven" echoes the old hymn "Alma Redemptoris Mater" by Hermann Contractus (1013–1054) of Reichenau, and finds its own perfect parallel in Wolfram's great steel door: the door that opens to permit the passage of Overflowing Happiness carrying the Grail as it makes the transition from one realm of time to another, from the gray aged man of the past to the present translucent table of Anfortas, and in the future to Parzival. Thus the Grail uninterruptedly provides the banquet of bliss for all throughout the passage of time, *per omnia saecula saeculorum.* The presence of the Gate of Heaven in the inscription and the inscription's identification of the Gate with the altar stone and the mention of the hall and the preparing of seats for those who die give support to the idea that Wolfram knew this altar, and imagined it lifted in benediction over the body of his Red Knight.

There is also an inner inscription that directly borders on the stone itself:

> *ara crucis Christi*
> *mense communicat isti,*
> *hac et enim rite*
> *sacratur victima vitae*

---

altar is precisely what Horgan says of the Holy Grail—both following 1 Cor 10:4, "for they drank from the spiritual rock that accompanied them, and that rock was Christ."

The altar of Christ's cross is one with this table, and this is therefore
the proper place for the sacrifice of the Victim who secures life.

This is the wood and the stone that guarantees the passage from Good Friday
to Easter Sunday, death to life, as do the Christian sarcophagus stones that
guarantee the future of life for Gahmuret, and for the fallen of Alischanz. The
portable altar, and perhaps this very portable altar, is Wolfram's special stone
of Resurrection, the phoenix stone in Wolfram's language, that was imagined
by him as being lifted in blessing over the body of Ither, the fallen Red Knight.

I had found my portable altar stone with the rivers of Paradise. Now I
looked at the side of the Paradise Altar, and what to my eyes should appear but
a beautifully enameled thin winding blue stream of water making its way along
the edge around the entire periphery of the upper altar table. It was as near as
an artist could come to illustrate that the four rivers of this stone's Paradise
were overflowing, encircling the whole world, entwining themselves around
the golden line marking the *limes*, the final border, the edge of the earth. No
wonder the water from the urn of the river on the right is flowing all the way
to the edge of the tabletop; it then overflows onto the side. Wherever the Paradise river flows all along the edge, the artist has placed green vegetation
emerging on both sides of the streaming water. This harks back not only to
the Paradise of Eden but to the heavenly Paradise as well:

> Then the angel showed me the river of the water of life, as clear as
> crystal, flowing from the throne of God and of the Lamb down the
> middle of the great street of the city. On each side of the river stood
> the tree of life, bearing twelve crops of fruit, yielding its fruit every
> month. And the leaves of the tree are for the healing of the nations.
> . . . They will not need the light of a lamp or the light of the sun, for
> the Lord God will give them light. And they will reign for ever and
> ever. (Rev. 22:1–5, NIV)

There is nothing like this water-centered presentation anywhere else; it is
unique among surviving portable altars. Most artists simply marked the edges
of the altar table with abstract or geometric designs, with no attempt made to
do more than provide decorative color—though some others have inscriptions
on the outside edge. This altar has a clearly depicted overflow of the streams
of Paradise encircling the whole world. Now I felt sure that this stone played
a role in Wolfram's poetry of the Grail of sacramental and emotional overflow.
As I looked closer, I saw another most unusual design, not in enamel, but in
brass relief on the beveled edges that connect the altar table, and the

The Bamberg Altar of Paradise. The portable altar is about 10 inches long and about 6 inches wide, and is dated to the second half of the twelfth century. Around the edge of the upper table, most unusually, water is depicted as a blue stream flowing with green plants growing on both sides of it as in the river of the heavenly Paradise. The lower edge of the altar seems to depict floods of water in waves under the feet of the apostles. The altar stone itself, the lid of the sepulchrum, is of green serpentine. *Diözesanmuseum, Bamberg.*

base table, to the central altar: moving along in a regular pattern, canted at a slight angle away from being perpendicular to the side of the altar, row after row of waves. The overflowing water seems even to have contributed to all the oceans and water of the earth, so that even the twelve apostles who surround the central altar have to have come through the water and are now in the midst of it—all flowing from under the central stone. This stands in such concord with the filling of the font in book 16 that I believe it further confirms the identification of the Bamberg Paradise Altar as the inspiration for the scene in which the miraculous water that comes into the ruby baptismal font for Feirefiz's baptism comes from the Grail stone. It also stands parallel to the priest's sermon on the power of water to give fructification and sight. Only after baptism does Feirefiz look back and see the stone from which the waters of Paradise flow to the font of baptism. This is Wolfram's Grail.

Because one of these inscriptions was deciphered with the help of one of the portable altars at Siegburg, I decided to travel north up the Rhine to that town and visit the treasury of the church of St. Servatius. There I was welcomed by a very friendly custodian, who not only let me examine the famous Gregorius portable altar but also insisted that I first look at the valuable collection in the treasury's drawers. I could not imagine anything but coins in such flat drawers, but what should be on display in them but medieval Byzantine and oriental silks! At first I was impatient, but then I thought—*which of these that*

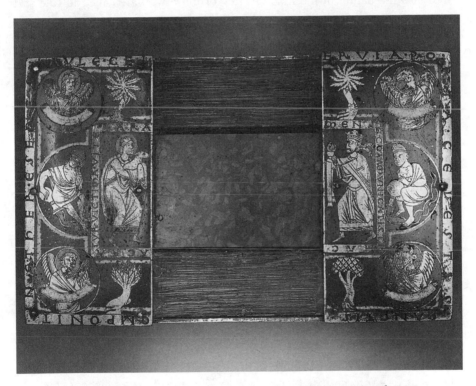

The Bamberg Altar of Paradise seen from above. The green serpentine altar stone covers the sepulcher in the middle. In the four corners, the four evangelists look to the stone, as on either side of the stone, Abel brings his lamb as an offering and Melchisedech brings his bread and wine. The four trees of Paradise are at the four corners of the stone. On the left and right center, two of the four personified rivers of Paradise look back to the stone as their source while they pour out their streams of water which overflow around the entire edge of the altar. Two plaques are missing but it is possible to reconstruct what they depicted, among which would have been the other two rivers of Paradise. *Diözesanmuseum, Bamberg.*

I am looking at might be an example of the pfellel silk that Wolfram is always writing about? The gifts of silk cloth were many and of great value, coming from the emperor at Constantinople to the chancellor of his Western counterpart. And, of course, one was of colored silk with interwoven gold thread. Then I was shown into the next room with several beautiful *portatilia* and left to myself. There was the Gregorius, which, I think, has some mysterious connection to the Paradise Altar in Bamberg. In any case, when I examined it I saw something on it that may also have been connected to Wolfram's striking notion that a gravestone inscription, an *epitafium* (*epi*, upon, + *taphos*, tomb), can be seen on the Grail. Calling the inscription an "epitaph" suggests strongly the nature of the Grail as a kind of stone tomb or sepulcher and equally strongly indicates the nature of the final journey of those who are called to rule and extend the Land of Salvation:

> Hear now how those called to the Grail are made known. On the stone, around the edge, appear letters inscribed [*von karacten ein epi-tafium*; 470, 24], giving the name and lineage of each one, maid or boy, who is to take this blessed journey. . . . When life dies for them *here* they are given blissful happiness [*wunsch*] there [*swenne in erstir-bet* hie *daz leben / sô wirt in* dort *der wunsch gegebn*]. (471, 13–4; Mustard, 252, modified)[9] (See illustration, p. 167)

Who then is called to "take this blessed journey," that is, to begin to realize through human feelings the true nature of the Holy Grail and then to be rewarded after death with bliss in heaven? To answer the question in terms of the Gregorius altar's inscribed writings, one must examine each of the four sides of the altar. Each of the four sides of the tabletop of the Gregorius altar has a row of people on it with their names written above them on the Grail.

On the top of the altar are the twelve apostles (with St. Paul) standing in a row, looking toward the altar's *sepulchrum* stone. Facing them, at the bottom, is the line of their successors, saints who followed them, human frailty succeeding human frailty—Peter who denied thrice; Paul who held cloaks and persecuted—Anfortas is not far from here. The line of twelve bishops standing side by side begins with St. Cunibert and ends with St. Augustine. Parzival will succeed Anfortas. Both lines are facing the central altar stone, which is, once again, a green serpentine. Under the stone is the familiar rectangular recess for relics of the saints and the Body of Christ. On the stone's left are

---

9. The concept *wunsch* unites Wolfram's description of the future bliss, *wunsch*, of those who go to Heaven with his description of the Grail stone as the present bliss of Paradise, *wunsch von pardîs* (235, 21) and his view of bearing the Grail as the overflow of earthly happiness, *erden wunsches überwal*, Repanse de Schoye.

the "maids," Saints Cecilia, Ursula, Agatha, and Catherine. To the stone's right are the "boys," Saints Maurice, Gereon, George, and Mercury (?!), all called to "take the blessed journey."

It seems to me probable that Wolfram was also acquainted with examples of this type of altar stone, perhaps this one, and included one of its character-istics, the written names of those called to the service of the Grail in the Land of Salvation, in describing the nature of the Grail. On the second altar at Sieg-burg, the Mauritius portable, there is a poignant theological representation on the left panel showing the Father and the Holy Spirit above the crucified Christ, whose blood is dripping down into an opened rectangular sepulcher. In this grave, the blood touching him, Adam is rising up. The inscription above the entire panel says *Trinitas*, the Trinity. I made a happy journey back to Frankfurt.

I should relate one more thing related to the silks that had made an im-pression on me at St. Servatius in Siegburg. Beforehand, when I had visited Bamberg, just before I left, I returned to the director's office and offered him my thanks. Later arrangements would be made to have a professional photog-rapher supplement my poor efforts. I decided to let him know my reason for my interest in the Bamberg Paradise Altar, and mentioned Wolfram von Es-chenbach's unusual notion of the Grail. He seemed not to know what to say, it was not his field, he was probably inclined to disagree, and I was not sur-prised at that. When I then got up to leave, he said, somewhat abstractedly, as if thinking aloud, that when the Paradise Altar was examined they had found some green threads still attached to its base. Silk, no doubt, I thought, and mumbled, half to myself, "achmardi."

It is hard to visit Bamberg without thinking that there is some connection here to Wolfram's spirituality. The Paradise Altar is the main reason, but it is not alone. I looked for a while at the statue of Pope Clement II (1046–1047 AD) and noted again the presence of the breastplate of Aaron, the ornament of the high priest that the pope was wearing as a pectoral.[10] The twelve gemstones were originally colored, and must have been very prominent. The jeweled breastplate is worn on top of the pallium itself, a clear statement that as pope he is the new Aaron, the new high priest—a liturgical use of jewels I had not seen before. Could Wolfram have seen this statue and its powerful association of the twelve gemstones with priestly mediation between heaven and earth? The statue is dated to the thirteenth century, but usually a bit later than Wolf-ram, about 1240. Such dating is not precise. Could Wolfram's use of gems be circumstantial evidence that the statue was from a few decades earlier and had

10. See *Clemens II, der Papst aus Bamberg, 24. Dezember 1046– 9. Oktober 1047*, published by the Archdi-ocese of Bamberg (Bamberg: St. Otto-Verlag, 1997), pp. 7, 49.

The tomb of Pope Clement II in the cathedral of Bamberg. On the far end of the side
panel, the original river of Paradise pours out its stream from an urn, which becomes
the four headwaters of divine virtue: temperance is to the left of the river, and justice
is next. The other two virtues are on the other side. In Augustinian language the
tomb says that the interred Pope Clement is in Paradise. *Diözesanmuseum, Bamberg.*

had an influence on him? Or, the opposite, did his widely read masterwork
influence it?

Even more intriguing are the gravestones of the sepulcher of Pope Clement II.[11] The gravestones have stood in their present position since about the
year 1240. The symbolic pictures that decorate the sides and the base of the
tomb seem, once again, somehow related, through St. Augustine's reading of
Genesis 2, to Wolfram's Grail stone. On one end, the sleeping pope is being
awakened by the angel of death; at the other, John the Baptist, with his obvious
connection to the Jordan River and baptism, is holding the sword of his decapitation above the silver platter and has a shield in the other hand with his
designation of Jesus as the Lamb of God. On the north side of the tomb, the
river that rises in the center of Paradise is depicted in the classical manner,

11. *Clemens II, der Papst aus Bamberg*, pp. 32–3, 45–6.

The statue of Pope Clement II in Bamberg Cathedral. He is wearing the pectoral of Aaron with its 12 gemstones. *Diözesanmuseum, Bamberg.*

pouring water out of a large urn, as on the Bamberg Paradise Altar. Next is the first headwater of Augustine's reading of the symbolic meaning of the four rivers: Temperance, mixing water into wine. The third figure on the north side of the tomb is Justice, holding the scales in balance in one hand and the sword in the other. On the south side of the tomb is Fortitude, wrestling, Samson-style, with a lion, and finally there is partially veiled Prudence engaged in a much more careful face-off with a dragon. These are the four cardinal virtues that Augustine read as Eden's flowing stream of Divine Pleasure as it divided into four on leaving the Garden of Paradise. The tomb thus enclosing the pope says in Augustinian language that the pope from Bamberg has returned by death, as did John who baptized in the water of the Jordan, to the source. He is now at the place from which all the waters of Divine Happiness flow: the Garden of Paradise.

The theme of vegetation growing from the flowing water of Paradise, heavenly or earthly, is found both on the sides of the Paradise Altar and on the tomb of Pope Clement. As you examine closely the stone base into which the tomb sides have been placed, you notice that emerging tree leaves have been sculpted into the stone itself, peeping out, as it were, between foundation stone and the six small base pillars that mark the four corners and the midpoints of the sarcophagus. Not only is it clear that the pope is in Paradise but the very plants that grow on both sides of the river of life that flows from the throne are there. This is very close to the spiritual thought that is embodied in the portable Paradise Altar about the Holy Sepulcher, and about the abundance of life that radiates from the phoenix stone, the Grail. Wolfram was surely a part of and a contributor to this world of spiritual poetry.

Is there a literary theological source from which Wolfram got this idea of the real nature of the Grail? Wolfram himself, of course, says it came from Kyot, and indescribable floods of unhappy ink have been put on paper attempting to establish or discredit such a person's possible reality. I am not going to attempt to rehabilitate the idea that Kyot was a real poet from Provence or from Provins, or attempt to refute it. I am instead much taken with the notion of Professor William McDonald, who once suggested to his students that Kyot was not to be understood as "Guiot" but as the phonetically similar rhetorical question "Qui autre?"—"Who else?" I agree, it is surely Wolfram himself— who else, indeed! Nonetheless, I do attach some value to what Wolfram describes under this "Kyot" as being a bent bowstring that may be charged with some indirect information. First of all, if there is any allusion at all in the name "Kyot" to Guiot of Provins, then it must have been to suggest to the contemporaneous reader some recollection of the title of his satiric work: *La Bible*. This work takes everyone to task in all of Christendom from the pope down, much in the style of Erasmus, leaving only the Knights Templar in a hopeful light. Perhaps from Guiot of Provins came the concern for a positive, if dolorous, role for the Knights Templar. More important, through the name Guiot and, above all, the title of his book comes a careful suggestion of Wolfram's ultimate source for the true nature of the Grail: the Bible.

The "Kyot" passage in book 9 can be read as a description of Wolfram's use of the Bible, and most especially of Matthew's Gospel, given in Wolfram's usual startlingly ecumenical terms. "Who else" but Wolfram found the book written in heathen, non-Christian tongues? These, I would venture, are the Hebrew and Greek of the Old and New Testaments rather than the Arabic that has been suggested. Flegetânîs, the fictive scholar who wrote the stone Grail story, came from the Israelite clan, but "who else" could not read the text without baptism.[12] This is not an unusual claim—surely one could not easily accept the story of the stone of the phoenix-like Resurrection of Christ without faith and baptism. As with Wolfram's depiction of Feirefiz, there is no seeing beyond the cloth veil into the real presence of Christ in the Grail stone without baptism. Once again, Wolfram is reminding his readers, as he did in Gyburc's plea for mercy toward the heathen, that we are all pagan in origin. Moreover, *mirabile dictu*, Wolfram now maintains in carefully clothed language: so also are our inspired Christian Scriptures, which were written by unbaptized heathen whose (Hebrew) fathers once, as Scripture admits and Wolfram bemoans, worshiped a calf.

Nonbaptized status is true not only of Old Testament figures such as Moses and Isaiah but also of Matthew and the evangelists of the New Testament. They, too, were once unbaptized. Wolfram thus in the middle of the discussion of his ultimate source in book 9 broaches the baptismal theme that is such a concern in the books 1 and 2 and 15 and 16 of the frame story. Daringly and ingeniously, in book 9 he claims that his ecumenical approach is fully justified by the very heathen origin and nature of Scripture itself. No wonder he carefully disguised his claim with his bent bowstring!

Flegetânîs was able to read the message of the Grail in the stars and knew the story of the coming of the Grail stone to earth. This sounds very much like Matthew's version of the Christmas story, marked as it is by the coming of the Magi, heathen astrologers from the East who read God's message in the sky. The allusion to the fact that the stone that covers the mortality of all people, and covers the death of Christ, was and is a property of the whole human race

---

12. It has been suggested that Wolfram created Flegetânîs from the title of an actual Arabic treatise on astronomy/astrology called *felek thani* (*"altera sphaera"*) meaning the "Second Sphere," possibly indicating the crystalline sphere of the stars, just below the "primum mobile."

is simply mentioned in the fact that the original keeper of the Grail stone was not the current Christian Anfortas but his ancestor, "Mazadan," which is surely "MacAdam," son of Adam. But then, as Queen Ampflise points out at the vesper games in book 2, we are all sons of Adam, and some of the sons of Adam, heathens, read the speech of God in the stars.[13]

I would like to venture the suggestion that this thought is very much in the *Heliand* tradition. The *Heliand* is never given as a possible source for *Parzival*, and I would like to suggest that it well might have been. The positive attitude toward the pagan Magi as being heathen who could read God's message in the stars is presented very extensively in the *Heliand*, with two whole songs, the seventh and the eighth, being devoted to them. The *Heliand* author, moreover, invents an "ancestor" in the East, who is suspiciously similar to the invented Flegetânîs. This "ancestor" of the Magi was

> a wise man, a man of experience and great wisdom—this was a
> long time ago—our ancestor there in the East. . . . He was able to
> interpret God's speech, because the Lord of mankind had granted
> him the ability to hear the Ruler's words up above from down on
> earth. For this reason this thane's knowledge was very great. When
> the time came for him to depart, to leave the earth and the throng of
> his relatives, to give up the comings and goings of men and to travel
> to the other light, he told his followers, his heirs and his earls, to
> come closer, and told them truthfully in soothsaying everything that
> came afterwards. . . . Then he said that a wise king was to come here
> to the middle world. He said that it would be God's Son, and that
> He would rule this world forever, both the earth and the heavens,
> for days without end. He said that on the same day on which his
> mother gave birth to him blessedly in the middle world, in the East
> there would shine a bright light in the sky such as we had never had
> between the earth and the heavens nor anywhere else—never such a
> baby and never such a beacon! . . . He said that we were to follow it
> as it goes before us, in a westerly direction, over this world.[14]

In other words, the author of the *Heliand* is perfectly at home, in the ninth century, saying that there was divine revelation and communication with God in the heathen East. Though one cannot prove it, it seems clear to me that when Chrétien's *Perceval* story was received in Germany by Wolfram, it was

13. Though queen of France, Ampflise considers all the knights at the tourney, no matter what their place of origin, her relatives, "for by Adam's rib they are all my kinsmen" (Mustard, 47).

14. *The Heliand: The Saxon Gospel*, trans. G. Ronald Murphy, S.J. (New York: Oxford, 1992), pp. 22–3.

received in an area that already had a Christian literary tradition that was quite open to divine revelation in pagan religions. This is the *Heliand*'s interpretation of Matthew's Magi and their following the rules of astrology to find Christ. Such acceptance of the validity of pagan religion is not far from Wolfram's redoing of Flegetânîs from a book of astrology to a pagan-Jewish-Christian scholar of the stars and writer of Scripture. Such a degree of sympathy and respect for heathen spirituality is striking, and it must be noted that it already had a basis in Germanic tradition. This gracious tradition had already been in existence for four hundred years at the time of Wolfram. And Wolfram himself may also have been engaged in reading the message of the Grail in the stars when he reflected on the meaning of Saturn and observed the ominous conjunction of Mars and Jupiter in Leo.

The other possible influence from the *Heliand* is the interrelatedness of the feeling of happiness with the radiation of light and with faith. The central point of the *Heliand* epic is the Transfiguration; in it the unknown author combines pagan and Christian images of bliss, and unites the green meadows of Valhalla with the Garden of Eden:

> The Son of God was shining! His body gave off light, brilliant rays
> came shining out of the Ruler's Son. There was a beautiful conver-
> sation, good words among men, as God's Son willed to talk there
> with the famous men [Moses and Elijah]. It became so blissful up
> on the mountain—the bright light was shining, there was a magnifi-
> cent garden there, and the green meadow, it was like Paradise![15]

There is no association made between people and gems, but the stone is emphasized, and there is an association between loyal faith, in Saxon *triuuue*, and the radiant beauty of happiness as in *Parzival,* and it is also connected with the women in the story, as in *Parzival.* In the scene of the Resurrection on Easter morning, the author fills the air with light.

> It was not long until: there was the spirit coming, by God's power,
> the holy breath, going *under the hard stone* to the corpse. Light was
> at that moment opened up for the good of the sons of men; the
> many bolts on the doors of Hel were unlocked; the road from this
> world to heaven was built. Brilliantly radiating, God's Peace-Child
> rose up! . . . The women were on their way, walking to the grave, the
> Marys most lovely. . . . They were concerned about who could roll
> the huge stone off to one side of the grave. They had seen the men

---

15. *The Heliand*, pp. 102–3. The last phrases are *gard godlic endi groni uuang, paradise gelic.*

lay it over the corpse when they had buried the body *in the rock*.
[The angel comes and removes the stone.] The women saw him sitting there on top of the stone which he had removed and terror
came over them because of the nearness of such radiance. . . . "I
know you long to look *inside this rock*. The places are clearly visible
where His body was lying." The pale women felt strong *feelings of
relief* taking hold in their hearts—*radiantly beautiful women*. (emphasis mine)[16]

The *Heliand* author had to find a Germanic equivalent for the Latin *fides*,
"faith." There were two possibilities open to him, *gilobo* and *triuuue*. The first
implies an option or preference between two teachings; it refers, therefore, to
"what" is believed. The second means "faithfulness," loyalty to a person rather
than a teaching, and this is the word most often used in the *Heliand* as being
closer both to Scripture and to the Saxon culture. It is this version of the nature
of faith, that it is a fidelity to a person, loyalty, that is taken up again in both
of Wolfram's epics. If he did not know the *Heliand*—and I think there is a
good chance that he did—then he was clearly one of those to whom its tradition
was passed on as a major influence. In Wolfram's hands, it reaches a point
near perfection that is hard to surpass. Until Parzival learns to keep faith, be
loyal to his suffering uncle, until he learns to be faithful to God who is fidelity
itself, until he learns to feel shame for his times of faithlessness to his mother,
to the Red Knight, until he learns that fidelity to kin implies that no sword
may be raised against Gawain, his Christian brother, or against his pagan
brother, Feirefiz—in short: until he feels the happiness and the compassion of
a relative toward all, he will not realize that the Grail is already his.

     When he does realize that all are related, and laughs together with Anfortas
at the suggestion that the Grail could be attained by fighting, it is at that moment that he genuflects three times to the Trinity in his realization that within
the Creator is kinship, absolute loyalty, both in the Godhead itself and toward
Adam and Eve and their children. The sepulcher stone gives witness to the
fidelity of the Trinity to his relatives, the human beings made in the image and
likeness of the Triune God.

16. *The Heliand*, pp. 191–3. The addition of the feelings and emotion to the scriptural text as well as the
enhancement of radiant light and the insistence on burial in the rock are perhaps further indications that Wolfram
was aware of the *Heliand* or its tradition.

Afterword

Aftermath

Was he understood? With such refined opposition to crusading as a violation of kinship, and such a lofty conception of the role of human feelings and their relationship to gemstones, with such a sacramental idea of the Grail, together with so leading a role for women in locating the Grail, and a loyalty-based Trinitarian ecumenism as his theology, the question is a legitimate one. Was Wolfram's concept of the Grail understood? Did his readers/listeners enter through the sixteen gates of his epic and come to find and appreciate what he had realized about the Grail's nature? Wolfram himself seems to have been very aware of the spiritual nature of his book. He divided his epic into sixteen books, just the number of gates he gave to the walled city of Belacane at the beginning of the work. His foreign hero is black and white and appears different at first, but actually is an endearing member of the family; Wolfram's parchment is also black on white, a book that may appear foreign at first but is an endearing writer's vision of the extended human family as relatives of the Triune God. As Albrecht Classen wrote, "Wolfram and Dante fully grasped the significance of the book as the ultimate catalyst for self experience and the experience of God, the original creator and scribe."[1]

In the realm of spirituality and the expression of human emo-

---

1. See his "Reading, Writing and Learning in the *Parzival*," in *A Companion to Wolfram's Parzival*, ed. Will Hasty (Columbia, S.C.: Camden House, 1999), pp. 189–202.

tions, the historian Bernard Hamilton commented that the Crusades of the twelfth century, the pilgrimages to Jerusalem, created a new piety that wanted to identify with the human feelings felt by Jesus, the apostles, and Mary in the events that happened to them in the Holy Land. This thirteenth-century "affective piety," so evident in Wolfram's insistence on feelings, is very different from the "eleventh-century quest for perfection of Apostolic life." Thus Wolfram participated and participates in one of the great movements of Western spirituality.[2] The new affective piety "passed from the Franciscans to the Brethren of the Common Life, whose . . . *Devotio Moderna* was influential in shaping the thought of both Luther and Ignatius Loyola, and which came to form part of the devotional traditions of Catholics and Protestants alike."[3]

In the political realm, I have already mentioned that one of the subsequent Crusades, the Sixth, may actually have been affected much to the good because of the Muslim-friendly attitude of the well-read and intellectual German emperor Frederick II, who restored Jerusalem through peaceful negotiation to crusader administration. I believe it is possible that he may have been influenced by Wolfram's sensationally popular work. I have already shown that Arnoldus Saxo seems to have been so aware of the stone Grail that he added Wolfram's sacred stone to his otherwise secular Aristotelian lapidary as a powerful precious stone containing a *sacrarium*, a recess for containing holy things. Another contemporary, the poet Heinrich von dem Türlin, writing about ten to twenty years after Wolfram, seems to have made extensive use of *Parzival* in his curious and wild romance *Diu Crône* (The Crown). This romance is especially interesting here since it demonstrates that Wolfram's contemporaries understood that he was speaking of a reliquary-style portable altar. Heinrich even mentions that it is a common sight to see such a consecratory reliquary placed upon an altar. His hero is Gawein—Heinrich has no patience with Parzival's failure first time and changes his Grail hero to Gawein. As opposed to Wolfram's gradual approach through the example of the women, there is no second chance here based on changed or acquired feelings, and so he brings in Gawein to find the Grail and ask the Question. As Gawein and his companions approach the Grail country, a sign appears that lets the reader know that what Gawein is approaching is Eden:

2. For a magnificent retrieval of the origins and nature of this movement see Rachel Fulton's detailed and insightful work *From Judgment to Passion, Devotion to Christ and the Virgin Mary, 800–1200* (New York: Columbia University Press, 2002).

3. This observation is taken from Bernard Hamilton, "The Impact of Crusader Jerusalem on Western Christendom," *Catholic Historical Review* 80, 4 (October 1994): 695–713.

Just before he entered the country, Gawein encountered something remarkable and beautiful, which pleased him greatly. He saw a very broad sword of fire that guarded a road leading to a strong tower in front of a charming castle the walls of which were as bright and transparent [*durchsichtic unde lieht*] as glass.[4]

The allusion to the flaming sword designed to prevent Adam and Eve, and their descendants, from returning identifies the nature and location of the strange and transparent castle whose walls are made of a stone, like those of Paradise, and can be seen through—they are completely transparent.[5] Heinrich's Grail procession shows that Wolfram was read and understood as speaking of the Grail as sacramental mystery:

On gold-embroidered silk she [the most beautiful lady God created]
held something that looked like a small gaming board of red gold,
on which was as splendid an object as has ever been wrought, *made*
of gemstone and the finest gold; it resembled a reliquary on an altar [*ge-*
stein was es und goldes rich / einer kefsen was es glich, / diu uf einem
alter stet; 29, 384–6]. (Thomas, 327, modified; emphasis mine)[6]

Heinrich von dem Türlin further elaborates his awareness of the sacramental relationship of the Grail stone to Communion by having the host, equivalent to Anfortas, first consume three drops of blood from the lance. Then the lid from the reliquary is removed. This must be the altar stone, since Gawein is then able to look into the compartment of the reliquary, where he sees a piece of bread (*einen brosem;* 29, 429), "of which his host broke off the third part and ate it" (*des dirre alt abe brach / daz dritte teil und az daz;* 29, 431). The mention of "one-third" hints at the three particles of the Body of Christ reserved in the *sepulchrum* and constitutes a reference both to the ritual emplacement of three particles of the Host therein when the *kefse* or *lapis* is consecrated and to the reception of Communion at Mass. It is at this point of holy Communion that the hero finally asks the saving Question. He does it in a form that many subsequent scholars would have wanted to put it to Wolfram

4. Heinrich von dem Türlin, *The Crown: A Tale of Sir Gawein and King Arthur's Court*, trans. and intro. J. W. Thomas (Lincoln: University of Nebraska Press, 1989), p. 323.

5. Gen. 3:23–24: "So the Lord God banished him [Adam] from the Garden of Eden to work the ground from which he had been taken. After he drove the man out, he placed on the east side of the Garden of Eden Cherubim and a flaming sword flashing back and forth to guard the way to the tree of life" (NIV).

6. *Diu Crône von Heinrich von dem Türlin*, trans. Gottlob Heinrich Friedrich Scholl (Stuttgart: Litterarischer Verein, 1852).

himself, namely, Tell us just *was daz wunder bediute*—what this miracle means! Though there are critics who feel that Heinrich as poet is too derivative, for my purposes his imitativeness is quite helpful. Heinrich knows and identifies a Grail that he must have gotten from Wolfram's *Parzival* as a reliquary that sits on top of an altar and contains the three particles of Bread. He confirms, therefore, that his understanding is that the Grail is a portable altar, housing a sepulcher beneath the stone that contains the Body of Christ.

Four hundred years after Wolfram, Europe began to turn its violent crusading spirit on itself. The Thirty Years' War pitted Christian against Christian, Reformed against Catholic, in a completely devastating and incredibly prolonged conflict fought on the soil of the Germanies. One voice was raised powerfully against this conflict in another of the masterpieces of German literature: Grimmelshausen's *Simplicissimus*. The hero is, like Parzival, a fool, a simpleton, with the wisdom gradually acquired that he wishes to be simple, simply Christian, neither Petrine nor Pauline. This is hardly achievable in a world that demands commitment to Christ in Catholic or Protestant form by military action against the other side. Grimmelshausen reached back to Wolfram for a way to express his opposition, in the name of Christ, to Christian warfare.

The main scene occurs in book 1, chapters 15–8. In these chapters, Simplicissimus has a dream, a vision that explains to him what is happening in the Thirty Years' War. It is a vision of a tree with a slippery trunk, one that keeps the lower classes from climbing higher. Down below, the tree presses hard on the roots for its support, which is the farmer and peasant class. The tree sways in the heavy wind and smashes into other trees as they busily attend to knocking off each other's branches. The nobility are in the upper branches where they can more easily catch the funds that stream from higher branches. This insane war of trees against trees, the wild flailing, causes arms, and branches, limbs, to litter the floor. In a moment of insight in the dream, Simplicissimus sees that all the trees are really one tree, and that at the pinnacle of the tree is, not Christ, not the pope, not Martin Luther, but rather the ruddy god Mars. Anfortas is suffering once again in the Thirty Years' War, despite the familiar belief of acting in Christ's name, by acting in service to the same pagan entity whom Wolfram had labored to expose: the war god Mars.

> All the trees that I saw were like one tree on whose peak sat the war god Mars, and the tree covered all of Europe with its branches. . . .
> [the following rhyme is written on the trunk of the tree that is breaking its own branches as the wind moves and hurts it]

"Through internal warfare and fraternal fighting / everything is turned upside down, causing nothing but suffering."

Alle diejenige Bäum, die ich sahe, wären nur ein Baum, auf dessen Gipfel saße der Kriegsgott Mars und bedeckte mit des Baums Ästen ganz Europam. . . . "Durch innerliche Krieg und brüderlichen Streit / Wird alles umgekehrt, und folget lauter Leid." (translation mine)[7]

Toward the end of his story, Grimmelshausen brings in the other pagan entity troubling Christendom, and that is a flea-bitten, Woden-like bum, who in tones shockingly presaging those of the hero of 1930s National Socialism, offers Germany a chance at absolute control and dominance if only the German people will, of course, lop off the head of any worthless people who disagree with the Christendom of their great German hero who is to come. This ranting entity, whom Grimmelshausen ridicules as an obsessed and very dirty ideologue, declares himself to Simplicius to be none other than the god Jupiter. Thus it seems clear to me that Grimmelshausen accepted and reimagined Wolfram's insight that Christendom needs the "simple fool" in order to come back to itself and to the recognition of human kinship; and that its militarily induced suffering is the result of its enthralldom to the values and methods of the gods of war and dominance, the conjunction of Mars and Jupiter at their zenith.

Another way Wolfram's work has come down to us may be surprising. Wilhelm Grimm, the great revisor and writer of *Grimms' Fairy Tales*, was an avid reader and teacher of German medieval literature. When I was doing research on his work, I found his classroom copy of *Parzival* in the Hessian state archives at Marburg.[8] It was full of detailed notes in his minute, precise script. He was impressed by the role of the Holy Spirit as transmitting the relatedness, the Father and the Son, within the Godhead to the human family. In this textbook, he underlined the Trinitarian lines that follow Parzival's happy musing after the cure of Anfortas at Mt. Salvation:

> God is human, and also the father's Word,
> God is father and son:
> this spirit of God can be of great help (translation mine)

---

7. Hans Jacob Christoph von Grimmelshausen, *Der Abenteuerliche Simplizissimus Teutsch* (Stuttgart: Reclam, 1997), p. 68. In this version the German has been modernized. For an English version, see *The Adventures of Simplicius Simplicissimus*, 2nd ed., trans. with intro. George Schulz-Behrend (Columbia, S.C.: Camden House, 1993), p. 28.

8. See my *The Owl, the Raven, and the Dove: The Religious Meaning of the Grimms' Magic Fairy Tales* (New York: Oxford University Press, 2000), pp. 9–15, 24, 65, 123.

Got ist mensch unt sîns vater wort

got ist vater unde suon

sîn geist mac grôze helfe tuon. (797, 28–30)

The Spirit of God in Wilhelm Grimm's writing becomes the spirit of harmony, one that united in love not just the eternal Father and Son of the Trinity
but Cinderella's tears with the grave of her dead mother, from which the living
tree grows. There is a most remarkable harmony here present between the
medieval and the romantic author of the nineteenth century. The lack of feelings, which is so important to *Parzival*, is transformed into a perfectly inappropriate lack of feelings in the *Fairy Tales:* the father of Cinderella, who feels
nothing for his daughter, nor for his dead wife; the (step)mother of Hansel
and Gretel, who suggests, without any feelings, that the children be abandoned
in the forest. The father of Hansel and Gretel is treated a bit better, and survives
to see the happy end of the story, since at least he had some feelings—he felt
bad for his children, and felt shame for his own weakness. These virtues are
added and embellished by Wilhelm Grimm, I believe, following in the path
laid down by Wolfram von Eschenbach. The Grimms felt, in any case, that
they were restoring these tales to their original medieval condition, and what
could be a surer guide to the restorers than that they follow the example of
Parzival?

But did they have the Grail in any of the classical fairy tales? If one thinks
of the Grail in the traditional terms, those of Chrétien's serving dish or of
Robert de Boron's chalice, the answer is no. Should one remember, however,
that if in *Parzival*, if I am right, the Grail is the portable altar with its stone-
covered *sepulchrum*, parallel to the sepulchers of Gahmuret, of Ither, and of
Christ in Jerusalem, then it is in the Grimms' description and role of the
sarcophagus that one should look for the Grail. The Grail signifies the death
and the Resurrection from the Sepulcher, stone that is transparent to the fidelity of the Trinity. Snow White's casket is made of gold, and it is of glass,
translucent and transparent. The Grimms far exceeded both Musäus and their
Norwegian source in their version of glass casket.[9] The medieval predilection
of Wilhelm Grimm for Wolfram's *Parzival* and its Grail stone may be the
reason why the casket of Snow White has such a long pedigree and deep
attraction for the reader, the film audience, and the prince.

We cannot leave the nineteenth century without mentioning Richard Wagner. Wagner's work deserves to be considered in its own right, so let it only be
mentioned here that Wagner's relationship to Wolfram's version of the story

---

9. Murphy, *The Owl, the Raven, and the Dove*, pp. 114–32.

was a very critical one. Wagner rejected Wolfram's notion of the Grail as a stone and embraced Robert de Boron's chalice from the Last Supper and the Crucifixion. He wrote of Wolfram as a thoroughly immature phenomenon from a barbaric age and praised Frederick the Great's rejection of such things.[10]

Finally, in the twentieth century, in the writing of Bertolt Brecht stands another part of the long aftermath of Wolfram's *Parzival*: Brecht's play *Mother Courage and Her Children*.[11] Brecht was as anxious to protest World War II as Grimmelshausen to protest the Thirty Years' War, and Wolfram the Crusades. To express his feelings, he fell back on a character of Grimmelshausen's invention, a canteen woman named "Courage," and placed his play back in that era, locating it in another religious war. In an era conspicuously without a Grail, Mother Courage lives from her wagon and her necessary complicity with war. This wagon is not on a religious level with the Grail but, in a demythologized manner, shares its portability, its hidden relationship to crucifixion, and serves its hauntingly familiar function; it preserves life and distributes food, without being able to preserve beauty. What I believe Brecht brought forward from *Parzival* through Grimmelshausen is the family tragedy of human feelings in time of war. As opposed to Wolfram's hero, who simply did not think you should express your feelings if the rules of proper decorum are against it, Brecht's heroine does not dare to express human feelings if she wishes to survive. Human relatedness becomes a threat to life. As one of her children is brought before her by Catholic soldiers in an attempt to implicate her as part of the Protestant war effort, Mother Courage denies her kinship to him. She denies that she ever knew him, her own son. The incident echoes the kinship denial of Wolfram's Parzival and alludes to the scene of Peter's painful three-fold denial of ever having known Jesus. As with Wolfram, warfare and killing, even in the name of crusading for Christ, is a denial of the family relatedness of all the children of Adam and Eve. All three of Mother Courage's children die in religious warfare in ways that reflect the Passion of Christ.

Brecht may have known something of the importance of feelings in *Parzival*, but Brecht does not in this play give any hope to the phoenix stone. He stops at the tarpaulin placed over the body and puts no translucent gems above the grave stone. In his early play, *Baal*, however, despite the provocative biblical title, Brecht does let himself go just one step further.[12] The pagan-god hero, at

---

10. See the very revealing letter on the subject he wrote to Mathilde Wesendonck, in Ulrich Müller, "Wolfram, Wagner, and the Germans," in *A Companion to Wolfram's Parzival*, ed. Will Hasty (Columbia, S.C.: Camden House, 1999), pp. 252–4.

11. See my *Brecht and the Bible: A Study of Religious Nihilism and Human Weakness in Brecht's Drama* (Chapel Hill: University of North Carolina Press, 1980), pp. 68–87.

12. *Brecht and the Bible*, pp. 24–48.

the end of the play, dying, drags himself to the doorway so that he can look out one last time and see the stars. As he sees them he makes his final comment, the rather unheroic "Hmm." The audience of the twentieth century is left alone in the doorway with the Question of whether or not the sky above the grave is transparent. Perhaps a distant echo of the Grail story may still be there, eight hundred years later, in that indecipherable remark, neither statement nor question.

Enter the twenty-first century. The ancient and deadly hostilities that were present at the beginning of the thirteenth century are back again: Christian versus Muslim versus Jew in the Holy Land and beyond. The reader may be surprised that I did not mention the Ring Parable of Lessing's *Nathan the Wise* (1778) as an appropriate piece and a descendant of the frame story of *Parzival*. This is because I feel Wolfram's writing is far more appropriate to our present situation than Lessing's. Lessing assumes the stance of the noncommitted, a position of presumed superiority vested in his belief in detached reason. This is a stance that no person committed to a religion adopts. Lessing posits an almost quantitative standard for determining which of the three religions actually possesses the "ring." And then he also says that the true ring—which has the familiar ability to make one pleasing to God and men—has probably been lost anyway, meaning all three religions should strive for the maximum performance of good works to determine which of their most likely counterfeit rings is possibly the true ring; the true ring of the father probably being nonexistent. This is the stance of the noncommitted, the stance of the rationalist observing and judging, but not partaking. This is not a stance anyone within the three religions could take. Wolfram knows better.

Lessing ignores the fact that religion is not based on counting good deeds to prove anything. Religion is based, and here Wolfram is completely right, on *triuwe*, faith understood as personal loyalty. This personal fidelity to Moses, to Christ, to Muhammed almost always shows up in an attachment to small objects, things—accidentals—with which this great faithfulness is associated: the Christmas tree, a Passover plate, the head scarf, very small things. Religion is far closer to marriage, to family, to a love affair, to the overflow of feelings of loyalty, to commitment, than to a rationally worked out set of good deeds. Therefore, the appeal to the religions to be peaceful with one another has to be based on knowing what religions are, not on the judicious, well-intentioned suggestions of the a-religious rationalist. Wolfram's insights in *Parzival* are far more relevant to today's committed people of faith than Lessing's didactic suggestion of epistemological insecurity, and his reduction of loving fidelity to the socially useful function of good works.

The appeal to love between religions has to acknowledge the heart's fidelity to things that outsiders might consider mere accidentals: to an uncovered altar stone with a great candle shining beside it at Easter; to a pilgrimage once in a lifetime to Mecca—Muhammed did it; to unleavened bread at Passover (because the women did not have enough time to let the bread rise—so fast was the Exodus). In this critical aspect, *Parzival* presents the far more relevant and realistic view, when Wolfram uses the Trinity, for example, to acknowledge that *triuwe* must extend to the acknowledgment that those of other fidelities are sons and daughters of the same Father. Tolerance is easy from the noncommitted, but Wolfram points to a way for committed Christians to see as part of their Trinitarian fidelity that they should be fully appreciative of the love that those of other forms of fidelity enjoy from the Father. The way to the Grail is led by Condwiramurs, and Parzival is told he cannot go to it without a companion. He picks his pagan brother, and they are both well received by the Grail community, both the one who genuflects three times to the Trinity and the one who speaks of Jupiter and Juno but who admires the beauty of the Grail community's Repanse de Schoye.

Feirefiz is fed from the Grail even before he can see it. There is no attempt made to force Feirefiz to acknowledge the Trinity, no conversion by force. He himself wants to come to the waters of baptism, not because he has been persuaded by the force of reason or by the example of good deeds, but because he falls in love with a newly restored Christianity's Overflowing Happiness, Repanse de Schoye, and, one might add, this is the better way. In pure happiness alone is it appropriate to carry the stone of Resurrection, the altar of the rebirth of the Phoenix, the gem-like bliss of Paradise. If Christians wish to convert others, or, following Lessing, wish to demonstrate that they have the real ring, let them do it not by force—no one can attain the Grail by force of arms, and that is why people have lost interest in it—but by inviting the non-baptized members of the family to share the table of the Father's life, and to see, and become enamored of, the Grail stone and its Overflowing Happiness.

APPENDIX I

Etymological Excursus

The Meaning of the Five Women's Names

A great deal of work has been done identifying many origins—medieval, biblical, Arabic, and classical—of the many names that populate Wolfram's *Parzival*.[1] When it comes to commenting on the meaning of the five critical names that are Wolfram's poetic invention, and are of great importance to an understanding of the text—Herzeloyde, Sigûne, Condwîramurs, Cundrîe, and Repanse de Schoie—there is linguistic division. I believe this is because of an inappropriate methodology used in approaching the names. Linguists and etymologists often treat each name in isolation, as a standard word whose derivation is to be discerned according to the rules of linguistics, and whose internal composition is to be perceived according to known etymological rules. Some of the results will be seen later. Actually, the five names are not derived at all in the strict sense but are fictional: poetic multilingual compositions. With some poetic freedom, words are borrowed and altered to create an air of suspended unfamiliarity, so that the reader can have the pleasure of feeling his or her way to realizing what they mean.

The meaning of the names can be perceived and felt by the reader because of a poetic device used by Wolfram and first described by Jean Fourquet as "reprise."[2] I believe, however, that in relying on the poetic device of reprise, a repetition with some variation, to determine meaning, the location of the reprise can and should be expanded methodologically beyond simple repetition to include an examination of the immediate environment of the

---

1. See Werner Schröder, *Die Namen im "Parzival" und im "Titurel" Wolframs von Eschenbach* (Berlin: de Gruyter, 1982), for an exhaustive categorization of sources.

2. See Jean Fourquet, *Wolfram d' Eschenbach et le Conte del Graal, Les divergences de la tradition du Conte del Graal de Chrétien et leur importance pour l'explication du texte du Parzival* (Paris: Presses Universitaires de France, 1966).

word in the text, looking especially to appropriate synonym and rhyme, to identify the clues Wolfram has given as to his intent in creating the fictional name. Sometimes Wolfram actually defines the name directly, making the task of interpretation easy, and sometimes he defines it indirectly by placing significant actions or synonyms in the surrounding text. If the immediate context of Wolfram's newly created names is examined, their meaning and function can become clear enough to confirm a poetically intuitive reading. If poetic context is not considered, the puzzlement faced by a reader whose overall understanding of a passage is being influenced by a linguistic reading of a name is increased. The translator, who confronts both word and its context, will have to remain in an uncomfortable ("sour" Wolfram would say) state of doubt.

This situation was expressed well by the obviously perplexed translators Helen Mustard and Charles Passage in their comment on the name Herzeloyde: "The text seems to imply an etymology for 'Herzeloyde' as 'Heart's Sorrow' (herz + leide), but linguistic analysis will not support this poetically appropriate interpretation."[3]

I believe that Wolfram's narrative takes Parzival to emotional maturity, that is, the capacity to feel sufficient compassion to break convention, and he does this by having Parzival follow the path of exemplification given in the form of the five women. The path goes from the loyal heart's sorrow (Herzeloyde) through kinship fidelity (Sigune) and continues with love leading the way (Condwiramurs) on to painful self-knowledge and appropriate shame (Cundrie) and finally to overflowing happiness (Repanse de Schoye). I will examine the five in that order.

Herzeloyde. Chrétien gives her no name, but calls her "la veve dame de la gaste forest" (the widow lady from the waste forest). The name "Herzeloyde" is Wolfram's creation.

> Herzeloyde in kuste und *lief im nâch.*
> der werlde *riwe* aldâ geschah.
> dô si *ir sun niht langer sach.* . . .
> dô *viel* diu frouwe valsches laz
> ûf die erde, aldâ si *jâmer sneit*
> sô *daz se ein sterben niht vermeit.* (128, 16–23)

[Herzeloyde kissed him and ran after him. Then the sorrow of the world befell. When she no longer saw her son . . . then the lady without falsity fell upon the ground, where grief stabbed her until she died.] (Mustard, p. 72)

> deiswâr du heizest Parzivâl.
> der nam ist rehte enmitten durch.
> grôz liebe ier solch *herzen* furch
> mit dîner muoter *triuwe*:
> dîn vater liez ir *riuwe*. (140, 16–20; emphases mine)

3. Mustard, 78, n. 9.

[In truth, your name is Parzival, which signifies *right through the middle*. Such a furrow did great love plow in your mother's heart with the plow of her faithfulness. Your father bequeathed her sorrow.] (Mustard, p. 78)

In the first passage, I have emphasized the words that give rise to the interpretation of the name as a compound of "heart" and "sorrow." She runs after her child after kissing him. The world's sorrow then befalls her. When she can see him no longer as he rides away, she falls down on the ground, where agonized sorrow so stabs her that she dies. The stabbing of a furrow through the heart betokens her total commitment in love to her son. In the second passage, Parzival's own name is explained to him by Sigûne as "right through the middle." Then Sigûne explains his mother's name as parallel to her fate, a result of her faithfulness in love; great love plowed a furrow through the heart of your mother's faithfulness: your father left her sorrow. From these passages, including just a hint of the old Germanic belief in fate concealed in the name, passages with their metaphors and synonyms for the cutting pain of sorrow, *jâmer, sneit, riuwe*, I believe it is clear what Wolfram intended Herzeloyde to mean, and thus *loyde* must be *Leid*, and the name can be translated Sorrowful Heart.

A useful summary of etymologists' research is given by Frank Chandler.

Already Schulz pointed out that, owing to the consistent spelling of the ending *oy* in Parzival . . . it is impossible for this name to be derived from *Leid*, as would seem at first sight the most obvious etymology. Schulz suggested a derivation from Welsh *erch*, "dismal," and *llued* or *lluydd*, "warfare." Bartsch suggested that the ending *oyde* is derived from the German name-ending *hilt*, through *haut*, *l* in conjunction with *hilt* being common in names (cf. Godalhildis beside Godahildis). *Herze-* he would derive from *hardo*, "hard." Alternatively Bartsch suggests that the original form of the name might be Harchehildis (*harc-* from OHG *haruc, fanum*) for Harchehildis, the former giving OF Herceleude. Gaston Paris disagrees entirely with the suggestions made by Bartsch, and asserts that Herzeloyde is a form of the OF name Herselot, a view which is held also by Golther and Bruce. Martin agrees with Bartsch that the second half of the name seems to contain the German *hilde* (cf. Rischoide and Mahaute), and he therefore doubts the etymology suggested by Gaston Paris. Martin has no explanation for the former half of the name (*Herzel-*).[4]

By ignoring the poetic context of the name, the linguistic etymologists end up with a strange division of the word into Herzel- and -oyde that leads nowhere, not even into the waste forest. What goes completely unnoticed in the etymological discussion is the wonderful and telling rhyme of faithful love with sorrow, of *triuwe* with *riuwe*, in 140, 19–20, and the presence, unsurprisingly, in the preceding verse, of the love-furrowed *herzen*.

4. Frank Chandler, *A Catalogue of the Names of Persons in the German Court Epics* (London: Kings College, Centre for Late Antique and Medieval Studies, 1992), p. 124.

Sigûne. Chrétien has no name for the young woman holding her decapitated knight-lover, but he does refer to her as a young girl, "pucele," and has her identify herself to his Perceval as "ta germaine cosine," your cousin on your mother's side. It seems that her function is to show loyalty, as did Herzeloyde; she mourns loving wedding ties even when the marriage did not take place. Her reproof of Parzival and his reply are as follows.

> ir lebt, und sît an sælden tôt.
> dô sprach er "liebiu *niftel* mîn. . . ." (255, 20–1)

[you are alive, and yet as far as salvation is concerned you are dead. Then he said, "My dear cousin . . ."] (transl. mine)

> *der rehten ê diz vingerlîn*
> für got sol mîn geleite sîn.
> daz ist ob mîner triwe ein slôz,
> *vonme herzen mîner ougen vlôz.* (440, 13–6)

[This ring of true marriage will be my escort before God. This ring is a castle defending my loyalty—the tears that flooded my eyes came from my heart.] (transl. mine)

Sigûne accuses Parzival of hardheartedness, risking his ultimate happiness, *sælde,* and all he can say in reponse is to ask her not to be so harsh on him, and he begins this by calling her his *niftel* (his cousin)—Wolfram using German for Chrétien's French. The second citation shows Sigûne's wanting the ring to be her escort before God, proof that she treated the dead knight with fidelity and that the tears in her eyes really flow from her heart. This is her function, to show Parzival what compassion in the family-initiating world of wooing and lovers is. Thus I think it reasonable to treat the name Sigûne as an anagram for "cosine." Parzival's cousin.

The linguistic approach is:

Schulz suggested a derivation of this name from *cygne,* "swan," whilst Bartsch sees in it the feminine of the Old French name Seguin, from OHG Siguwin, a view which Singer shares. Martin compares Sigûne with with Signý, the faithful wife of Loki.[5]

While "swan" may have some charm, I cannot imagine Wolfram associating Sigûne with Signý, since that would make her anointed lover into a highly improbable and unpalatable Loki. "Siguwin" might mean "friend of victory" and seems rather curious for the name of the weeping gem of a woman named Sigûne. None of these three suggestions really fits the poetic context of Sigûne's iconic role in the epic as Parzival's thoughtful relative and embodiment of the Pietà.

Conwiramurs. Chrétien gives her a name, "Blancheflor," "White Flower," which

---

5. Chandler, *A Catalogue of the Names of Persons,* p. 259–60. Other researchers note that the name Sigûne became an extremely popular name in Germany from 1286 onward.

Wolfram obviously did not take over into his epic poem. In the case of the name "Cond-wiramurs," we have an explanation by Wolfram of the meaning of the name just as in the case of "Parzival." In describing the bravery of Parzival's brother, Wolfram writes:

> diu *minne condwierte*
> in sîn manlîch herze hôhen muot,
> als si noch dem minne gernden tuot. (736, 6–8)

[Love conducted, led, escorted high courage into his manly heart, just as it still does for those who yearn for love.]

The translator should consider that love is the subject of the action, not the object, in Wolfram's formulation. "Condwiramurs" means "Love Leads" (leads courage into his heart) and not "Leads to Love." Love is thus the source of en-courage-ment, of high–spiritedness, for the warrior, whether he be Feirefiz or Parzival, pagan or Christian.

The linguistic reflections on the name are not very far off:

> Golther explains this name as an invention from Wolfram from an infinitive plus noun, put together in German style.[6] Bartsch, trying to avoid the infini-tive plus noun construction, suggested derivation from *coin de voire amors*, i.e. "ideal of true love," a suggestion which is ridiculed by Gaston Paris. Ac-cording to Singer, the name occurred in Kîôt, who had sometimes *Conduire amors*, "escort of love" [Geleitung der Liebe] and sometimes *Conduire en amors*, "escort into love" [Geleitung in die Liebe], thus accounting for the form *Kondwiren âmûrs* in *Parzival* 327, 20.[7]

Though the observations do consider both love and the idea of escorting or con-ducting, instead of examining the context, for example, 736 earlier, Bartsch resorts to idealism and Singer to two projected forms in a text of the story, Kyot's, that we simply do not have and probably did not exist. We do have Trevrizent's remark, however, re-ferring to the woman he once served for love, which gives another useful example: "ir minne condwirte / mir freude in daz herze mîn" (495, 22–3), "her love conducted joy into my heart."

Cundrîe. Chrétien has no name for the hideous maiden, but simply describes her as "une demeisele qui vint sor une mule fauve," a maiden who came on a tawny mule. "Cundrîe" is therefore again a name-creation of Wolfram. I believe we can trust the intuition that her name is associated with the immense learning and knowledge she displays. Thus Cundrîe is properly associated by the reader with *kund*, to be aware, or to know about. In view of her being aware not only of the names of all the planets, in Arabic and Latin but also of Parzival's shameful failure, and since she "lets him know," this is a very appropriate creation based on *kund*.

6. Chandler mentions that Golther thought that Wolfram had explained the meaning of the name in 495, 22f., *A Catalogue of the Names of Persons*, p. 164, n. 35.

7. Chandler, *A Catalogue of the Names of Persons*, p. 164.

The linguistic approach bypasses her function in the story and goes instead to her appearance:

> Schulz derived this name from the Old French *contruit,* "misshapen," whilst Bartsch thought that the Old French *conrée,* "flame [or tan] colored" (die Lohfarbige) was the root, a derivation with which Gaston Paris disagrees, but which is supported by Martin, who translates *conrée* by the more usual "woman adorned with jewelry" (die Geschmückte).[8]

If we look at the text surrounding her appearance in the story, we can come closer to determining the name's intent:

> der meide ir *kunst* des verjach,
> *alle sprâche si wol sprach,*
> *latîn, heidensch, franzoys.*
> si was der *witze kurtoys,*
> *dîaletike* und *jêometrî:*
> ir wâren ouch die *liste* bî
> von *astronomîe.*
> si hiez Cundrîe:
> *surziere* was ir zuoname; (312, 19–27)

[The maiden was so learned that she spoke all languages well, Latin, French, and heathen (i.e. Arabic). She was versed in dialectic and geometry and even in the science of astronomy. Cundrie was her name, with surname *la sorcière.*] (Mustard, p. 169)

> diu maget *witze rîche.* (313, 1)

[the maiden rich in intelligence] (transl. mine)

Repetition of her abilities is not only in the "reprise" that she is the maiden rich in intelligence, *witze rîche,* but also in all the synonyms for intelligence and skills, *kunst, witze, liste,* all parallel to *kunt,* the root, I believe, of her name. The context surrounds her as a sorceress of cultivated mind by detailing an impressive list of her abilities in the arts and sciences: she has command of Latin, Arabic, and French, she knows dialectics and geometry; all contribute to explaining the significance of her name as designating a person of awareness and knowledge. No contextual gesture is quite as fine, however, at suggesting the meaning of her name as Wolfram's taking her premier knowledge, that of the planets and the stars in their courses, and rhyming her astrological knowledge with her name: *astronomîe: Cundrîe!*

---

8. Chandler, *A Catalogue of the Names of Persons,* p. 168. The verb *conreer* in medieval French meant to arrange, to equip, to put in order, to furnish what is necessary, to prepare; *conreé* 'equipped. It could be used of soldiers or horses being furnished with equipment for battle, of hides being prepared (tanning) for use, or, in the case of women, *couvrer et vestir,* to cover, dress and adorn. From Frédéric Godefroy, *Dictionnaire de l'ancienne Langue Française et des tous ses dialects du IXe au XVe siècle* (Paris: F. Vieweg, 1884).

> ir wâren ouch die liste bî
> von astronomîe,
> si hiez Cundrîe. (312, 24–6)

[she knew well the science of astronomy, her name was Cundrie.] (transl. mine)

Repanse de Schoye. Chrétien does not give a name to the young girl carrying the Grail. He simply refers to her as "une pucele." There is agreement on all sides that the name Wolfram gives her is his creation in French. There is further agreement that Schoye is *joie*, joy or happiness. The difficulty arises in determining the intention of Wolfram in using "Repanse." Could Repanse mean "fullness" so that the name might mean the "Fullness of Joy"? The linguists offer several suggestions:

> Schulz thought that the form in *Titurel*, "Urrepanse," was the original, and
> he derived this from the Old French *ourer* "to pray," and *pens*, "thought," i.e.
> "sunk in reverence." Martin is more inclined to Lachmann's explanation
> that it is derived from the Old French *répenser*, "to think again," i.e. "remem-
> brance of joy."[9]

Though these are possible, I think once again it is more than useful to look at the context. At her first appearance carrying the Grail, Repanse is described in the section that contains some of the most famous lines in the poem:

> nâch den kom diu künegîn.
> *ir antlütze gap den schîn,*
> *si wânden alle ez wolde tagen.*
> man sach die maget an ir tragen
> pfellel von Arâbî.
> ûf einem grüenen achmardî
> truoc si den *wunsch* von pardîs.
> bêde wurzeln *unde rîs.*
> daz was ein dinc, daz hiez der Grâl,
> erden *wunsches überwal.*
> Repanse de schoy si hiez. (235, 15–25)

[After them came the queen. So radiant was her face that everyone thought the dawn was breaking. She was clothed in a dress of Arabian silk. Upon a deep achmardi (green silk cloth with gold thread) she bore the perfect bliss of Paradise, both root and branch. That was a thing called the Grail, the over-flow of earthly bliss. Repanse de Schoye was her name.] (Mustard, p. 129, modified)

The images in the text suggest that there is an exuberant expansion of light and happiness that come out of her and the Grail. First, her face is so radiant with light that

---

9. Chandler, *A Catalogue of the Names of Persons*, p. 245.

people think the dawn is breaking. Then the Grail is described in similar terms; it is the blissful happiness of Paradise, not in its static primal form alone but blissful happiness both in its root and in its expansion from its root into its branches. Finally, the Grail itself is described as blissful joy, *wunsch*, in *überwal*, literally: overflow.[10] The image of expansion and overflow is the dominant one, and helps determine the image behind Wolfram's creation of "Repanse de Schoye." The French word at its base must be, then, *respanche* (modern French *épancher, répandre*) a spilling over, an overflow, and the whole name would then mean "Overflow of Happiness."[11]

To confirm this, a close examination of the text reveals another reprise, similar to that in the case of "Cundrîe" earlier. Immediately preceding the words "Repanse de Schoy" in line 25, we find hidden in plain sight in line 24 the two-word explanation of her name: *wunsches überwal. Wunsches überwal: Repanse de Schoy*—"Overflow of Happiness." She is thus closely connected to the outflow of divine pleasure pictured in the Augustinian view of the rivers of Paradise.

The inner sequence of the story, the stages of Parzival's slow progress to emotional maturity, his passing from childish self-centeredness to spontaneously felt compassion, is written in the names of the women of his story: Herzeloyde, Sigûne, Condwîramurs, Cundrîe, and Repanse de Schoye—maternal affection and pain, constant fidelity to lover and kin, the guiding commitment of husband and wife, painful self-knowledge and shame, and finally, arrival in fraternal style with compassionate tears at overflowing happiness.

---

10. Translators often give this as some form of "transcending earthly happiness." Using the abstract "transcendence" instead of the more concrete "overflow" is philosophically interesting, but it costs the reader the enjoyment of one of the fundamental metaphors of the work.

11. The word *respanche* (mod. Fr. *épancher*) is ultimately based on a form of *(ex-)pandere*, the classical Latin verb for opening wide, spreading, or expanding [its Old French synonym *respandre (re + pandere)* has the same meaning]. *Respanche* is used for an overflow, a pouring out, or spilling of a liquid, e.g., "Ils respancherent tout le vin," in one case, and in another, for generous flow of libations for a sacrifice: "et respanche avec du laict . . . du vin, du miel." Godefroy has an elegant definition, albeit with household overtones, of *respandre*: letting a liquid flow onto a space on which it expands, "laisser couler un liquide sur un espace où il s'étend." This fits quite well with Wolfram's accompanying images of expansion: light radiation, plant growth, and overflow. See Godefroy, *Dictionnaire de l'ancienne Langue Française*, 7:108 and 10:558.

APPENDIX 2

Two Medieval Texts on the Consecration of the Altar and the Veneration of the Sepulcher

The two early medieval texts from England show the close analogy felt between the altar (in this case a fixed altar) and the Holy Sepulcher. The first is excerpted from the liturgy for the consecration of an altar as given in the Egbert pontifical. It antedates the First Crusade, coming from approximately 950 AD or a bit later. The second text is excerpted from the Middle English version of William of Tyre's account of the crusaders' first visit to the Sepulcher after the fall of Jerusalem in 1099. To William of Tyre's aristocratically distanced account, the Middle English version has added several lines rooted in fidelity, *triuwe*, about feeling the presence of the body of Christ in the Sepulcher. Both texts show congruence with Wolfram's presentation of the Grail.

FROM THE EGBERT PONTIFICAL

Benedictio tabulae: "Dominum deum omnipotentem patrem artificem et immensae molis admirabilem conditorem . . . deprecemur . . . lapis Christus unigenitus excissus sine manibus . . . compage angulari solidaret. Ut adtollere caput sciret in caelum, quae de caelo acceperat fundamentum. Lapidem quoque hunc ad conficienda vitae sacramenta compositum, ita chrismate divinae sanctificationis suffundat, et aeterni luminis benedictione illustret, quatenus efficiatur altare sacrum caelesti impetu fluminis irrigatum."

Oratio ad corporale benedicendum. "Benedic omnipotens deus pater domini iesu christi pannum istum lineum benedictione caelesti ad capienda mysteria caelestia corporis et sanguis domini nostri iesu christi filii tui, sicut per evangelia in sindone linea et munda sepultam cognovimus carnem domini nostri iesu christi . . . atque in sindone ioseph lino texta totum te involvi permisisti." . . .

Deinde vadunt ad eum locum in quo reliquiae per totam noctem preteritam cum vigiliis fuerunt et dicit sacerdos orationem hanc antequam inde levantur: "Aufer a nobis quaesumus domine iniquitates nostras ut et sancta sanctorum puris mereamur mentibus introire."

Finita vero oratione elevant eas sacerdotes cum feretro, et cum honore dignissimo, cum crucibus et thuribulis atque candelabris et luminibus multis, laudes deo decantando, cum his antifonis. "De hierusalem exeunt reliquiae et salvatio de monte sion; Ambulate sancti dei ad locum destinatum quod vobis praeparatum est ab origine mundi." *Dum autem pervenerint ad ianuam ecclesiae canatur litania. Expleta vero dicit episcopus:* "Ingredere benedicte domine praeparata est habitatio sedis tuae."

Venientes autem ante altare et extenso velo inter eos et populum, facit episcopus crucem de sancto chrismate intus in confessione in medio ubi ponende sunt reliquiae, et per iiii angulos ipsius ita dicendo, "In nomine patris et filii et spiritus sancti. Pax tibi. Et cum spiritu tuo." *Deinde ponit tres portiones corpus domini intus in confessione et tres de incenso et recluduntur intus reliquiae, canentes:* "Sub altare domini sedes accipitis. . . ." *Deinde ponatur tabula desuper id est mensa altaris.*[1]

Translation:

The blessing of the altar table: "Lord God, almighty Father, designer and wondrous creator of this massive [stone], we beseech you that this stone, Christ your only Son, cut out without the help of human hands, will be the solid, unifying cornerstone. May this stone [altar] be able to lift its head into the heavens—the place from which its foundation came. May this stone, put together for the purpose of carrying out the sacraments of life, be flooded with chrism, the oil of divine sanctification, and may it be radiant with the blessing of eternal light—since it is becoming the sacred altar flowing with the river whose source is in heaven."

Prayer for blessing the corporal. "Almighty God, Father of Our Lord Jesus Christ, bless this linen cloth with your heavenly blessing so that it may hold the body and blood of Our Lord Jesus Christ, your Son, for we know from the gospels that the flesh of Our Lord Jesus Christ was buried in a clean linen shroud . . . God, the Word who became flesh and lived completely among us, you permitted yourself to be wrapped up completely by Joseph in a linen shroud."

Then they go to the place where the relics were kept throughout the entire preceding night with vigils, and the priest says this prayer before the relics are lifted up and carried: "Take away our sins, we ask you, Lord, so that with we may deserve to enter with clear consciences into the Holy of Holies."

---

1. *Two Anglo-Saxon Pontificals (the Egbert and Sidney Susses Pontificals)*, ed. H.M.J. Banting (London: Henry Bradshaw Society, 1989), pp. 46–50.

When he is finished the prayer, the priests lift them up and carry them in
the portable reliquary, the feretory, with the greatest honor, with crosses and thuri-
bles, with candelabra and with many lights, as they sing the praise of God with
the following antiphons: "The remnants [here understood as parallel to relics]
went forth from Jerusalem and salvation went forth from Mount Zion;
Saints of God, walk to the place which has been destined and prepared for
you from the foundation of the world." *When they have made their way to the*
door, they chant the litany [of the saints]. When they are finished the bishop says:
"Come in, blessed Lord, the place for your throne has been prepared."

When they come before the altar a veil is extended between them and the
people. The bishop makes a cross using holy chrism inside the cavity at the top of
the altar base [the *confessio,* "place for witnesses," also called the *sepulchrum*]
where the relics are to be put, and also on the four corners of the same, saying [to
the altar]: "In the name of the father and of the son and of the holy Spirit.
Peace be with you. And with your spirit." *After this he places three particles of*
the Body of Christ inside, in the compartment, then three of incense, and then the
relics are enclosed within while he sings: "Beneath the altar of the Lord you
have received your thrones." . . . *Afterwards the table, that is, the altar* mensa
is secured on top."

THE MIDDLE ENGLISH CHRONICLE (THE CAXTON ERACLES)

Thenne began they goo bare foot, and in wepyings and teers [tears], into the
holy places of the Cyte [city] where our sauyour Ihesu Criste had ben bodyly.
They kyssed the place moche swetly [sweetly, devoutly] where his feet had
touched. The Crysten peple and the clergye of the toun, to whom the turkes
had many tymes don [done] grete shames for the name of Ihesu Criste, cam
with procession & bare [bore] such relyques as they had ayents [toward] the
barons; and brought them, yeldyng [yielding, giving] thankes to Almychty
God, into the Sepulcre. And there it was a pytous thing to see how the peple
wepte for joye and pyte. And how they fylle doun a crosse to fore [fell down
prostrate before] the sepulcre. It seemed to everyche of them that eche [each
one] sawe there the bodye of onr lord there deed [dead]. There were so many
teers and wepyings that every man thought certaynly oure lord was there.

Select Bibliography

PRIMARY SOURCES

Chrétien de Troyes. *Le Conte du Graal (Perceval)*. In *Les Romans de Chrétien de Troyes, édités d'apres la copie de Guiot (Bibl. Nat. Fr. 794)*. Edited by Félix Lecoy. Paris: Librairie Honoré Champion, 1973.

Wolfram von Eschenbach. *Parzival: Studienausgabe, Mittelhochdeutscher Text nach der sechsten Ausgabe von Karl Lachmann*. Translated by Peter Knecht with an introduction by Bernd Schirok. Berlin: de Gruyter, 1998.

———. *Willehalm: Text der sechsten. Ausgabe von Karl Lachmann*. Translated with a commentary by Dieter Kartschoke. Berlin: de Gruyter, 1968.

PRIMARY SOURCES IN ENGLISH TRANSLATION

Chrétien de Troyes. *Arthurian Romances*. Translated by William W. Kibler. New York: Penguin, 1991.

Wolfram von Eschenbach. *Parzival, a Romance of the Middle Ages*. Translated with an introduction by Helen Mustard and Charles E. Passage. New York: Vintage Books, 1961.

———. *The Middle High German Poem of Willehalm*. Translated into English prose by Charles E. Passage. New York: Ungar, 1977.

———. *Parzival*. Translated by A. T. Hatto. London: Penguin, 1980.

———. *Titurel and the Songs*. Edited and translated by Marion E. Gibbs and Sidney M. Johnson. New York: Garland, 1984.

———. *Parzival with Titurel and the Love-Lyrics*. Translated by Cyril Edwards. Cambridge: D. S. Brewer, 2004.

SECONDARY LITERATURE

Adamnan. *De Locis Sanctis*. Edited by Denis Meehan. Dublin: Dublin Institute for Advanced Studies, 1958.

Albertus Magnus [St. Albert the Great]. *Book of Minerals*. Translated with commentary by Dorothy Wyckoff. Oxford: Clarendon, 1967.

Andrieu, Michel. *Ordines Romani du haut Moyen-Âge*. Louvain: Spicilegium sacrum lovaniense, 1931.

———. *Pontifical Romain au Moyen-Âge*. Vatican City: Biblioteca apostolica vaticana, 1938.

Aquinas, St. Thomas. *Summa Theologiae, Latin Text and English Translation, Notes, Appendices and Glossaries*. London: Blackfriars, 1975.

———. *Tractatus de lapide philosophico* (chap. 2). Available on the Internet at www .alim.it/alim/; ALIM, Archivo della latinità italiana del Medioevo.

Arnoldus Saxo [Arnold the Saxon]. *Die Encylopedie des Arnoldus Saxo, zum ersten Mal nach einem Erfurter Codex*. Edited by Emil Stange. Erfurt, Germany: Fr. Bartholomäus, 1905.

Augustine of Hippo, St. *Sancti Augustini Opera: De Genesi Contra Manichaeos*. Edited by Dorothea Weber. Vienna: Österreichische Akademie der Wissenschaften, 1998.

Barber, Richard. *The Knight and Chivalry*. New York: Harper and Row, [1970] 1982.

———. *The Holy Grail, Imagination and Belief*. Cambridge, Mass.: Harvard University Press, 2004. Presents an overview of the French, English, and German Grail romances; establishes the universal connection of the Grail and the Eucharist, until the Reformation. In Wolfram's case, defends the poet's humaneness and orthodoxy, and posits Wolfram's possible misunderstanding of Chrétien's description of the Grail. Barber ends up multivalent on the nature of the Grail in Wolfram. Barber mentions the possibility of it being an altar stone, but unfortunately is misled by mistaken history: he writes that altar stones were "Carolingian."

Barbero, Adriaan Hendrik. *Christendom and Christianity in the Middle Ages: The Relations between Religion, Church, and Society*, trans. Reinder Bruinsma. Grand Rapids, Mich.: Eerdmans, 1994. Original: *Christenheid en Christendom in de Middeleeuwen. Over de verhouding van godsdienst, kerk, en samenleving*. Kampen: Kok Agora, 1986. Confirms the importance of medieval devotion to the Holy Sepulcher in the West, especially as a monument to the Resurrection rather than to the Passion of Christ.

Bartlett, W. B. *An Ungodly War: The Sack of Constantinople and the Fourth Crusade*. Phoenix Mill, England: Sutton, 2000.

Baumgärtel-Fleischmann, Renate. *Ausgewählte Kunstwerke aus dem Diözesanmuseum Bamberg*. Bamberg: Bayerische Verlagsanstalt Bamberg, 1992.

Bayerschmidt, Carl F. "Wolfram von Eschenbach's Christian Faith." *Germanic Review* 29 (1954): 214–3.

Biblia Sacra, Vulgatae Editionis. Edited by P. Michael Hetzenauer, O.F.M.Cap. Regensburg, Germany: Pustet, 1929.

Biddle, Martin. *The Tomb of Christ.* Phoenix Mill, England: Sutton, 2000. A thorough and accessible review of the shape and condition of the Holy Sepulcher from the earliest times to the present with many illustrations from its history.

Bishop, Morris. *The Horizon Book of the Middle Ages.* Edited by Norman Kotker. New York: American Heritage, 1968.

Bliley, Nicholas. *Altars According to the Code of Canon Law.* Washington, D.C.: Catholic University of America, 1927.

Boron, Robert de. *Joseph d'Arimathie, A Critical Edition of the Verse and Prose Versions.* Edited by Richard O'Gorman. Toronto: Pontifical Institute of Medieval Studies, 1995.

———. *Merlin and the Grail: Joseph of Arimathea, Merlin, Perceval, The Trilogy of Prose Romances attributed to Robert de Boron.* Introduced and translated by Nigel Bryant. Rochester, N.Y.: Boydell and Brewer, 2001.

Braun, S.J., Joseph. *Der christliche Altar in seiner geschichtlichen Entwicklung.* vol. 1 (Arten, Bestandteile, Altargrab, Weihe, Symbolik). Munich: Guenther Koch, 1924. This is the unsurpassed work in its field. Braun is the one who proposed that the portable altar, with its top-mounted stone and excavated chamber, was a development from the portable reliquary or "feretory." See also vol. 2.

———. *Die Reliquiare des christlichen Kultes und ihre Entwicklung.* Freiburg im Breisgau: Herder, 1940.

Bredero, Adriaan H. *Christendom and Christianity in the Middle Ages: The Relationship between Religion, Church, and Society.* Grand Rapids, Mich.: Eerdmans, 1994. (First published in 1986 as *Christenheid en Christendom in de Middeleeuwen: Over de verhouding van godsdienst, kerk, en samenleving.*)

Bremness, Lesley. *Herbs.* Smithsonian Handbook. London: Dorling Kindersley, 2002.

Budde, Michael. *Altare Portatile, Kompendium der Tragaltare des Mittelalters 600–1600.* Vol. 1, Text; Vol. 2, Catalogue 1; Vol. 3, Catalogue 2. Münster in Westfalen: Eigenverlag des Autors, 1998. Available at the Marquand Library of Art and Archaeology at Princeton University. The author has compiled an exhaustive catalogue of 150 known portable altars, with individual bibliographies, detailed descriptions, and the varying interpretations of the iconography and inscriptions to be found on each one. Included are the portable altars that can be seen in the United States: one at the Cleveland Museum of Art, one in the Dumbarton Oaks Collection in Washington, D.C., and one at the Walters Art Gallery in Baltimore.

Bull, Marcus. *Knightly Piety and the Lay Response to the First Crusade: The Limousin and Gascony, c. 970-1130.* Oxford: Clarendon Press, 1993.

Bumke, Joachim. *Wolfram von Eschenbach.* 5th ed. Stuttgart: Metzler, 1981.

Burdach, Konrad. *Der Gral: Forschungen über seinen Ursprung und seinen Zusammenhang mit der Longinuslegende.* With a foreword by Johannes Rathofer. Stuttgart: Kohlhammer, 1938; reprint, Darmstadt: Wissenschaftliche Buchgesellschaft, 1974.

Cecchi Gattolin, Enrichetta. *L'Altarolo Portatile nel Duomo di Modena.* Modena, Italy: Banco S. Geminiano e S. Propero, 1984. Explores some of the unique features, including the feet, of Modena's portable altar.

Chandler, Frank W. *A Catalogue of Names of Persons in the German Court Epics: An*

Examination of the Literary Sources and Dissemination, together with Notes on the Etymologies of the More Important Names. Edited with an introduction and an appendix by Martin H. Jones. London: King's College Centre for Late Antique and Medieval Studies, 1992. Gives a useful overview of the history of the often quite varied opinions, including the latest, on the etymologies and possible meanings of the important names in *Parzival* (and other works). In the case of Wolfram, on occasion cites scholars who give the meaning of a name as that which is expressed in parallel statements or clarifications made by Wolfram in the epic.

Classen, Albrecht. "Reading, Writing, and Learning in Wolfram von Eschenbach's *Parzival*." In *A Companion to Wolfram's Parzival*, edited by Will Hasty. Columbia, S.C.: Camden House, 1999.

————. "Jewish-Christian Relations in the German Middle Ages." In *Amsterdamer Beiträge zur Älteren Germanistik*, vol. 58. Amsterdam: Rodopi, 2003.

————. "Self and Other in the Arthurian World: Heinrich von dem Türlin's 'Wunderketten.' " *Monatshefte* 96, 1 (spring 2004): 20–39.

Clemens II, Der Papst aus Bamberg, 24. Dezember 1046–9. Oktober 1047. Published by the Archdiocese of Bamberg, revised by Liutgar Göller und Alfons Dechant. Bamberg: St.-Otto Verlag, 1997.

Crosby, Sumner McKnight. *The Royal Abbey of Saint-Denis from Its Beginning to the Death of Suger, 475–1151*. New Haven: Yale University Press, 1987.

Currer-Briggs, Noel. *The Shroud and the Grail: A Modern Quest for the True Grail*. London: Weidenfeld and Nicholson, 1987.

Dalman, Gustaf. *Das Grab Christi in Deutschland*. Leipzig: Dieterich'sche Verlagsbuchhandlung, 1922.

Daniel, Abbot. *The Pilgrimage of the Russian Abbot Daniel in the Holy Land 1106–1107 AD*. Translated by W. Wilson. London: 1888. Available at www.holyfire.org, under "Orthodox Christian" and "Daniil."

DeVries, Kelly. *Medieval Military Technology*. Peterborough, Ontario: Broadview Press, 1992.

Dizionario dei Concili. Under the direction of Pietro Palazzini. Rome: Città nuova editrice, 1963–1968.

Edbury, Peter W. *The Conquest of Jerusalem and the Third Crusade, Sources in Translation*. Aldershot, Hants, England: Scolar Press, 1996.

Enchiridion Symbolorum Definitionum et Declarationum de Rebus Fidei et Morum. 1st ed. edited by Henricus Denzinger, revised by Adolfus Schönmetzer, S.J. Freiburg im Freiburg im Breisgau: Herder, 1967.

Fourquet, Jean. *Wolfram d' Eschenbach et le Conte del Graal: Les divergences de la tradition du Conte del Graal de Chrétien et leur importance pour l'explication du texte du Parzival*. Paris: Presses Universitaires de France, [1938] 1966.

France, John. "The Destruction of Jerusalem and the First Crusade." *Journal of Ecclesiastical History* 47, 1 (January 1996): 1–21.

Fulton, Rachel. *From Judgment to Passion: Devotion to Christ and the Virgin Mary, 800–1200*. New York: Columbia University Press, 2002. A medieval historian's remarkable tour de force tracing the development of religious devotion beginning with origins in the *Heliand*.

Gentry, Francis G. "Gahmuret and Herzeloyde: Gone but Not Forgotten." In *A Companion to Wolfram's Parzival,* edited by Will Hasty. Columbia, S.C.: Camden House, 1999.

Gibbs, Marion E. "Ideals of Flesh and Blood: Women Characters in *Parzival.*" In *A Companion to Wolfram's Parzival,* edited by Will Hasty. Columbia, S.C.: Camden House, 1999. Loyal devotion, *triuwe,* is the intrinsic virtue of women and of God. Men, Parzival, have courage, but acquire loyal devotion led by love, Condwiramurs, and then can achieve the Grail.

Godefroy, Frédéric. *Dictionnaire de l'ancienne Langue Française et des tous ses dialects du IXe au XVe siècle.* Paris: F. Vieweg, 1884.

Green, D. H. "Homicide and Parzival." In *Approaches to Wolfram von Eschenbach,* edited by Dennis Howard Green and Leslie Peter Johnson. Bern: Peter Lang, 1978.

Green, Dennis Howard, and Leslie Peter Johnson, eds. *Approaches to Wolfram von Eschenbach: Five Essays.* Bern: Peter Lang, 1978.

Griffin, Justin E. *The Holy Grail: The Legend, the History, the Evidence.* Jefferson, N.C.: McFarland, 2001.

Grimm, Jakob and Wilhelm. *Deutsches Wörterbuch.* Leipzig: Hirzel, 1877.

Grimmelshausen, Hans Jacob Christoph, von. *Der Abenteuerliche Simplizissimus Teutsch.* Stuttgart: Reclam, 1997. The German, especially the spelling, has been modernized. For an English version, see *The Adventures of Simplicius Simplizissimus.* 2nd ed. Translated with an introduction by George Schulz-Behrend. Columbia, S.C.: Camden House, 1993.

Groos, Arthur. "Time Reference and the Liturgical Calendar in Wolfram von Eschenbach's *Parzival.*" *Deutsche Vierteljahrsschrift* 49 (1975): 43–65.

Gross, Arthur. *Romancing the Grail: Genre, Science, and Quest in Wolfram's Parzival.* Ithaca: Cornell University Press, 1995. Detailed research on the astrological, medical, and calendrical aspects of *Parzival.*

Gübelin, Eduard, and Franz-Xaver Erni. *Gemstones, Symbols of Beauty and Power.* Tucson: Geoscience Press, 2000.

Guibert de Nogent. *The Deeds of God through the Franks: Gesta Dei per Francos.* Translated by Robert Levine. Woodbridge, Suffolk, England: Boydell Press, 1997.

Guiot de Provins. *Les Oeuvres de Guiot de Provins, Poète Lyrique et Satyrique.* Edited by John Orr. Manchester, England: Imprimerie de l'Université, 1915. Contains *La Bible,* Guiot's satirical attack on Rome, on the religious orders—except the Templars—and on the professions, for corruption and greed.

Haage, Bernhard Dietrich. *Studien zur Heilkunde im "Parzival" Wolframs von Eschenbach.* Göppingen: Kümmerle Verlag, 1992. Contains a useful identification of each of the gemstones in Wolfram's list, p. 99.

Hall, Cally. *Gemstones.* 2nd ed. Smithsonian Handbook. London: Dorling Kindersley, 2002.

Hall, Clifton D., comp. *A Complete Concordance to Wolfram von Eschenbach's Parzival.* New York: Garland, 1990.

Hamilton, Bernard. "The Impact of Crusader Jerusalem on Western Christendom." *Catholic Historical Review* 58, 4 (October 1994): 695–713.

Hasty, Will. "At the Limits of Chivalry in Wolfram's *Parzival.*" In *A Companion to Wolfram's Parzival,* edited by Will Hasty. Columbia, S.C.: Camden House, 1999.

———, ed. *A Companion to Wolfram's Parzival.* Columbia, S.C.: Camden House, 1999.

Hatto, Arthur T. "On Chrétien and Wolfram." *Modern Language Review* 44 (1949): 380–5. Finds contrastive parallels: "God," in Wolfram, versus "Church," in Chrétien; likewise "orthodoxy" versus "personal grasping."

Heinrich von dem Türlin. *Diu Crône von Heinrîch von dem Türlîn.* Published for the first time by Gottlob Heinrich Friedrich Scholl. Stuttgart: Der litterarische Verein, 1852.

———. *The Crown, a Tale of Sir Gawein and King Arthur's Court.* Translated with an introduction by J. W. Thomas. Lincoln: University of Nebraska Press, 1989.

Heliand, The: The Saxon Gospel. Translated with commentary by G. Ronald Murphy, S.J. New York: Oxford University Press, 1992.

Hildegard of Bingen. *S. Hildegardis Abbatissae Subtilitatem Diversarum Naturarum Creaturarum Libri Novem. Liber Tertius (Quartus), "De Lapidibus."* In *Patrologia Latina,* edited by Jacques-Paul Migne. Paris: Migne, 1844; reprint, Turnhout, Belgium: Brepols, 1982, vol. 197, cols. 1247–9.

Horgan, A. D. "The Grail in Wolfram's *Parzival,*" *Medieval Studies* 36 (1974): 354–75. Horgan identifies the Grail stone with the stone that is used as a metaphor for Christ in the Bible.

Huber, Hanspeter Mario. *Licht und Schönheit in Wolframs "Parzival."* Zurich: Juris Druck Verlag, 1981.

Huntley-Speare, Anne Margaret. "The Symbolic Use of a Turtledove for the Holy Spirit in Wolfram's *Parzival.*" In *Arthurian Literature and Christianty: Notes from the Twentieth Century,* edited by Peter Meister. New York: Garland, 1999.

———. "Wolfram's Willehalm and Triuwe: A Model for Society." Ph.D. diss., Pennsylvania State University, 2001. (Available from UMI Dissertation Services, Ann Arbor, Mich.)

Isidore of Seville. *Isidori Hispalensis Episcopi Etymologiarum sive Originum, Libri 20.* Vol. 2, bk. 16. Revised with a brief critical commentary by Wallace M. Lindsay. Oxford: Clarendon, 1911.

Jackson, William H. "Tournaments and Battles in *Parzival.*" In *A Companion to Wolfram's Parzival,* edited by Will Hasty. Columbia, S.C.: Camden House, 1999.

Jackson, William T. H. "The Progress of Parzival and the Trees of Virtue and Vice." *Germanic Review* 33 (1958): 118–24. Traces Parzival's fall and rise in accordance with the tree scheme of Hugh of St. Victor, from root to branch, and in accord with Hugh's definition of despair.

Johnson, Leslie P. "Parzival's Beauty." In *Approaches to Wolfram von Eschenbach: Five Essays,* edited by Dennis Howard Green and Leslie Peter Johnson. Bern: Peter Lang, 1978.

Johnson, Sidney. "Doing His Own Thing: Wolfram's Grail." In *A Companion to Wolfram's Parzival,* edited by Will Hasty. Columbia, S.C.: Camden House, 1999.

Joinville and Villehardouin, Chronicles of the Crusades. Translated with an introduction by Margaret Shaw. New York: Penguin Books, 1963.

Jung, Emma, and Marie-Louise von Franz. *The Grail Legend*. 2nd ed. Translated by
Andrea Dykes. Princeton: Princeton University Press, [1960] 1998. Jungian approach: the Grail is concerned with the psychic development that carries on
Christ's "effectiveness" in this world after his earthly death. The Grail stone is "a
particle of God concealed in nature."

Kolb, Herbert. *Munsalvaesche: Studien zum Kyotproblem*. Munich: Eidos Verlag, 1963.

Kordt, Christa-Maria. *Parzival in Munsalvaesche, Kommentar zu Buch V/1 von Wolframs
Parzival*. Herne, Germany: Verlag für Wissenschaft und Kunst, 1997.

Kratz, Henry. "The Crusades and Wolfram's *Parzival*." In *Arthurian Literature and
Christianity: Notes from the Twentieth Century*, edited by Peter Meister. New York:
Garland, 1999.

Kühn, Dieter. *Der Parzival des Wolfram von Eschenbach*. Frankfurt am Main: Insel Verlag, 1986.

Kunz, George Frederick. *The Curious Lore of Precious Stones, being a description of their
Sentiments and Folk Lore, Superstitions, Symbolism, Mysticism, Use in Medicine,
Protection, Prevention, Religion, and Divination. Crystal Gazing, Birthstones, Lucky
Stones and Talismans, Astral, Zodiacal, and Planetary*. Philadelphia: Lippincott,
1917; reprint, New York: Dover, 1971. The author was the professional gemologist
for Tiffany, and has a gemstone, kunzite, named after him. The book is a gem
showing the range of his curiosity beyond the lens of his loupe, containing lore
from the sixteenth to the twentieth century, not omitting some of the ancients
and medievals. His subtitle says it all.

Lasko, Peter. *Ars Sacra 800–1200*. 2nd ed. New Haven: Yale University Press, 1994.
Plentiful illustrations enable the reader to visualize the function of gemstones
and development from the reliquary and plain altar stone to portable altar with
central stone.

Loomis, Roger Sherman. *The Grail: From Celtic Myth to Christian Symbol*. Princeton:
Princeton University Press, 1991.

Mansi. See *Sacrorum Conciliorum*.

Marbode of Rennes, Bishop. *Marbode of Rennes' (1035–1123) De Lapidibus, Considered
as a Medical Treatise with Text, Commentary, and C. W. King's Translation, Together
with Text and Translation of Marbode's Minor Works on Stones*. Edited with commentary by John M. Riddle. Wiesbaden: Franz Steiner Verlag, 1977.

Markale, Jean. *The Grail: The Celtic Origins of the Sacred Icon*. Translated from the
French by Jon Graham. Rochester, Vt.: Inner Traditions International, [1982]
1999.

McConnell, Winder. "Otherworlds, Alchemy, Pythagoras, and Jung: Symbols of Transformation in *Parzival*." In *A Companion to Wolfram's Parzival*, edited by Will
Hasty. Columbia, S.C.: Camden House, 1999. Sees the story as an attempt to
restore harmony in the individual and collective consciousness. Considers the
shining pillar to be a temporal binary opposite to the transcendent Grail.

Meier, Christel. *Gemma Spiritalis, Methode und Gebrauch der Edelsteineallegorese vom
frühen Christentum bis ins 18. Jahrhundert*. Munich: Wilhelm Fink Verlag, 1977.
The author systematically details historical allegorical use of precious stones, in-

cluding the interpretations of red and green gems given by Augustine, Bede, and Gregory the Great.

Meister, Peter, ed. *Arthurian Literature and Christianity: Notes from the Twentieth Century*. New York: Garland, 1999.

Mergell, Bodo. *Der Gral in Wolfram's Parzival, Entstehung und Ausbildung der Gralsage im Hochmittelalter*. Halle: Max Niemeyer Verlag, 1952.

Messerer, Wilhelm. *Der Bamberger Domschatz in seinem Bestande bis zum Ende der Hohenstaufen-Zeit*. Munich: Hirmer Verlag, 1952.

Middle English Chronicle of the First Crusade, The Caxton Eracles. Vol. 2. Edited with an introduction by Dana Cushing. Lewiston, N.Y.: Edwin Mellen Press, 2001. William of Tyre's account, brought to England. It describes in English the intense feelings of the first crusaders as they reached the Holy Sepulcher: they came, bearing their reliquaries, "bare suche relyques as they had," and brought them "yeldyng thankes to Almyghty God, into the Sepulcre, and there it was a pytous thyng to see how the peple wepte for joye and pyte." They "fylle doun" prostrating themselves before the Sepulcher. "It semed to everyche of them that eche sawe the bodye of onr lord there deed." "There were so many teers and wepyings that euery man thought certaynly oure lord was there."

Mohr, Wolfgang. "Wolframs Kyot and Guiot de Provins." In *Wolfram von Eschenbach, Aufsätze*. Göppinger Arbeiten zur Germanistik no. 275. Göppingen: Kümmerle, 1979. Notes with surprise the positive treatment accorded to the Templars by Guiot in the midst of his bitter satire of most of society, and compares this positively with Wolfram's treatment.

Müller, Ulrich. "Wolfram, Wagner, and the Germans." In *A Companion to Wolfram's Parzival*, edited by Will Hasty. Columbia, S.C.: Camden House, 1999.

Murdoch, Brian. "*Parzival* and the Theology of Fallen Man." In *A Companion to Wolfram's Parzival*, edited by Will Hasty. Columbia, S.C.: Camden House, 1999.

Murphy, S.J., G. Ronald. "Brecht's Pocket Bible." *German Quarterly* 50, 4 (November 1977): 474–84.

———. "A Ceremonial Ritual: The Mass." In *The Spectrum of Ritual: A Biogenetic Structural Analysis*, edited by Eugene d'Aquili, Charles D. Laughlin, Jr., and John McManus. New York: Columbia University Press, 1979.

———. *Brecht and the Bible: A Study of Religious Nihilism and Human Weakness*. Chapel Hill, N.C.: University of North Carolina Press, 1980.

———. *The Saxon Savior: The Transformation of the Gospel in the Ninth-Century Heliand*. New York: Oxford University Press, 1989.

———. "Yggdrasil, the Cross, and the Christmas Tree." *America* 175, 19 (December 19, 1996): 16–20.

———. "The Light Worlds of the *Heliand*." *Monatshefte* 89, 1 (spring 1997): 5–17.

———. "From Germanic Warrior to Christian Knight: The *Heliand* Transformation." In *Arthurian Literature and Christianity: Notes from the Twentieth Century*, edited by Peter Meister. New York: Garland, 1999.

———. *The Owl, the Raven, and the Dove: The Religious Meaning of the Grimms' Magic Fairy Tales*. New York: Oxford University Press, 2000.

Noel, William, Daniel Weiss, and Deborah Horowitz for the Walters Art Museum,

eds. *The Book of Kings: Art, War, and the Morgan Library's Medieval Picture Bible.*
Lingfield, Surrey, England: Third Millennium, 2002. The outstanding reproductions in this affordable volume from the Maciejowski Bible are invaluable for visualizing the crusader warfare of the time of Wolfram and in much of *Parzival.*

Nordstrom, Folke. *Medieval Baptismal Fonts: An Iconographical Study.* Umeå Studies in the Humanities 6. Stockholm: Almquist and Wiksell, 1984. Gives examples of the baptismal font depicted as the Fountain of Life with the four rivers of Paradise.

Parzival of Wolfram von Eschenbach, The. Translated with an introduction by Edwin H. Zeydel. Chapel Hill: University of North Carolina Press, 1951. The introduction contains extensive material on *Parzival.* The translation is no longer much used.

Patrologia Latina. Jacques-Paul Migne. Paris: Migne, 1844–64; reprint, Turnhout, Belgium: Brepols, 1982.

Payne, Robert. *The Dream and the Tomb: A History of the Crusades.* New York: Cooper Square Press, [1984] 2000.

Peter, Michael. *Der Gertrudistragaltar aus dem Welfenschatz, Eine Stilgeschichtliche Untersuchung.* Mainz: Verlag Philipp von Zabern, 2001. Beautiful color photographs of the altar in the Cleveland Museum of Art.

Peters, Edward, ed. *The First Crusade. The Chronicle of Fulcher of Chartres and Other Source Materials.* Philadelphia: University of Pennsylvania Press, 1971.

Plinius Secundus, C. *Naturalis Historia.* Edited by Roderich König. Munich: Artemis, 1986.

Physiologus, latinus versio Y. Edited by Francis J. Carmody. Berkeley: University of California Publications in Classical Philology, 1941.

Pocknee, Cyril E. *The Christian Altar.* London: Mowbray, 1963.

Ranke, Friedrich. "Zur Symbolik des Grals bei Wolfram von Eschenbach." In *Wolfram von Eschenbach,* edited by Heinz Rupp. Darmstadt: Wissenschaftliche Buchgesellschaft, 1966. Good discussion of previous theories on the nature of the Grail; Ranke opts for the "stone of humility," as in the *Iter ad Paradisum* of the priest Lamprecht.

Read, Piers Paul. *The Templars.* New York: St. Martin's Press, 1999; reprint, Cambridge, Mass.: Da Capo Press, 2001.

Regan, Geoffrey. *Saladin and the Fall of Jerusalem.* London: Croom Helm, 1987.

Riddle, John M. *Quid pro Quo: Studies in the History of Drugs.* Aldershot, Hampshire, England: Variorum, 1992. Relates ancient and medieval lore and practice. Interesting treatment of *smaragdus,* the emerald.

Riley-Smith, Jonathan S. C. *What Were the Crusades?* Totowa, N.J.: Rowman and Littlefield, 1977. Clear exposition giving two motives: recovery and defense of Christ's property, Just War; and conversion and expansion of Christendom, Holy War. (Wolfram opposes these neatly: the portable altar as Christ's effective residence against the first; Adamic kinship and the expansion of happiness against the second.)

———. "Crusading as an Act of Love." *Journal of the Historical Association* 65 (1980): 177–220.

———. *The First Crusaders, 1095–1131.* Cambridge: Cambridge University Press, 1997.

Roach, William, ed. *The Continuations of the Old French Perceval of Chrétien de Troyes.* Vol. 1. Philadelphia: University of Pennsylvania Press, 1949.

Robert of Clari. *The Conquest of Constantinople.* Translated from the Old French by Edgar Holmes McNeal. New York: Columbia University Press, 1936.

Robert, Paul. *Le Grand Robert de la langue Française, Dictionnaire Alphabétique et Analogique de la Langue Française.* 2nd ed., expanded by Alain Rey. Paris: Le Robert, 1986. Concerning "Repanse" and "re(s)pandre," says that the word used normally of a liquid means "overflow"; if used as an abstraction means an "expansion," or "spreading."

Rock, Daniel. *The Church of Our Fathers: As Seen in St. Osmund's Rite for the Cathedral of Salisbury.* 4 vols. London: Hodges, 1903–4.

Röhrig, Floridus. *Der Verduner Altar.* 7. New, rev. ed. Klosterneuburg-Wien: Mayer, 1995. Careful examination of the images in this thirteenth-century masterpiece shows the effect of the Holy Sepulcher's actual shape on many scenes from the life of Christ, including the Nativity and the Enthronement, as well as the Deposition, Entombment, and Resurrection.

Rubin, Miri. *Corpus Christi: The Eucharist in Late Medieval Culture.* Cambridge: Cambridge University Press, 1991.

Runciman, Steven. *The First Crusade.* Cambridge: Cambridge University Press, [1951] 1992.

Sacker, Hugh. *An Introduction to Wolfram's "Parzival."* Cambridge: Cambridge University Press, 1963. Believes that the change from chalice to stone precludes precise identification of the Grail ceremony with the Mass; concludes, however, that the Grail ceremony is indeed analogous to the Mass. He is mystified that the Grail community kneels and faces the Grail "as Christians face the altar," and concludes that the Grail must be "sacramental in nature."

Sacrorum Conciliorum Nova et Amplissima Collectio. Edited by Joannes Dominicus Mansi. Venice: Antonius Zatta, 1767; reproduction, Paris: H. Welter, 1902.

Scavone, Daniel C. "Joseph of Arimathea, The Holy Grail and the Turin Shroud" Available at www.shroud.com/scavone2.htm.

Schmid, Elisabeth. "Wolfram von Eschenbachs 'Parzival.' " In *Interpretationen: Mittelhochdeutsche Romane und Heldenepen.* Edited by Horst Brunner. Stuttgart: Reclam, 1993.

Schröder, Walter Johannes. *Der dichterische Plan des Parzivalromans.* Halle: Max Niemayer Verlag, 1953. Sees the internal schema as reflecting three spatial dimensions and thus also the three identifying characteristics of the Holy Trinity: power, loving loyalty, truth.

Schröder, Werner. *Die Namen im "Parzival" und im "Titurel" Wolframs von Eschenbach.* Berlin: de Gruyter, 1982.

———. *Wolfram von Eschenbach, Spuren und Werke.* Stuttgart: S. Hirzel Verlag, 1989. Points out Wolfram's fascination with Christian paradoxes: e.g., as Christ was dying on the cross, he was actually getting better, *der al sterbende genas.*

Schumann, Walter. *Gemstones of the World.* Rev. and exp. ed. New York: Sterling, 1977.

Schwarzweber, Annemarie. *Das heilige Grab in der deutschen Bildnerei des Mittelalters.*

Freiburg im Breisgau: Eberhard Albert Universitätsbuchhandlung, 1940. This is a rare and effective study and makes the connection between the liturgy of Good Friday and placing the Host in the representation of the grave, but the reproductions are dated. The book deserves a successor.

Schwietering, Julius. "Parzivals Schuld." In *Philologische Schriften*, edited by Freidrich Ohly and Max Wehrli. Munich: Wilhelm Fink Verlag, 1969. Suggests Eastern Christian influence on Wolfram.

Sheingorn, Pamela. *The Easter Sepulcher in England*. Kalamazoo, Mich.: Medieval Institute, 1987.

Sources of the Grail: An Anthology. Selected and introduced by John Matthews. Hudson, N.Y.: Lindisfarne Press, 1997.

Stahlman, William D., and Owen Gingerich. *Solar and Planetary Longitudes for the Years −2000 to +2000 by Ten-Day Intervals*. Madison: University of Wisconsin Press, 1963.

Tax, Petrus W. "*Felix Culpa* und *Lapsit Exillis*: Wolfram's *Parzival* und die Liturgie." *Modern Language Notes* 80 (1965): 454–69. Interprets the Grail as intimately related to the liturgical celebration of Holy Week. Relates the Grail's radiance to that of the Easter candle and to that of the Resurrection through the phoenix imagery of the text, and connects it to the *felix culpa* of the "Exultet" hymn. Further, he associates *lapsit exillis* with Christ as the *lapis angularis*, that is, the (corner-)stone from which the Easter fire is struck "by the cross."

Theoderich of Würzburg. *Guide to the Holy Land*. Translated by Aubrey Stewart. 2nd ed. with new introduction, notes, and bibliography by Ronald G. Musto. New York: Italica Press, 1986.

Two Anglo-Saxon Pontificals. Edited by H.M.J. Manning. London: Henry Bradshaw Society, 1989. The Egbert pontifical, c. 950, describes the placing of the three particles of the Eucharistic Body of Christ, together with three grains of incense, and then the relics of saints (carried solemnly to the altar in a feretory, a portable reliquary), into the altar cavity during the consecration of a permanent altar.

Vetus Latina: Die Reste der altlateinischen Bibel. Newly compiled by Petrus Sabatier and published by the Archabbey of Beuron. Freiburg: Herder, 1949.

Walshe, Maurice O'C. *A Middle High German Reader*. Oxford: Oxford University Press, 1974.

Wapnewski, Peter. *Wolframs Parzival: Studien zur Religiösität und Form*. Heidelberg: Carl Winter, 1955. Attempts to describe an architectonic structure in *Parzival*, with books 3 to 9 seen as parallel to books 10 to 16. To make this analysis work, however, the author must leave books 1 and 2 out of consideration. Johannine and Augustinian spirituality are well shown as the basis for Parzival's development of Christian maturity and character.

Weigand, Hermann J. "Die epischen Zeitverhältnisse in den Graldichtungen Chrestiens und Wolfram." *Publications of the Modern Language Society* 53, 4 (December 1938): 917–50. Points to Wolfram's creation of a unified time sequence for the story's episodes, and to his meaningful unification of diverse elements, e.g., his linkage of the summer snowfall to the mystery of Anfortas's suffering.

————. "Wolfram's Grail and the Neutral Angels: A Discussion and a Dialogue." *Germanic Review* 29 (1954): 83–95.

Weston, Jessie Laidlay. *From Ritual to Romance*. Princeton: Princeton University Press, [1920] 1993.

William of Malmesbury. *Liber de Antiquitate Glastoniensis Ecclesiae*. In *Patrologia Latina*, edited by Jacques-Paul Migne. Paris: Migne, 1844–64; reprint, Turnhout, Belgium: Brepols, 1982, vol. 179, cols. 1698–1700A. Describes Glastonbury's famous portable altar stone, "The Sapphire," recounting its legendary origin in Jerusalem and attributing its many virtues to its consecration by containing the Body of Christ: "Dominicum corpus sacrabat." He uses *lapis* and *altare* interchangeably.

————. *The Early History of Glastonbury: An Edition, Translation and Study of William of Malmsbury's "De Antiquitate Glastonie Ecclesie."* Edited by John Scott. Woodbridge, Suffolk, England: Boydell Press, 1981.

William of Tyre. *Willelmi Tyrensis Archiepiscopi Chronicon*. Corpus Christianorum, Continuatio Mediaeualis 63. Turnhout, Belgium: Brepols, 1986.

Index

Page numbers in *italic* type indicate illustrations.